GENDER ASPECTS OF THE TRADE AND POVERTY NEXUS

A Macro-Micro Approach

Maurizio Bussolo

Rafael E. De Hoyos

Editors

A COPUBLICATION OF PALGRAVE MACMILLAN
AND THE WORLD BANK

©2009 The International Bank for Reconstruction and Development / The World Bank
1818 H Street, NW
Washington, DC 20433
Telephone: 202-473-1000
Internet: www.worldbank.org
E-mail: feedback@worldbank.org

1 2 3 4 12 11 10 09
A copublication of The World Bank and Palgrave Macmillan.

PALGRAVE MACMILLAN
Palgrave Macmillan in the UK is an imprint of Macmillan Publishers Limited, registered in
England, company number 785998, of Houndmills, Basingstoke, Hampshire, RG21 6XS.
    Palgrave Macmillan in the US is a division of St Martin's Press LLC, 175 Fifth Avenue,
New York, NY 10010.
    Palgrave Macmillan is the global academic imprint of the above companies and has
companies and representatives throughout the world.
    Palgrave® and Macmillan® are registered trademarks in the United States, the United
Kingdom, Europe and other countries.

This volume is a product of the staff of the International Bank for Reconstruction and
Development / The World Bank. The findings, interpretations, and conclusions expressed
in this volume do not necessarily reflect the views of the Executive Directors of The
World Bank or the governments they represent.
    The World Bank does not guarantee the accuracy of the data included in this work.
The boundaries, colors, denominations, and other information shown on any map in this
work do not imply any judgement on the part of The World Bank concerning the legal
status of any territory or the endorsement or acceptance of such boundaries.

ISBN: 978-0-8213-7762-8 (soft cover) and 978-0-8213-7764-2 (hard cover)
eISBN: 978-0-8213-7763-5
DOI: 10.1596/978-0-8213-7762-8 (soft cover) and 10.1596/978-0-8213-7764-2 (hard cover)

Library of Congress Cataloging-in-Publication Data
Gender aspects of the trade and poverty nexus : a macro-micro approach / Maurizio
Bussolo and Rafael E. De Hoyos, editors.
    p. cm.
Includes bibliographical references and index.
ISBN 978-0-8213-7762-8 (pbk.) — ISBN 978-0-8213-7764-2 (hardback) —
ISBN 978-0-8213-7763-5 (electronic)
1. Sex role. 2. Poverty. 3. Commerce. I. Bussolo, Maurizio, 1964- II. De Hoyos,
Rafael E.
    HQ1075.B88 2008
    339.4'6082—dc22

                                                                    2008044224
Printed in the United States

Contents

Part II. The Micro Approach: Household Models of Trade, Gender, and Poverty

Figures

Tables

Foreword

What is the impact of trade liberalization on the well-being of women and children? This important question is one of a set of questions that links macroeconomic policy instruments to the microeconomic-level consequences of their deployment. The linkages are complex and multifaceted, but we might make analytical headway by breaking the causal chain into two stages. The first stage links the operation of the policy instrument to consequences for factor incomes earned by individuals in the marketplace. In the context of gender and trade liberalization, for example, the specific question would be, What is the impact of trade liberalization on the factor incomes of men and women? Particular attention would focus on men and women as earners of labor income—skilled and unskilled.

However, poverty depends on how these factor incomes are turned into individual consumption through the sharing of factor incomes between individuals. This can happen through the tax and expenditure instruments of the state or, perhaps more importantly for poor economies, through sharing within households. Thus, to get at the consequences for poverty, patterns of household formation, and then intrahousehold allocations, have to be superimposed on the macro policy–induced changes of factor incomes. This is intricate enough if the allocation rules are given and unchanging. The analysis is further complicated if the macro-level changes themselves alter the micro-level intrahousehold allocation processes, or even household formation processes.

The above brief discussion of the structure of the problem should make clear that theory, although important in helping us construct the analysis, can only take us so far in providing an answer to the basic question posed. Ultimately the impact of trade liberalization on the well-being of women and children is an empirical issue, depending on the specifics of how each link in the chain of causality plays out. Certainly the early, unalloyed optimism on gender-specific distributional consequences of trade liberalization was misplaced—or at least empirically unverified. A gloom-and-doom scenario is not warranted either. What is needed is a careful, case-by-case analysis of specific situations, paying due attention to the structure of the economy in addressing the first stage of the causal link and due attention to the economic implications of a range of sociocultural factors in the second stage. In situations where the well-being of women and children can be shown to have worsened or where gender inequality has increased, there is a strong case for trade liberalization to be accompanied by complementary measures.

This excellent volume brings together a collection of papers in the macro and micro traditions and then puts the arguments together in the introductory section. What I particularly like about it is that it does not take an a priori position "for" or "against" trade liberalization but is willing to be led by the empirical analysis. In some cases, the answer comes out one way, in other cases, the opposite. So be it. What is important is that the methods explored and illustrated in the chapters allow us to have a structured discussion; they permit policy makers to see the trade-offs involved in undertaking trade liberalization, and encourage them to design country-specific policy packages to address their development challenges encompassing gender and trade.

Ravi Kanbur
T. H. Lee Professor of World Affairs
International Professor of Applied Economics and Management
Professor of Economics
Cornell University
December 2008

Preface

This book reports on the findings of a major international research project examining the links between trade, gender, and poverty. Trade liberalization can create economic opportunities, but women and men cannot take advantage of these opportunities on an equal basis. Women and men differ in their endowments, control over resources, access to labor markets, and their roles within the household. It may seem obvious that gender differences play an important role in transmitting the effects of trade expansion to poverty, especially in less developed countries, where gender inequality is usually more pronounced. However, very few studies have examined this issue directly. Although the literature includes numerous analyses on the links between trade and poverty and between gender inequality and poverty, it seems not to have combined these two sets of studies in a consistent empirical framework. The main objective for the research project documented in this book was to fill, at least in part, this gap in the literature.

Achieving this objective has been a complex task. In methodological terms, assessing how relevant gender differences are in the transmission of the effects of trade liberalization to poverty meant tracing and gauging the links between this macroeconomic policy and the microeconomic-level consequences of its implementation. Most of these links are not direct. They tend to be mediated by the characteristics of labor markets, household endowments, and intrahousehold allocation behavior. All of these elements are highly specific to individual countries, and that is why this project opted for a set of country-specific case studies. In choosing the country case studies, particular attention was paid to sub-Saharan Africa. In this region, many countries have adopted market-friendly reforms, including deep trade liberalization, but they have not universally reaped significant growth and poverty reduction benefits. As documented by ample evidence, gender inequality in Africa tends to be wider than that in other developing-country regions, another reason to study the links between trade, gender, and poverty on this continent.

Although no generally applicable policy prescriptions emerge from the research collected here, two relevant policy messages can be distilled. First, combining trade reforms with well-designed, gender-aware social policies can produce larger gains than can isolated trade reforms. The design of these social policies will depend on the characteristics of the specific country. Second, counterbalancing trade-related, widening gender disparities can have positive outcomes in the long run. In some cases, decreasing women's incomes are shown to have negative effects on investment in human capital and on output response in agriculture.

Ackowledgments

Many people have contributed in various important ways to the development of this book. First, we want to thank the Bank Netherlands Partnership Program (BNPP), which funded the entire three-year research project behind this book.[1] Second, our greatest recognition, clearly, goes to the authors of the nine chapters and the foreword. Some of them have been with us from the beginning, helping to shape the basic ideas and to steer the project in fruitful directions. Others joined at later stages, yet they provided indispensable support to our efforts. This book is really the product of the joint original work of a team of motivated and accomplished researchers. Their names and current affiliations are listed in the contributors section.

The core team of authors benefited from the support and advice of many colleagues, including those who contributed comments during the seminars and conferences where draft chapters were presented. At various stages of its development, the research work contained here was presented at worldwide conferences, meetings, and seminars, including the following: the Global Trade Analysis Project (www.gtap.agecon.purdue.edu) international conferences in Helsinki, Finland, and at Purdue University, West Lafayette, Indiana, U.S.; the Poverty and Economic Policy Research Network annual meeting in Lima, Peru (www.pep-net.org); the Poverty Reduction, Equity and Growth Network conferences (www.pegnet.ifw-kiel.de) in Berlin, Germany, and Accra, Ghana; a World Institute for Development Economics Research (United Nations) conference, also in Accra; the Latin American and Caribbean Economic Association conference (www.lacea.org) in Bogotá, Colombia, and Rio de Janeiro, Brazil; and several seminars organized at the World Bank. For their remarks, suggestions, and peer review, we thank in

---

[1] The Bank Netherlands Partnership Program (BNPP) was established in June 1998 to address concerns of the Minister of Development Cooperation for a more coordinated and prioritized approach in the use of trust fund resources. The aim is to provide financing and a priority-setting framework for analytical, policy, sector, and research activities financed by the Ministry of Foreign Affairs.

particular Ataman Aksoy, Orazio Attanazio, John Baffes, Elena Bardasi, François Bourguignon, Uri Dadush, Louise Fox, Basudeb Guha-Khasnobis, Catalina Gutierrez, Rebecca Lessem, Andre Martens, Will Martin, Denis Medvedev, Lars Christian Moller, Jacques Morisset, Cristina Savescu, Hans Timmer, Eric Thorbecke, and Alan Winters.

Special thanks go to Helena Nkole, World Bank BNPP Administrator; Philip Schuler, World Bank BNPP Trade Focal Points; and Kathy Rollins, program assistant, who provided superb administrative support and assistance during various critical phases of this project.

We are very grateful to Janet Sasser for her dedication and professionalism in assisting the editors at the key final stages of the production of this volume and in particular for managing its editing, typesetting, proofreading, cover design, and indexing; and to Santiago Pombo-Bejarano for his support during the long life of this project and for his keen commitment to converting the manuscript into a finished volume. Production of this book occurred in the World Bank Office of the Publisher.

Contributors

Editors

Maurizio Bussolo | Senior economist in the Latin America and Caribbean Economic Policy Sector at the World Bank, Washington, DC

Rafael E. De Hoyos | Chief of advisers in the Under Ministry of Education of Mexico

Other Contributing Authors

Charles Ackah | Research fellow in the Institute of Statistical, Social, and Economic Research at the University of Ghana, Accra

John Cockburn | Codirector of the Poverty and Economic Policy (PEP) research network and associate professor in the Department of Economics at Laval University, Québec, Canada

Bernard Decaluwé | Full professor in the Department of Economics at Laval University, Québec, Canada, and lead adviser in the Poverty and Economic Policy (PEP) research network

Ismael Fofana | Researcher in the Department of Economics at Laval University, Québec, Canada

Marzia Fontana | Research fellow in the Globalisation Team at the Institute of Development Studies, Sussex, UK

Jennifer Golan | Researcher in the School of Social Sciences at the University of Manchester, UK

Ravi Kanbur   T. H. Lee Professor of World Affairs,
                             International Professor of Applied
                             Economics and Management, and
                             professor of economics at Cornell
                             University, Ithaca, NY, US

Jann Lay   Senior economist and head of the
                             Poverty Reduction Equity and
                             Development Research Area at the
                             Kiel Institute for the World Economy,
                             Germany

Jean-Pascal Nganou   Economist in the Africa Poverty
                             Reduction and Economic Manage-
                             ment Sector at the World Bank,
                             Washington, DC

Oscar Núñez   Consultant in the Development
                             Economics Prospects Group at the
                             World Bank, Washington, DC

Juan Carlos Parra   Consultant in the Development
                             Dialogue on Values and Ethics
                             Department at the World Bank,
                             Washington, DC

Véronique Robichaud   Researcher in the Department of
                             Economics at Laval University,
                             Québec, Canada

Quentin Wodon   Adviser in the Development Dialogue
                             on Values and Ethics Department at
                             the World Bank, Washington, DC

Abbreviations

$	All dollar amounts are U.S. dollars unless otherwise indicated
CAFTA	Central America Free Trade Agreement
CBI	Caribbean Basin Initiative
CBTPA	Caribbean Basin Trade Partnership Act
CET	common external tariff
CFAF	Commaunité Financière Africaine franc (Senegal)
CGE	computable general equilibrium
cif	cost, insurance, and freight
COMESA	Common Market for Eastern and Southern Africa
CPI	consumer price index
DID	difference-in-difference
DR–CAFTA	Dominican Republic–Central America Free Trade Agreement
ECOWAS	Economic Community of Western African States
EPHPM	Encuesta de Permanente de Hogares de Propositos Multiples (Honduras nationally representative household surveys)
EPZ	export-processing zone
ESAM	Enquête Sénégalaise auprès des Ménages (Senegalese Household Survey)
FDI	foreign direct investment
fob	freight on board
GDP	gross national product
GPRS	Ghanaian Poverty Reduction Strategy

IFPRI	International Food Policy Research Institute
IV	instrumental variables
NIC	newly industrializing country
NTAE	nontraditional agricultural export
OECD	Organisation for Economic Co-coperation and Development
OLS	ordinary least squares
SAM	social accounting matrix
SAP	Special Access Program
SUR	seemingly unrelated regressions
UEMOA	West African Economic and Monetary Union
WTO	World Trade Organization

1

Gender Aspects of the Trade and Poverty Nexus: Introduction and Overview

Maurizio Bussolo and Rafael E. De Hoyos

This volume introduces the gender dimension into the empirical analysis of the links between trade and poverty. Its main claim is that considering this dimension can shed light on the trade and poverty debate, possibly improving policy making.

Various arguments justify this claim. First, gender disparities, an important component of overall inequality, may limit the gains from trade. This view is supported by the robust finding that growth—the major vehicle for lifting people out of poverty—is more likely to be pro-poor when initial inequality is low (Ravallion 2001; Bourguignon 2002). High inequality also directly reduces the rate of poverty reduction by hampering growth. Ample evidence shows that, despite recent improvements, large gender disparities persist. In the developing world as a whole, women account for 56 percent of adults with no formal education and represent just 46 percent of people who have completed secondary or higher education (table 1.1). Social norms and discrimination outside as well as inside the household mean that women and men differ not only in terms of education but also in terms of access to labor markets, remuneration, sectoral employment, control over resources, and roles within the households. Because of these disparities, men and women cannot uniformly take advantage of the opportunities created by trade liberalization.

Table 1.1 Global Gender Disparities in Education
(percentage of total)

Group	Not educated	Completed primary school	Completed at least secondary school
Adult population			
Male	44	56	54
Female	56	44	46
Adult poor population[a]			
Male	44	59	62
Female	56	41	38
Adult nonpoor population			
Male	43	53	51
Female	57	47	49

Source: Authors' calculations based on the Global Income Distribution Dynamics (GIDD) database (see Ackah and others 2008).

a. *Poor* is defined here as living on less than $2 a day.

Second, these gender-specific constraints appear to be especially binding for poorer households (Lipton 1983; Marcoux 1998; Filmer 1999). Among adults living below the $2 a day poverty line, just 38 percent of those with secondary or higher education degrees are women. This share is considerably lower than the 46 percent for the female population as a whole. Gender gaps in other dimensions, such as health, are also more pronounced among poorer households (World Bank 2001).

Third, some analysts have pointed out that women tend to be overrepresented among the poor. Until recently, female-headed households were believed to be poorer than male-headed ones; in assessing the impact of trade on poverty, accounting for gender-differentiated effects was therefore deemed crucial. Recent evidence has shown that female-headed households tend to be concentrated in urban areas, however, and are not necessarily poorer than households headed by males.[1]

It is true that women's worse economic opportunities are reflected in lower incomes and higher poverty rates among households with larger numbers of female adults. As a result of discrimination, the mere presence of more women in the household can be a disadvantage, even after controlling for income determinants such as age, education, sector of occupation, and area of residence (urban or rural). All else equal, for a household of five adult members, substituting one male adult for a female adult reduces the household's total income by 8 percent.[2]

Fourth, a large literature suggests that the assumption of a "unitary" model of household behavior is unfounded (see, for example, Haddad and Kanbur 1990; Bourguignon and Chiappori 1992; Alderman and others 1995). In most cases men and women do not pool resources or jointly make decisions about household spending. As Chao (1999, p. 11) notes:

> Household spending patterns are often closely linked to the levels of income generated by gender, with important implications for the allocation of resources for consumption, production, and investment. To the extent that men and women have different expenditures responsibilities, policies that affect men's and women's incomes differently will generate different welfare outcomes.

In particular, women's greater control over resources or income flows has been found to be strongly associated not only with improvements in their own welfare but also with increased levels of investment in their children's human capital (nutrition, health, and education) (Hoddinott and Haddad 1995). This suggests that neglecting intrahousehold inequality issues—ignoring gender bargaining within the household—could mean overlooking short-term and, more important, long-term, growth-reducing impacts of trade policy or other external shocks.

Trade can have strong effects on poverty through two main linkages: growth and distribution (see Winters 2002). Women can be engaged in or excluded by the economic transformation triggered by a trade shock, affecting the strength of these linkages. This volume focuses on the grey dashed connecting arrows in figure 1.1, in an attempt to answer the following questions:

- Does trade expansion increase women's employment opportunities relative to men's?
- How does trade affect gender earning gaps?
- How does trade liberalization, or an external shock such as a price increase of food or cash crops, affect the intrahousehold reallocation of resources?
- As a result of the above, what are the effects on poverty?

The volume approaches these questions by examining detailed single-country case studies. Cross-country regressions can identify some strong correlation between gender inequality and poverty (and even between gender inequality and growth) (Morrison, Raju, and Sinha 2007). But, as in the case of the cross-country analyses on trade and growth, strong correlation does not mean causation.

Figure 1.1 Trade and Poverty Links

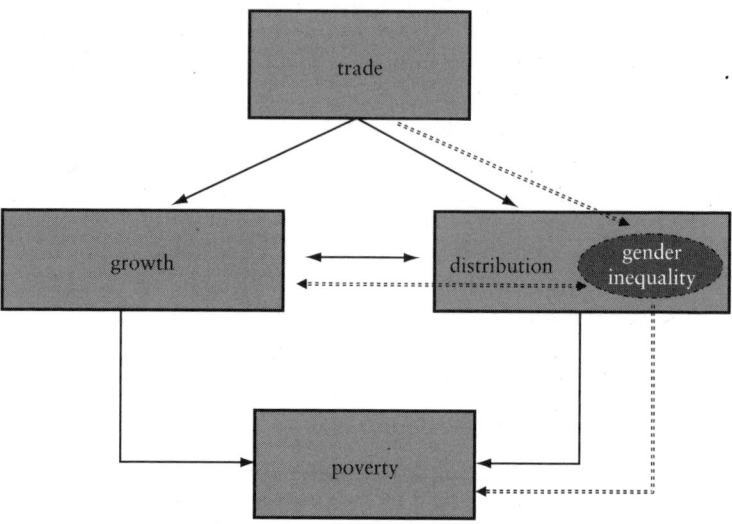

Source: Authors.

Most of this cross-country empirical literature has been strongly criticized (Durlauf 2001; Rodrik and Rodriguez 2001). Moreover, the policy relevance of the literature is minimal because the models used are usually in reduced form (and partial equilibrium), making it impossible to trace the direct effects of policy interventions on agents' behavior.

A better alternative, and the one chosen here, is to use country-specific structural models. In fact, given the macro nature of trade policy and the micro nature of poverty and gender issues, both macro and micro empirical lenses are needed to explore the complex links between trade, gender, distribution, and poverty. This volume thus includes two parts: one devoted to macro techniques and one devoted to micro techniques.

Analyzing Trade-Gender-Poverty Linkages

This section describes the simplest conceptual framework that can be used to analyze the linkages between trade and poverty through gender. It includes two parts. The first, based on standard international trade models, considers the linkages between trade and gender. The second, based mainly on the microeconomic models of household behavior, deals with the linkages between gender and poverty.

Trade and Gender

For any specific good or service, expanded trade can be thought of as the result of a reduction in the relative price of imports with respect to domestic output (or an increase in the relative price of exports with respect to domestic output). These relative price changes are usually the result of the liberalization of trade policy, but they can also be produced by productivity shocks or other exogenous shocks, such as the recent increase in the price of internationally traded commodities that began in the late 1990s as a result, among other things, of the rising demand for raw materials by fast-growing developing countries (particularly China and India) and the expanding use of biofuels. In standard trade models, assumptions about intersectoral mobility of factors and factor substitution in production determine how these changes in goods' relative prices are transmitted to changes in factor demands and remunerations.

In the Ricardo-Viner model, factors are sector specific; there is no factor mobility across sectors. In this setup the factor specific to the export industry benefits from an expansion of trade, while the factor specific to the import-competing industry loses. It is possible to find cases in which this is the relevant model for the study of the trade and gender linkages. In a study of female workers in tea-producing regions of China, Qian (2005) shows that "given their smaller stature, particularly in terms of their height, and the size of their hands, women have a comparative advantage over men in the production of tea" (cited by Duflo 2005, p. 4). This comparative advantage is equivalent to a barrier against the entry of male workers in the tea sector (low intersectoral labor mobility). As Qian reports, economic liberalization allowing households to grow cash crops instead of food crops, implemented as part of post-Mao agricultural reforms in rural China, has been accompanied by a marked reduction in female mortality in tea-producing regions, a clear sign that female workers benefited from trade liberalization.[3]

An alternative to the Ricardo-Viner model is the factor proportion (Heckscher-Ohlin) model. In this model factors are mobile across sectors; what matters for the final effect on factor prices are the degree of factor substitutability in production and the relative endowment of different factors. The standard prediction of this model is that trade liberalization will induce countries to specialize in the production of goods that use the more abundant factor more intensively. In a typical developing country, the more abundant factor is unskilled labor. Expanded trade would thus mean that such a country would specialize in exporting unskilled labor–intensive products and that wages for unskilled labor would increase relative to the returns of other factors.

How could women benefit from trade in this setting? For such a positive effect to be realized, a few additional assumptions, not implausible for the developing world, must hold. In particular, it must be the case that unskilled and skilled labor are imperfect substitutes in production, that female and male workers are perfect substitutes, and that female workers have, on average, lower qualifications than male workers. Under this set of assumptions, unskilled workers, the majority of whom are women, will benefit from expanded trade.

Empirical observations appear to validate the factor proportion model. This model's main prediction—that women will be overrepresented in the export sector—is supported by the well-known empirical regularity that large segments of developing countries' export-oriented manufacturing (textiles and garments, electronic products, and export-processing zones) are intensive in their employment of female workers. In a study of 35 developing countries, Wood (1991) finds that the integration in global trade of the South is strongly correlated with the increase in female intensity of its manufacturing. Artecona and Cunningham (2002), Paul-Mazumdar and Begum (2002), and Nicita and Razzaz (2003) confirm that women employed in export-oriented manufacturing typically earn more than they would have in traditional sectors. Milner and Wright (1998) find that trade liberalization in Mauritius increased the employment and relative wages of female and unskilled labor in the exportables sector. De Hoyos (2006) finds that a significant proportion of the increase in female labor participation observed in Mexico during the second half of the 1990s was attributable to the North American Free Trade Agreement (NAFTA).

In the models just described, trade can improve the gender-related employment and wage disparities in an environment of perfect competition (that is, in a situation in which no agent is able to use its market power to influence prices). Links between trade and gender inequality can also be found when the assumption of perfect competition is relaxed. In his seminal work on the economics of discrimination, Becker (1971) claimed that noncompetitive product markets can be associated with labor market discrimination. Given their preferences, he argued, monopolistic employers may be able to pay male workers wages in excess of their productivity. The positive earnings differential between men and women thus created would be maintained through market power and higher price-setting in the product markets. When barriers to entry are removed and competition increases, however, less-discriminatory firms enter the market and hire women, taking advantage of their lower initial wages. All else equal this should lead to lower wage or employment gaps between men and women. Empirical research (Artecona and Cunninghan 2002; Black and Brainerd 2002; Santos and Arbache 2005) shows that, triggered by trade liberalization, increased competition from imports has indeed contributed to smaller gender gaps.

Gender and Poverty

Expanded trade can affect both the employment opportunities and earning potentials of women. The trade theories illustrate the explicit channels—sector-specific skills, unskilled female abundance, and greater competition—that may explain the correlation between the recent wave of globalization, growing participation of women in the labor markets, and narrowing gender earnings gaps. But what about the relation between gender and poverty? How can the potentially positive trade-to-gender effects be translated into faster poverty reduction? The second part of the conceptual framework is needed to answer these questions.

The welfare effects of the trade-related changes identified in the first part of the framework—in particular, the changes in women's income with respect to men's—depend on a household's composition, its sources of income, and its consumption preferences. Ultimately, the poverty effects depend on how the household adjusts to these changes.

Microeconomic theory has devised two quite different household behavior models: the unitary and the bargaining model.[4] In the unitary model, the members of the household (for simplicity, men, m, and women, f) share the same set of preferences, and the household's economic choices (its consumption and labor supply decisions) are made as if the household were a single optimizing agent. In this case the household utility function depends on the consumption of a bundle of goods $\mathbf{x}$, including leisure, and household characteristics γ. Its utility can be written as

$$U(\mathbf{x}, \gamma).$$

From the maximization of this utility, subject to the following budget constraint (where y_j, y_m, and y_f are joint, male, and female income components, respectively)

$$\mathbf{p} \cdot \mathbf{x} = Y = y_j + y_m + y_f,$$

standard demand functions are derived:

$$x_i = x_i(\mathbf{p}, Y; \gamma).$$

The key prediction of the unitary model is that, given the common set of preferences, the household optimal choices do not depend on who brings resources into the household but only on the total amount (Y) of those resources (income pooling). Welfare changes—as well as poverty effects—caused by trade-related shocks (basically relative price changes) can be straightforwardly estimated using the following equation:[5]

$$\frac{dW_h}{Y_h} = \underbrace{\sum_i -\theta^c_{h,i}\hat{p}_i}_{\text{consumption}} + \underbrace{\theta^l_h \hat{w}}_{\text{labor income}} + \underbrace{\theta^{kap}_h \hat{\pi}}_{\text{profits}} + \underbrace{(1-\theta^l_h - \theta^{kap}_h)\hat{y}^o}_{\text{other income}},$$

where the relative gains or losses (W represents welfare) for each household (h) depend on changes in three factors:

- prices for purchased goods, p_i, where a hat represents percentage change and $\theta^c_{h,i}$ represents the initial share of expenditure on each good;
- factor returns, where w stands for returns to labor (male/female, skilled/unskilled), π represents returns to capital (or net revenues from sales of output directly produced by the household), and θ^l_h and θ^{kap}_h represent the shares of total initial income by source; and
- transfers and other income sources, which depend, among other things, on the change in government revenues caused by trade reform.

Income by source is calculated for each member of the household. To keep notation simple, the above equation shows results after aggregating incomes for each individual in the same household. In the unitary model, income flows from all members of the household are pooled to finance the common consumption and savings choices. A household is deemed poor when its per capita postshock welfare falls below the poverty line, where per capita welfare is estimated as the total household welfare divided by the household size.[6]

By ignoring intrahousehold inequality issues, the unitary model makes the estimation of poverty effects of (trade- and nontrade-related) price changes straightforward. This model is not very useful if one is interested in assessing the gender–poverty links, however (Haddad and Kanbur 1990).

By explicitly tackling intrahousehold inequality issues, the bargaining model is a more appropriate model (Browning and Chiappori 1998). In this model household members differ in their preferences, with individual utility functions accounting for this difference: $U_i(\mathbf{x}_i, \mathbf{x}_j; \gamma)$ with $i = m, f$ and $j = f, m$. The household optimization problem can be rewritten as

$$\max \mu U_m(\mathbf{x}_m, \mathbf{x}_f; \gamma) + (1 - \mu)U_f(\mathbf{x}_m, \mathbf{x}_f; \gamma),$$

where μ is a weight that represents a sharing rule. As in the case of the unitary model, the optimal choices of the household depend on prices, household characteristics, and the total level of resources. But in addition, they depend on the weight μ:

$$x_i = x_i \, (\mathbf{p}, Y, \mu; \gamma).$$

The weight μ can be interpreted as the "rule" by which individuals within the household share their incomes. This rule is likely to be influenced by individuals' relative bargaining power: a more powerful individual would control a larger share of the household's resources and thus be able to influence more strongly the final consumption choices. To explicitly take into account the bargaining power that is affecting μ, we rewrite these optimal choices as

$$x_i + x_i \, (\mathbf{p}, Y, \mu(\alpha_m, \alpha_f); \gamma),$$

where α_m and α_f are proxy measures for men's and women's bargaining power. This formulation provides a direct test of the unitary model. Holding everything else constant, the effect of the change of an individual's bargaining power on demand for good i should be equal to zero:

$$\partial x_i / \partial x_j = 0 \quad \text{with } j = m, f.$$

In the bargaining model, consumption and labor supply decisions are derived from a bargaining process that depends on the negotiating power of the members of the households; these partial derivatives are not equal to zero. Variants of this model have been used to explain observations such as the increases in households' expenditures on child nutrition, health, and education after women's incomes have risen relatively more than those of their male spouses (Hoddinott and Haddad 1995; Duflo and Udry 2004). Another empirical observation rationalized by the bargaining model is the weak agricultural supply response in household characterized by large asymmetric intrahousehold bargaining power (Udry 1996).[7]

The relevance of the bargaining model for the theme of this volume should be clear: expanded trade can directly affect women's incomes and thus increase or decrease their negotiating power. This change in the balance of power within the household has consequences for its consumption and investment choices. In particular, a reduction in women's revenues can reduce human capital accumulation for their children and thus affect long-term growth and poverty reduction.

Finally, a change in women's opportunities for remunerated activity outside the household has important effects on the division of labor inside the household. By changing the relative price (or remuneration) of market activities with respect to household work, trade reforms can affect labor supply—and even produce welfare-inferior outcomes (see Ghosh and Kanbur 2008). Because of data limitations—properly accounting for these effects requires households surveys that collect data on time use—the studies included in this volume do not incorporate this important gender aspect of the trade and poverty nexus (a good collection of studies on these issues is found in Blackden and Wodon 2006).

From Theory to Practice: Data and Methodology

Economic theory offers various hypotheses on the sign and magnitude of the gender-related links between trade and poverty. The next step—empirically verifying the theory—is not straightforward. Explicit testing of some of the hypotheses is difficult because of measurement issues and the fact that it is almost impossible to find historical cases in which trade shocks are the only shock. Isolating trade-related shocks from other simultaneous shocks, accurately measuring change in incomes and poverty rates, and identifying true causality from a macro shock to its micro consequences are complex tasks (Bourguignon, Bussolo, and Pereira da Silva 2008).

Cross-country econometrics captures some empirical regularities, suggesting that some of the theoretical links mentioned above actually operate in the real world. These correlations and regression analyses cannot prove causality, however, or discriminate among the different hypotheses advanced by competing theories. More important, even if the crucial measurement and simultaneity issues could be resolved, the results obtained from such cross-country analyses would not be very useful to policy makers, because such analyses do not provide any insights on how policy interventions can take advantage of the established cross-country relations. To achieve policy relevance, empirical analysis needs to be based on structural models in which agents' behavior, policy levers, or both are explicitly included and country specificity is taken account of, as it is in detailed single-country case studies.[8]

Adopting this approach—by applying the methods of the parallel literature on the evaluation of microeconomic policies (such as conditional cash transfers and unemployment benefits), for instance—represents a step forward, but additional methodological challenges need to be overcome. Both ex ante and ex post appraisals of the gender and poverty effects of a macroeconomic policy such as trade reform require that three distinct issues be addressed.

First, because of its general equilibrium effects, trade policy affects the entire economy, directly and indirectly. It is therefore not possible to identify a control group of nontreated individuals. A policy can still have different effects on heterogeneous individuals, however; individual level analysis is needed to capture these differential impacts. Second, a proper evaluation of the gender and poverty effects of a macro policy needs to include micro and macro counterfactuals, with macro counterfactuals usually examined in a general equilibrium setting. Third, not only are different models used to tackle macro and micro issues, different datasets are employed to evaluate those models. Aggregate national accounts data, or sectorally disaggregated ones, are normally used to investigate international trade questions; micro data from household surveys are used in gender and poverty analyses.

Reconciliation between these two data sources is almost never attempted, creating a fierce debate. The central issue in this debate has been that consumption in household surveys, which are used to measure poverty, has been growing less rapidly than consumption estimated in national accounts. This is the case for the world as a whole and for large developing countries, such as China and India. Plausible explanations account for this growth differential. For example, richer households tend to be underrepresented in household surveys, leading to lower consumption growth rates. Conversely, some rapidly growing items, such as increased marketization of personal services such as food preparation, tend to boost growth of consumption in national accounts.

Researchers have not settled on a common methodology to resolve this debate. Consequently, they disagree on the pace of poverty reduction in the recent era of growth and globalization.[9] Although not central to this volume, readers should be aware of this debate and the fact that some of the methods used here rely on national accounts data and others on household surveys.

The collection of chapters in this volume comes very close to an ideal macro-micro evaluation technique that explicitly confronts the issues just described. A first set of contributions deals with ex ante general equilibrium methods. Rather than the typical statistical testing of hypotheses, these methods, by embedding general equilibrium theory with data and econometrically estimated or calibrated parameters, allow different scenarios to be formulated. The value added consists of identifying the different direct and indirect channels of transmission between trade shocks, gender, and poverty and quantifying their relative importance. If the theory behind them is accepted, these models offer a very useful experimental setting within which different policies, including trade reforms and corrective interventions, can be simulated and their simultaneous effects on women and poverty readily observed.

This first part of this volume contains a set of studies focused on the macro linkages between trade and gender. The labor market structure, in terms of the initial employment levels by gender, sector, and skill, and how this market is functioning are the main factors affecting the links between trade and poverty via the gender dimension. Trade-related dynamics effects and their gender-differentiated impacts are also considered in part I.

The second group of contributions is based on microeconometric models of households. These chapters attempt to discern ex post traces of the trade shock in the micro data. These models are designed to address the heterogeneity observed at the household level and to answer questions about the changes in within-household inequality caused by improved economic opportunities for women.

A word on the specific countries analyzed in the following chapters—Ghana, Senegal, Uganda, and Honduras—completes the description of the empirical strategy adopted in this volume. The geographical emphasis is on sub-Saharan Africa, for several reasons. First, following almost to the letter the so-called Washington Consensus, countries in this region implemented wide-ranging market-friendly reforms, including trade liberalization. The growth and poverty reduction results have been disappointing (Chen and Ravallion 2001; Rodrik 2005).[10]

Second, prices of internationally traded agricultural commodities, both food and export crops, rose significantly between 2003 and 2007. Given the economic structure of African economies and the fact that a large share of poor people is concentrated among the rural and agriculture-dependent population, these price increases can have significant effects on poverty.

Third, women in sub-Saharan Africa are among the most "time-poor" women in the world. In all countries women combine household tasks with formal and informal market work; because of lower average incomes and higher young dependency rates, African women have to work harder than women in other regions.[11] Although not explicitly analyzed in this volume, this time constraint affects African women's adaptability and ability to take advantage of the new opportunities arising from trade expansion (as mentioned above, special surveys are needed to analyze this).

Within this regional context, Ghana, Senegal, and Uganda were identified as attractive case studies because they have recently experienced significant poverty reductions—in contrast to the general regional trend—and have been fairly active in their reforms of trade policy.[12] These three countries have low incomes (in 2004 gross national incomes per capita were $380 in Ghana, $630 in Senegal, and $250 in Uganda).[13] They are also aid and import dependent, with very large agriculture sectors that remain the most important employers of their large unskilled young populations (cocoa, groundnuts, and coffee are their main export crops). Manufacturing plays only a small role in these countries, with very little in the way of diversified merchandise exports.

The three countries also share features that distinguish them from the rest of the region. Growth and poverty trends in Ghana, Uganda, and, to a somewhat lesser extent, Senegal have been impressive. Between 1990 and 2002, GDP in Ghana rose by an average annual rate of 4.3 percent (1.8 percent in per capita terms). GDP growth in Uganda averaged 6.0 percent a year (3.3 percent in per capita terms), while Senegal grew at an average rate of 2.9 percent (0.3 percent in per capita terms). This growth has helped spur massive declines in poverty. At the international poverty line of $1 a day, poverty headcounts fell from 51.7 percent in 1991–92 to 39.5 percent in 1998–99 in Ghana, from 55.7 percent in 1992–93 to 37.7 in 2002–03 in Uganda, and from 67.8 percent in 1994 to 57.1 percent in 2001 in Senegal. In contrast, progress for the Sub-Saharan region between 1990 and 2002 regional averaged just 2.7 percent a year—about equal to population growth, implying stagnant per capita income. The poverty headcount ratio remained roughly constant (rising from 44.6 percent in 1990 to 45.7 percent in 1999), and inequality slightly worsened (see Chen and Ravallion 2001).

Analysts have advanced various hypotheses to explain the significant poverty reductions observed in Ghana, Senegal, and Uganda. One is the increase in commodity prices. The coffee boom of the mid-1990s brought tangible benefits to poor people in Uganda (Bussolo and others 2006). World Bank (2007) provides evidence of a sharp reduction of poverty among cocoa producers in Ghana, thanks to a growing stock of human capital and an improving investment climate. Although most studies qualify the overall progress and point out areas of concern—Azam and others (2007) note that Senegal's growth has not been pro-poor, for example, and World Bank (2007) highlights widening inequality in Ghana—there is very little evidence on the role played by gender following trade liberalization and growth.[14]

The studies in this volume attempt to fill this gap. They try to isolate what happens to sectoral employment by women and to wage gaps in response to trade liberalization and enhanced growth. In the micro-based studies, the main focus is on tracing the effect of the shocks to agricultural prices on poverty through changes in

rural incomes and the related adjustment of intrahousehold allocation of resources.

A country from a different region was added for comparability
purposes. Honduras is among the poorest ones in Latin America and
the Caribbean, with per capita income of $1,040 in 2004 ($2,980 in
purchasing power parity terms). About 20.7 percent of its population lived on less than $1 a day in 1999.[15] Since the beginning of the
1990s, Honduras has been implementing trade liberalization measures, culminating with the signature of the Central America Free
Trade Agreement (CAFTA) with the United States in 2005. With an
openness ratio of more than 90 percent, Honduras is one of the most
trade-dependent countries in the region.

Including Honduras among the case studies in this volume allows
illustration of mechanisms by which the trade, gender, and poverty
linkages operate in formal labor markets outside the agriculture sector. The female employment structure and income sources are quite
different in Honduras and the sub-Saharan African countries examined: about two-thirds of all working women have a job in the tertiary
sector, and many of them participate in the *maquila* segment, which
is directly linked to international markets. Therefore, the main focus
in the Honduras case is on gender discrimination in labor markets, an
important and complementary issue to the intrahousehold women
bargaining power dealt with in the African case studies.

Overview of the Volume

This volume opens with a review of the literature on trade and gender. This survey offers interested readers an extensive list of references and places the studies in this collection in the context of the
empirical literature on this subject.

Part I The Macro Approach: Social Accounting Matrices and Computable General Equilibrium Models of Trade, Gender, and Poverty

Part I includes four ex ante macro studies that consider the effects
of expanding trade flows on gender employment and wage gaps.
From these effects, these analyses infer the potential poverty consequences of the trade shocks.

The first two contributions use the simplest available method: multiplier analysis applied to Social Accounting Matrices (SAMs). The
first SAM multiplier model is applied to Kenya (chapter 3). Rather
than exploring the standard effects of a demand shock on production

and income levels, this case uses the multiplier model to assess the impact of a price shock on the cost of goods consumed by households. This chapter estimates the impact of an oil price shock on different households based on their poverty status and the gender of their heads. It shows that a 25 percent increase in the price of oil would cause a 9.1 percent increase in the cost of living for the average Kenyan household. Because of differences in consumption patterns, richer households are likely to suffer larger changes in their cost of living (9.3 percent) than poor households (8.8 percent); households with male heads could also be slightly more affected (with their cost of living rising 9.2 percent) than households with female heads (for whom the cost of living would rise 9.0 percent).

In chapter 4, a SAM–based multiplier model for Senegal is used to assess how increased demand in various sectors of the economy—especially a boom in tourism—could affect the incomes of women and men. The authors find that the impact on female labor income of an expansion in tourism is weaker than that of some other sectors, such as agriculture and financial services, although among export- oriented sectors, tourism is the sector in which women could gain the most from growth. For an increase in demand for tourism services equivalent to CFAF 1.0 (Commaunité Financière Africaine franc), female labor incomes increase by CFAF 0.37. Were the additional demand originating from the agriculture or financial services, the increases in female incomes would be CFAF 0.43 and CFAF 0.36, respectively. The direct impact of tourism expansion on female labor incomes is significant because this sector employs a large share of female workers. Indirect impacts of tourism growth, through multiplier effects, are also relevant, however. In fact, almost two-thirds of the labor income gains come from indirect as opposed to direct effects.

The results obtained with the SAM multipliers model used in these case studies are useful, but they depend on some strong assumptions. No behavioral response is taken into account, and the model cannot be used to simultaneously simulate price and quantity shocks (when a price shock is simulated, quantities are held constant; when a quantity shock is simulated, prices are held constant). By considering both the direct and the indirect effects, a SAM multipliers model produces general equilibrium results, but it also assumes that agents do not reoptimize their choices following a shock. In fact, a strong and long-lasting increase in the price of oil would almost certainly produce adjustments in the consumption and production structure of an economy, with consumers and producers trying to substitute their use of oil with other inputs for their energy needs. Because these substitutions are not accounted for in the multipliers model, the estimates obtained should be interpreted more as short-term initial effects than as long-term effects. With these caveats in mind, one can also say that the simplicity of the multipliers model is also its strength, because such a model is easy to understand and its results can be easily communicated and replicated.

Chapter 5 uses a computable general equilibrium (CGE) model to overcome the main limitation of no behavioral responses of SAM models. While many additional extensions to the modeling framework, more data work, and more realistic trade policy scenarios for specific trade reforms are required before any policy lessons can be drawn, the analysis in this chapter provides a number of interesting findings.

First, trade liberalization exacerbates existing gender wage gaps in all three African countries considered here, especially among unskilled workers. In contrast, in Honduras it has a small equalizing effect on the gender wage gap. This reflects the fact, already highlighted for Senegal by the simpler SAM multiplier analysis, that the African countries are more agricultural and that female workers in agricultural economies are more involved in import-competing activities such as food crops whereas male workers are better able to take advantage of expanding export opportunities (in cocoa and mining, for example). In contrast, female workers are relatively more involved in export activities in the semi-industrial Honduran economy. Related to this is an increase in the wage premium to urban and skilled workers. To the extent that the poor are more likely to be female, rural, and unskilled, these results raise concerns that trade liberalization may hurt the most vulnerable (or disproportionately benefit the least vulnerable).

Second, productivity/efficiency gains—directly linked to increased openness brought about by trade liberalization—generally increase the gender wage gap. This is because, in the country cases studied here, a majority of male workers earn wages from sectors in which openness increases most under trade liberalization, because of either high initial tariff rates or a strong export response. These impacts vary between and within countries, underscoring the importance of country-level analysis.

The first main result from this CGE analysis is driven by the data: the gender intensity of the tradable sectors. Taking account behavioral responses yields more precise and reliable results than those obtained from multipliers models. But CGE models do not normally generate very large changes in factor intensities. Moreover, the full employment assumption as well as the degree of substitutability between male and female workers strongly influence the results and thus need to be verified for the specific country cases.

The second main result—that the productivity increase caused by the trade policy change further hurts women—depends on parameters borrowed from the econometric literature; their applicability to the specific cases can be challenged. Sensitivity analysis of the results with respect to these key assumptions and parameter values, which could confirm how robust the results are, should be part of future research.

Part II The Micro Approach: Household Models of Trade, Gender, and Poverty

The second part of the volume comprises four ex post studies based on microeconometric techniques. It is often argued that men control incomes from export crops within rural households. It is also argued that consumption preferences differ between men and women, with women allocating a larger share of their resources to the well-being of their children (through greater spending for education, for example). Changes in producer prices for export crops may therefore redistribute resources within the household, leading to a decrease in the share of spending (and perhaps even the level of spending) allocated to investments in human capital for children. This decline in investment in education could in turn lead to a reduction in long-term prospects for poverty reduction, especially in rural areas.

Chapter 6 tests whether this is the case in Senegal. The results suggest that an increase in groundnut income through higher producer prices could lead to a decrease in education spending through a lower share of household income controlled by women. The effect is not large, however, and is likely to be compensated for by the positive impact of higher total income.

To the extent that trade expansion changes women's employment opportunities or their relative wages—and the income pooling hypothesis does not hold—trade should have an effect on the intrahousehold allocation of resources. But the case of Uganda, analyzed in chapter 7, seems to yield different conclusions. Recent household-level data show that the income derived from coffee, the country's main cash crop and export product, has been increasingly pooled between men and women. A similar conclusion can be reached by analyzing the evidence for Ghana (chapter 8), which shows that cocoa income is being spent on goods preferred by the household, not only by men, as traditionally believed. In both Uganda and Ghana, trade expansion would increase the gaps in gender earning, but the asymmetries would be eliminated within households. Trade expansion in agricultural-based African economies increases growth and gender earning gaps, but, in two out of three African countries analyzed, the gender disparities do not translate into an unfavorable reallocation of resources within the household.

Chapter 9 considers the case of Honduras, where the focus on gender inequality shifts from intrahousehold bargaining issues to the labor market. This chapter attempts to identify and estimate the strength of the reduction in poverty caused by the improved opportunities the expanding *maquila* sector offered women. *Maquila* firms appear to be less discriminatory than other firms, with a narrower gender wage gap. The overall gender wage gap is falling over time—at least partly as a result of the growing *maquila* sector. A simulation exercise shows that, at a given point in time, poverty would have been about 1.5 percentage points higher had the *maquila* sector not existed in Honduras. Of this increase in poverty, 0.35 percentage points can be attributable to the wage premium paid to *maquila* workers, 0.1 percentage points to the wage premium received by women in the sector, and 1 percentage point to employment creation by the sector. Given that female *maquila* workers represent only 1.1 percent of the active population in Honduras, this contribution to poverty reduction is significant.

Overall, the messages of this volume are very clear: trade expansion exacerbates gender disparities in agricultural-based African economies and reduces them in manufacturing-based economies like Honduras. For a constant rate of growth, a deterioration in household income distribution triggered by further gender disparities results in less poverty reduction. Gender disparities are an important determinant of the short-term poverty elasticity of growth. Through their effect on human capital investment at the household level, they also determine long-term growth and hence the potential for long-term poverty alleviation. Admittedly, the magnitude of the links between trade shocks, producer prices, male versus female bargaining power, consumption decisions, future growth, and poverty reduction does not seem large. This should not be surprising, however, as crop prices are just one factor determining farmers' incomes (and an even smaller factor in determining the proportion of female income in total household income). Even within these limitations, however, in Senegal about 20 percent of the total effect on education expenditures generated by an increase in groundnut incomes is erased by the worsening distribution of power within the household.

Trade liberalization brings important gender effects, but the evidence presented in this volume suggests that these effects tend to be of a small and sometimes uncertain magnitude. Moreover, where trade liberalization exacerbates gender disparities, these effects are not strong enough to overcome the positive income effects triggered by higher exports.

In policy-relevant terms, this collection of macro and micro analyses advances the thesis that trade liberalization should not be halted because of concerns over potential negative effects on women, because overall income growth effects seem to compensate for these effects. This does not mean that trade-related gender inequality effects should be ignored. Reducing gender gaps with complementary policies before, during, and after implementing trade policy reforms could increase the gains achieved. This volume provides a set of methodologies that can help identify outcomes of trade reforms that affect males and females differently. It can thus help policy makers design complementary mechanisms that enhance the positive effect of trade liberalization for everyone.

Notes

1. A review by Buvinic and Gupta (1997) of 61 case studies finds female-headed households to be disproportionately represented among the poor in only 38 cases. Quisumbing, Haddad, and Pena (2001) find that the relation between female headship and poverty is strong in only 2 out of 10 countries examined.

2. These results are obtained using micro data from household surveys for more than 70 developing countries (see Ackah and others 2008 and www.worldbank.org/prospects/gidd). A regression of per capita incomes finds that the coefficient for an index of femininity of the household—namely, the share of adult females to total adults—is negative and highly significant, even when the mentioned controls and country fixed effects are included. A precedent of the use of such a femininity index and of similar findings is found in Haddad's (1991) study of Ghana.

3. Qian (2005, p. 5) shows that "the number of *missing women,* which is particularly high in China, decreased in tea-producing regions compared to other regions. For the same increase in total household income, an increase in female income of $7 per month (10 percent) translates into a 1 percentage point increase in the survival rate for girls."

4. The following paragraphs draw on Quisumbing and Maluccio (2003).

5. The equation is derived straightforwardly from the dual problem of maximization of consumption (see, for example, Deaton 1997). For a standard application of this model to rural households, see Singh, Squire, and Strauss (1986).

6. An equivalence scale, accounting for the fact that different members in the households have different needs, can also be used to estimate per capita welfare levels.

7. In his examination of farm households in Burkina Faso, Udry (1996) finds that yields on female-owned plots are substantially lower than yields on male-owned plots because they are less intensively farmed. Because of diminishing returns, households could increase production by reallocating inputs, primarily labor, from male to female plots. The fact that this does

not take place suggests that prevailing bargaining processes (sharing rules and negotiated compensations) do not lead to efficient outcomes. A key reason for this outcome is that women's property rights on their land tend to be weaker (or less protected) than those of men. In such a situation, women fear that a potential consequence of sharing their land with men could be losing the property rights over it (after a while, men could start claiming that their work on the land is proof of ownership over it).

8. For a discussion of the advantages of this approach, see Bourguignon, Bussolo, and Pereira da Silva (2008) on the micro effects of macro shocks and Srinivasan and Bhagwati (2001) for the specific case of the relation between openness and growth.

9. Key references on this debate include Bhalla (2002), Ravallion (2003), Deaton (2005), Sala-i-Martin (2006), and Bourguignon, Bussolo, and Pereira da Silva (2008). The debate is relevant for policy making. Deaton (2005, p. xx) reports on the well-known case of private consumption in India, noting that "consumption growth and poverty reduction rates calculated from the surveys appear to be much slower than the same rates estimated from national accounts. And so supporters of additional market-friendly reforms of the Indian economy appeal to the positive results from the national accounts, whereas opponents of the reforms use the sluggish poverty reduction shown in the survey as a proof against the recent or even further liberalizations."

10. Rodrik (2005, pp. 2–3) notes that "most people would agree that when we evaluate the nature of policies today in Latin America and in most of sub-Saharan Africa, then by the conventional standards of how much liberalization, how much privatization, how much macroeconomic stabilization, how much openness to trade has actually taken place, the quality of policies in these two important regions is much better than it was about two to three decades ago. A lot of reform *has* taken place.... it is now commonly accepted that the countries that adopted [the Washington Consensus] have under-performed."

11. As the World Bank reports (2001, p. 66), "Women tend to work significantly more hours than men when both market and household work are taken into account.... evidence suggests that gender disparities in time use tend to be greater among the poor than the rich."

12. Trade liberalization in Ghana, Senegal, and Uganda has included the almost complete removal of quantitative restrictions and considerable tariff cuts. In Ghana the elimination of constraints to international trade remains an important issue in the country's agenda, as presented in its Poverty Reduction Strategy (GPRS) II. Both Ghana and Senegal benefit from preferential access to the European and North American markets; as part of their subregions, they began negotiating an economic partnership agreement (EPA) with the European Union. Uganda is a member of many bilateral and regional trade agreements, notably the Common Market for Eastern and

Southern Africa (COMESA). It has implemented significant unilateral trade liberalization over the past decade in an attempt to eliminate the trade deficit through increased export earnings (Blake, McKay, and Morrissey 2002). Uganda has converted many nontariff restrictions (such as quotas and import bans) into tariff equivalents. Tariff rates of 0, 10, 20, 30, and 60 percent in 1995 were reduced to 0, 7, and 15 percent in 2001 (Morrissey, Rudaheranwa, and Moller 2003). The country currently has the lowest tariffs in COMESA, with an average tariff of 12 percent—far lower than the 33 percent average within COMESA.

13. In purchasing power parity terms, gross national incomes per capita were $1,060 for Ghana, $1,440 for Senegal, and $780 for Uganda in 2004.

14. An important exception is Chao (1999, p. 1), the main objective of which was to "support the government in its efforts to develop a strategy for removing the gender-based barriers to sustainable economic development and poverty reduction in Ghana."

15. This is almost twice the 10.5 percent poverty headcount ratio for Latin America and the Caribbean as a whole. In 1992 the poverty incidence in Honduras was 28.3 percent.

References

Ackah, C., M. Bussolo, R. De Hoyos, and Denis Medvedev. 2008. "A New Dataset on Global Income Distribution." World Bank, Development Prospects Group, Washington, DC. http://www.worldbank.org/prospects/gidd.

Alderman, H, P. A. Chiappori, L. Haddad, J. Hoddinott, and R. Kanbur. 1995. "Unitary versus Collective Models of the Household: Is It Time to Shift the Burden of Proof?" *World Bank Research Observer* 10 (1): 1–19.

Arbache, J., and M. H. Santos. 2005. "Trade Openness and Gender Discrimination." World Bank, Office of the Africa Region Chief Economist, Washington, DC. siteresources.worldbank.org/INTAFROFFCHIECO/Resources/Trade_Openness_And_Gender.doc.

Artecona, R., and W. Cunninghan. 2002, "Effects of Trade Liberalization on the Gender Wage Gap in Mexico." Gender and Development Working Paper 21, World Bank, Washington, DC.

Azam, J. P., M. Dia, C. Tsimpo, and Q. Wodon. 2007. "Has Growth in Senegal after the 1994 Devaluation Been Pro-Poor?" In *Growth and Poverty Reduction: Case Studies from West Africa*, ed. Q. Wodon, 45–67. World Bank Working Paper 79, Washington, DC.

Becker, Gary S. 1971. *The Economics of Discrimination.* Chicago: University of Chicago Press.

Bhalla, Surjit S. 2002. "Imagine There Is No Country: Poverty, Inequality, and Growth in the Era of Globalization." Institute for International Economics, Washington, DC.

Black, Sandra E., and Elizabeth Brainerd. 2002. "Importing Equality? The Impact of Globalization on Gender Discrimination." NBER Working Paper 9110, National Bureau of Economic Research, Cambridge, MA. www.nber.org/papers/w9110.

Blackden C. Mark, and Quentin Wodon, eds. 2006. "Gender, Time Use, and Poverty in Sub-Saharan Africa." World Bank Working Paper 73, Washington DC.

Blake, Adam, Andrew McKay, and Oliver Morrissey. 2002. "The Impact on Uganda of Agricultural Trade Liberalisation." *Journal of Agricultural Economics* 53 (2): 365–81.

Bourguignon, François. 2002. "The Growth Elasticity of Poverty Reduction: Explaining Heterogeneity across Countries and Time Periods." DELTA Working Paper, Département et Laboratoire d'Economie Théorique et Appliquée, Ecole Normale Supérieure, Paris.

Bourguignon, F., and P.-A. Chiappori. 1992. "Collective Models of Household Behavior: An Introduction." *European Economic Review* 36 (2–3): 355–64.

Bourguignon, François, Maurizio Bussolo, and Luiz Pereira da Silva. 2008. *The Impact of Macroeconomic Policies on Poverty and Income Distribution: Macro-Micro Evaluation Techniques and Tools.* Washington, DC: World Bank.

Browning, M., and P.-A. Chiappori. 1998. "Efficient Intra-Household Allocations: A General Characterization and Empirical Tests." *Econometrica* 66 (6): 1241–78.

Bussolo, M., O. Godart, J. Lay, and R. Thiele. 2006. "The Impact of Commodity Price Changes on Rural Households: The Case of Coffee in Uganda." *Agricultural Economics* 37 (2–3): 293–303.

Buvinic, M., and G. Rao Gupta. 1997. "Female-Headed Households and Female-Maintained Families: Are They Worth Targeting to Reduce Poverty in Developing Countries?" *Economic Development and Cultural Change* 45 (2): 259–80.

Chao, Shiyan. 1999. "Ghana, Gender Analysis and Policymaking for Development." World Bank Discussion Paper 403, Washington, DC.

Chen, Shaohua, and Martin Ravallion. 2001. "How Did the World's Poorest Fare in the 1990s?" *Review of Income and Wealth* 47 (3): 283–300.

Deaton, Angus. 1997. *The Analysis of Household Surveys: A Microeconometric Approach to Development Policy.* Baltimore, MD: Johns Hopkins University Press for the World Bank.

———. 2005. "Measuring Poverty in a Growing World (or Measuring Growth in a Poor World)." *Review of Economics and Statistics* 87 (1): 1–19.

De Hoyos, Rafael E. 2006. "Structural Modelling of Female Labour Participation and Occupation Decisions." Cambridge Working Paper in Economics 0611, Faculty of Economics, University of Cambridge.

Duflo, Esther. 2005. "Gender Equality in Development," BREAD Policy Paper 011, Bureau for Research and Economic Analysis of Development, Center for International Development, Harvard University, Cambridge, MA.

Durlauf, Steven N. 2001. "Manifesto for a Growth Econometrics." *Journal of Econometrics* 100 (1): 65–69.

Filmer, Deon. 1999. "The Structure of Social Disparities in Education: Gender and Wealth." Background paper for *Engendering Development*, World Bank, Washington, DC. www.worldbank.org/prr/filmer.pdf.

Ghosh, Suman, and Ravi Kanbur. 2008. "Male Wages and Female Welfare: Private Markets, Public Goods, and Intrahousehold Inequality." *Oxford Economic Papers* 60 (1): 42–56.

Haddad, Lawrence. 1991. "Gender and Poverty in Ghana: A Descriptive Analysis of Selected Outcomes and Processes." *IDS Bulletin* 22 (1): 5–16.

Haddad, Lawrence, and Ravi Kanbur. 1990. "How Serious Is the Neglect of Intra-Household Inequality?" *Economic Journal* 100 (402): 866–81.

Hoddinott, John, and Lawrence Haddad. 1995. "Does Female Income Share Influence Household Expenditures? Evidence from Côte d'Ivoire." *Oxford Bulletin of Economics and Statistics* 57 (1): 77–96.

Lipton, Michael. 1983. "Demography and Poverty." World Bank Staff Working Paper 623, Washington, DC.

Marcoux, Alain. 1998. "The Feminization of Poverty: Claims, Facts, and Data Needs." *Population and Development Review* 24 (1): 131–39.

Milner, Chris, and Peter Wright. 1998. "Modelling Labour Market Adjustment to Trade Liberalization in an Industrializing Economy." *Economic Journal* 108 (March): 509–28.

Morrison, A., D. Raju, and N. Sinha. 2007. "Gender Equality, Poverty and Economic Growth." Policy Research Working Paper 4349, World Bank, Washington, DC.

Morrissey O., N. Rudaheranwa, and L. Moller. 2003. "Trade Policies, Performance and Poverty in Uganda." Uganda Trade and Poverty Project, funded by the Department for International Development, London.

Nicita, A., and S. Razzaz. 2003. "Who Benefits and How Much? How Gender Affects Welfare Impacts of a Booming Textile Industry." Policy Research Working Paper 3029, World Bank, Washington, DC.

Paul-Mazumdar, P., and A. Begum. 2002. "The Gender Imbalances in the Export- Oriented Garment Industry in Bangladesh." Policy Research Report on Gender and Development Working Paper 12, World Bank, Washington, DC.

Qian, Nancy. 2005. "Missing Women and the Price of Tea in China: The Effect of Sex-Specific Income on Sex Ratios." Department of Economics, Brown University, Providence, RI.

Quisumbing, Agnes R., Lawrence Haddad, and Christine L. Pena. 2001. "Are Women Overrepresented among the Poor?" FCND Discussion

Paper 115, Food Consumption and Nutrition Division, International Food Policy Research Institute, Washington, DC.

Quisumbing, Agnes R., and John A. Maluccio. 2003. "Resources at Marriage and Intrahousehold Allocation: Evidence from Bangladesh, Ethiopia, Indonesia, and South Africa. *Oxford Bulletin of Economics and Statistics* 65 (3): 283–328.

Ravallion, Martin. 2001. "Growth, Inequality and Poverty: Looking Beyond Averages." *World Development* 29 (11): 1803–15.

———. 2003. "Measuring Aggregate Welfare in Developing Countries: How Well Do National Accounts and Surveys Agree?" *Review of Economics and Statistics* 85 (3): 645–52.

Rodrik, Dani. 2005. "Rethinking Growth Strategies." In *WIDER Perspectives on Global Development*, 201–25. London: Palgrave-Macmillan, in association with UNU-WIDER.

Rodrik, Dani, and Francisco Rodríguez. 2001. "Trade Policy and Economic Growth: A Skeptic's Guide to the Cross-National Evidence." In *Macroeconomics Annual 2000*, ed. Ben Bernanke and Kenneth S. Rogoff. Cambridge, MA: MIT Press for the National Bureau of Economic Research.

Sala-i-Martin, Xavier. 2006. "The World Distribution of Income: Falling Poverty and... Convergence, Period." *Quarterly Journal of Economics* 121 (2): 351–97.

Singh, Inderjit, Lyn Squire, and John Strauss. 1986. "A Survey of Agricultural Household Models: Recent Findings and Policy Implications." *World Bank Economic Review* 1 (1): 149–79.

Srinivasan, T. N., and Jagdish Bhagwati. 2001. "Outward-Orientation and Development: Are Revisionists Right?" In *Trade, Development and Political Economy: Essays in Honour of Anne O. Krueger*, ed. Deepak Lal and R. H. Snape, 3–26. London: Palgrave.

Udry, C. 1996. "Gender, Agricultural Production, and the Theory of the Household." *Journal of Political Economy* 104 (5): 1010–46.

Winters, L. Alan. 2002. "Trade Liberalization and Poverty: What Are the Links?" *World Economy* 25 (9): 1339–67.

Wood, A. 1991. "North–South Trade and Female Labor in Manufacturing: An Asymmetry." *Journal of Development Studies* 27 (2): 168–89.

World Bank. 2001. *Engendering Development.* New York: Oxford University Press for the World Bank.

———. 2007. "Ghana—Country Economic Memorandum: Meeting the Challenge of Accelerated and Shared Growth." Report No. 40934, World Bank, Washington DC.

2

The Gender Effects of Trade Liberalization in Developing Countries: A Review of the Literature

Marzia Fontana

Gender inequalities and trade interact. As with other economic policies, trade policies are likely to have gender-differentiated effects, because women and men have differential access to and control over resources and because they play different roles in both the market economy and the household. Gender inequality may limit the gains from trade, through its impact on the process of innovation or the terms of trade, for instance.[1]

This chapter explores one dimension of the relation between gender and trade: the impact of trade expansion on gender inequalities in developing countries. It focuses on the impact of increased trade in goods and services. It does not analyse studies in related areas, such as financial liberalization or labor standards.

Interest in the gender effects of trade policies has been growing. Since the first comprehensive review of empirical evidence in this area (Joekes and Weston 1994) was published, several initiatives have been promoted, in the form of lobbying, awareness campaigns, and training. These initiatives include various projects by the Commonwealth Secretariat (Atthill and others 2007) and by several women's nongovernmental organizations (NGOs), such as London-based One World Action and Washington, DC–based Women's

EDGE and the Center of Concern; creation of worldwide networks (such as www.genderandtrade.com); and research. The numerous reviews of the literature (Beneria and Lind 1995; Cagatay 2001; Fontana, Joekes, and Masika 1998; Joekes 1999a; Gammage, Jorgensen, and McGill 2002; and Tran-Nguyen and Beviglia-Zampetti 2004, to name a few) vary in emphasis and tone (Bell 2002 focuses mostly on studies documenting negative effects, for example, while El-Kogali and Nizalova 2002 overlook them). Despite intense debate, sound empirical evidence is sparse, with analyses still limited by the absence of gender-differentiated data in many areas and the difficulty of disentangling the effects of trade liberalization from those of other simultaneous changes.

Does trade liberalization reduce or reinforce gender inequalities? The rest of this section develops an analytical framework to help answer this question.

Gender inequalities have various dimensions. A frequently used approach is to distinguish macro-, meso-, and micro-level effects (Elson and Evers 1996). Macro-level analysis involves examining the gender division of the labor force across different productive market and reproductive nonmarket sectors. Meso-level analysis looks at the institutions that help structure the distribution of resources and activities at the micro level. It involves examining gender inequalities in public provision as well as gender biases in the rules of operation of labor, commodity, and other markets. Micro-level analysis examines in greater detail the gender division of labor, resources, and decision making, particularly within the household.

Trade liberalization alters the distribution of income between social groups and between women and men. The main mechanism through which it operates is changes in the relative prices of goods. By modifying incentives, prices may induce reallocation of factors of production across sectors that use them with different intensities and therefore changes in their employment, remuneration, or both. The same variations in relative prices bring about changes in real incomes, which affect groups differently because of differences in their consumption patterns. Trade liberalization is also likely to reduce tariff revenues, which may have group-specific effects on the size and composition of government expenditure.

Trade liberalization can thus affect gender inequalities at all three levels. Gender gaps in market participation may narrow, for example, if the sectors that expand are more female intensive than the sectors that contract (macro). Public provision of social services that favor women (such as health and education) may be undermined if loss of government revenue from reduced tariffs leads to cuts in such services (meso). Female control over household spending may be reduced or extended, depending on whether trade liberalization destroys or creates sources of independent income for women (micro).

The effects of trade liberalization on gender inequalities in a country may be either negative or positive. Many factors mediate the effects and are important in determining final outcomes. They include resource endowments, labor market institutions, systems of property rights, access to markets and information, and other socio-economic characteristics.

Resource endowments matter, because they may influence which factor of production gains from trade. Asian and African countries have experienced divergent outcomes mainly because of differences in their comparative advantage (abundant labor in Asia, abundant natural resources in Africa) (Wood 1994). Whether women benefit from a country's greater exposure to trade depends on which factors of production experience a rise in demand as well as the prevailing gender norms regulating ownership of the factors that stand to gain. Women are more likely to benefit from increases in labor-intensive production, because women's control over their own labor is less restricted than their rights over access to land and natural resources. Property rights in land and access to markets and infrastructure are more relevant to the gender distribution of gains from trade in Africa than in Asia (Joekes 1999b).

Whether changes in output structure translate into changes in employment, in wages, or in a mixture of the two will depend on the characteristics of the labor market.[2] The extent to which women will be able to relocate from contracting to expanding sectors will depend on the level of gender segmentation across sectors and occupations and on the availability of retraining. The extent of change in women's relative wages will be determined by the elasticity of their labor supply, the prevailing forms of wage determination, and the existence and enforcement of antidiscrimination laws. Some of these factors may themselves be affected by trade liberalization. Greater exposure to international competition, for example, may lead firms to intensify gender discrimination in labor markets as a way of cutting their costs (Seguino 2000).

The effects of trade are also likely to vary among women. If new opportunities are created, women's ability to seize them will depend on their education, skills, and age, as well as the social norms and obligations prevailing in their households and communities. Women with infants, for example, would be less likely to respond to new incentives than women with older children.

A useful distinction when analyzing the gender impact of trade policy is that between practical and strategic gender needs (Moser 1989). It is important to assess not only the impact on women's current material status given their tasks and responsibilities under the established gender division of labor but also whether outcomes contribute to more egalitarian gender relations in the long term, by reducing the basis of women's economic disadvantage and widening women's options.

The review of the evidence presented in this chapter is organized around three questions, which combine elements of the conceptual frameworks outlined above. The next section asks whether trade expansion increases women's employment opportunities relative to men's. It explores whether the creation of new jobs for women challenges the traditional division of labor in the market and whether such jobs provide stable and secure forms of employment in the long term. The following section reviews the evidence on the effects of trade on gender gaps in earnings. It also examines whether trade expansion helps women gain greater control over the income they earn. The third section examines the evidence on intrahousehold reallocation of resources, time, and tasks that may result from trade liberalization. The last section summarizes the chapter's main findings and offers some recommendations for future research.

Does Trade Expansion Increase Employment Opportunities for Women Relative to Men?

Women's participation in paid employment has risen in most countries in recent decades (ILO 2007). While factors other than trade have caused this trend, the increased openness of individual countries has contributed to it, although its effects on women's employment vary by sector and region. Most empirical work has looked at the formal manufacturing sector, partly because of the availability of data. Trade liberalization has led to the feminization of the manufacturing labor force in developing countries. The greater the share of garments, textiles, and electronics in a country's exports, the greater the employment-creating impact of trade has been for women. A cross-country study of formal sector employment in manufacturing in developed and developing countries over the period 1960–85 (Wood 1991) shows a strong correlation between increased exports and increased female employment in manufacturing in the South. Similar trends continued until the mid-1990s (Standing 1999).

Corroboration of these overall trends is found in many country case studies, mostly of export-processing zones (EPZs), which account for much of export-oriented manufacturing. The contribution of EPZs to women's employment has been the subject of much debate (for comprehensive reviews, see Baden and Joekes 1993 and Pearson 1999). While some researchers have focused on the positive impact of the expansion of wage employment for women, others have raised questions about working conditions, lack of training and promotion, and health hazards. The evidence on working conditions is inconclusive. Working conditions generally appear to be poor, but not usually worse than in most other jobs open to women. Some evidence also suggests that young single women, often new migrants to the cities, were the preferred workforce, at least initially, in Asia (Baden and Joekes 1993). But trends are varied and changing, with higher proportions of older, married, and better-educated women in the labor force in some countries (Pearson 1999).

The gains in manufacturing employment appear to have been particularly strong in Asia (not only in the four East Asian "tigers" but also in Bangladesh and Sri Lanka in South Asia and Indonesia, Malaysia, the Philippines, and Thailand in South East Asia), with limited expansion in Latin America (most notably in Mexico but also in Central America and the Caribbean). In sub-Saharan Africa no country has matched Mauritius, where employment in manufactures for export grew by more than a factor of 10 in seven years in the 1980s (Pearson 1999). Mauritius has a different economic structure, and different resource endowments, than the rest of sub-Saharan Africa (Wood and Mayer 2001).

Most recent evidence on the manufacturing sector of the African region reports declines in output and jobs caused by import displacement. Most of the industries affected, however, were not large employers of female labor, so the negative impact has not been borne disproportionately by women. There is some evidence that import competition has damaged activities in which women are involved, including basket weaving in Kenya (Joekes 1999a), textiles in South Africa (Valodia 1996), and the informal sector in urban Zimbabwe (Kanji and Jazdowska 1995). (Information available is limited to specific cases, so no assessment of economywide gains or losses is possible.)

The feminization of employment through export orientation appears to be more common in the manufacturing sector and in semi-industrialized economies than it is in agriculture-based economies. The agricultural export sector, which accounts for the bulk of women's trade-related economic activity in sub-Saharan Africa, remains underresearched. The sparse evidence, from Africa and elsewhere, shows that the impact of expanding agricultural exports is generally less favorable to women and varies according to prevailing sociocultural factors governing the gender division of labor (Joekes 1999b). But the picture is mixed, with differences between traditional export crop production and newer exports, such as horticultural products and agroindustry. Many women have recently found employment in agroindustry, but such jobs may not have improved their status as much as employment in manufacturing.

Expansion of traditional agricultural exports has created employment in some cases, both in the field and in processing and trading activities associated with increased commercialization. But the employment gains appear to be larger for men than for women. Women often work less on more commercialized crops than do men, and they are also less likely to work as hired laborers, most of whom are men (von Braun and Kennedy 1994). Women farmers may find it difficult to become independently involved in the production of export crops because of limited access to credit, technology, and marketing channels. Even if not independently involved, women often increase the amount of time they contribute to their husbands' crops—work for which they are not paid.

The effects of the expansion of agricultural exports vary with the gender intensity of the crops that expand, but this may itself be endogenous. There is evidence, for example, that even when a crop is traditionally female intensive, commercializing it causes men to enter the sector and take over production. This was the case for groundnuts in Zambia (Wold 1997), for example, and rice in The Gambia (von Braun, John, and Puetz 1994).

Nontraditional agricultural exports (NTAEs)—flowers, vegetables, and fruits, often produced on a contract basis for foreign buyers and air-freighted out—are a significant growth area in African agriculture, but they remain relatively small. NTAEs are developed in Kenya, South Africa, Uganda, and Zimbabwe (as well as in Chile, Ecuador, and most of Central America). The sector includes two types of production: small farm contract growers and large-scale commercial farms. On small farms women work as family labor and own-account farmers and are subject to similar constraints as in traditional agriculture. On large farms women work as "modern" agricultural wage labor, and their ability to participate is often unrelated to land rights. Their terms and conditions of employment are more akin to those of industrial workers (Barrientos and Dolan 2003).

There is some evidence that the expansion of exportable services is another source of employment for women, especially in the information and communication sector. The sector includes call centers and simple data entry in India, the Caribbean, and some of the newly industrializing countries (NICs) (Joekes 1995; Mitter, Fernandez, and Varghese 2004). This area is underresearched.

These varying patterns of female employment across regions and sectors support the hypothesis that factor endowments, systems of property rights, and access to resources are key determinants of women's opportunities from trade. Increases in women's employment are greatest in countries that are abundant in unskilled labor and have a comparative advantage in the production of basic manufactures. This is so because women are disproportionately represented among unskilled workers and because prevailing norms make their entitlements to the rewards from their own labor stronger than those of any other factor of production. Women's weaker property rights in land and limited access to the resources required to work on it (caused by strong disadvantages associated with gender biases) have limited the gains from trade to women in Africa. These forces are also likely to have contributed to the weak supply response of African agriculture to export opportunities.

Darity (2007) formalizes some of these aspects in a model of an archetype gender-segregated, low-income economy. He shows how different regimes of gender-related power affect the impact of export expansion. If women resist coercion and are unwilling to work without pay, they will not switch to production of export crops following devaluation, slowing export expansion. Empirical evidence that farm output from a given quantity of household labor is less than the maximum that could be produced can be found in Burkina Faso (Udry 1996; Smith and Chavas 1999), Tanzania (Tijabuka 1994), and Zambia (Wold 1997).

Weak marketing structures and lack of the technical expertise required to comply with regulations and output standards are other important factors preventing women small producers from enjoying the new opportunities created by trade liberalization. Evidence that female producers experience more constraints in accessing international markets than male producers and that women traders are often confined to local markets can be found in Samoa, Mozambique, and other sub-Saharan African countries (Carr 2004; Tran-Nguyen and Bevigilia-Zampetti 2004).

Another constraint that prevents women from seizing new opportunities, in both agriculture and wage employment, is the heavy burden of household responsibilities that falls disproportionately on them. Studies from settings as different as the cut flower industry in Ecuador (Newman 2001), EPZs in the off-farm informal sector in Guatemala (Katz 1995), NTAEs in Kenya (McCulloch and Ota 2002), and rural-urban linkages in Malaysia (Kusago 2000) all point to the presence of other female members in the household as a determinant of women's participation in new opportunities created by trade. These other female household members may be mothers or elder daughters who are available to take on household duties relinquished by women who go out to work. Very little is known about the circumstances of these other females and the impact of trade on their well-being.

Do the newly created jobs for women offer them sustainable gains? Do they challenge gender stereotypes? Determining whether women have benefited from increased work opportunities requires consideration of a range of labor market outcomes, including the type of jobs that women can access and the conditions of those jobs. The evidence suggests that most of these jobs do not appear to provide secure or long-lasting employment opportunities. Many researchers (Standing 1999; Barrientos and Dolan 2003; Kabeer 2003; Chen and others 2005) emphasize growing flexibility and vulnerability in working conditions in export-oriented sectors. The percentage of women in trade-related jobs with temporary or casual status—and few or no benefits—greatly exceeds that of men (Chen and others 2005).

Several studies (Tzannatos 1999; Gammage and Mehra 1999; UN 1999; ILO 2007) find little decline in employment segregation by gender over the past two decades. Female workers have remained confined to female jobs, with little opportunity to enter previously male-dominated sectors and occupations. Women continue to be employed in low-skill and low-pay jobs. Within the manufacturing sector, women are concentrated in assembly line and production work that is semiskilled and short term.

There is evidence of a moderate decline in horizontal segregation in some countries. In the NICs, for example, women are increasingly employed in export-oriented services, such as information processing, tourism, and financial services (ILO 2007). But vertical segregation appears to be persistent, and within-sector hierarchies have become more pronounced. Such is the case in Bangladesh (Paul-Majumder and Begun 2000), Madagascar (Nicita and Razzaz 2003), and Mexico (Fleck 2001), where women are increasingly occupying bottom occupations and men taking up supervisory roles.

In Bangladesh female employment in manufacturing has remained highly concentrated in a single activity (ready-made garments), while other textile subsectors remain predominantly male. In knitwear, for example—the sector with seemingly the best prospects in the post–Multifiber Agreement phase—women constitute only 14 percent of the labor force (Bhattarchaya 1999; Kabeer and Mahmud 2004). In Mexico *maquila* employment has risen significantly more for men than for women in recent years, because of the increased importance of sectors such as transportation equipment. Women's share of the total labor force in EPZs declined from 77 percent in 1980 to 57 percent in 1998 (Fleck 2001). Similar declining trends in the share of female employment in EPZs are found in the Republic of Korea, Malaysia, Mauritius, and Singapore (Kusago and Tzannatos 1998; Gammage and Mehra 1999).

These trends indicate that, over time, the process of feminization of export employment may decline. It is not clear, however, what prevents women from benefiting from upgrading and shifting production toward skill-intensive goods, because gender educational gaps are narrowing in many countries. The number of educated female workers is significant in Malaysia, Singapore, and Sri Lanka, for example, but there is evidence of increasing levels of female unemployment (Malhotra and De Graff 1997). This evidence on educational patterns stresses that it is not just the level of education that counts but also its content, which still has a strong gender bias in many countries. On-the-job training is even more relevant than formal education, and there is evidence that firms continue to prefer investing in training male workers. Whether these processes of defeminization differ across countries could be an interesting area for research.

How Does Trade Affect the Gender Earnings Gap?

Evidence on changes in female and male wages associated with trade liberalization is even sparser than that on employment. It is limited to formal manufacturing and to a few (mainly middle-income) countries. Data exclude the informal sector and at times also small firms in the formal sector, where many women work, thus providing an incomplete picture even of the manufacturing sector. The information on wages is rarely comparable over time or across countries because of problems in definitions. Wage data for males and females are often not disaggregated by skill level. The effects of trade expansion on women's relative wages are not straightforward theoretically, for reasons outlined earlier; empirically, no general conclusions can be drawn from the few studies that have been conducted. Overall, the gender wage gap remains large in most countries, even, surprisingly, where there has been rapid growth in exports that rely on female labor, a fact for which different studies offer different interpretations.

In one of the few cross-country studies of female–male relative wages over the past 20 years, Tzannatos (1999) finds that there has been a more rapid convergence between women's and men's wages in developing countries than was experienced historically in industrial countries. Tzannatos, however, looks at general trends and does not explicitly link wages to trade. It is not clear from this study whether the narrowing of the gender wage gap occurred mainly because wage discrimination has declined or because the educational attainment of women has increased relative to men. Future research should try to disentangle the wage effects of increased educational attainment of women from the effects of trade and other factors.

Trade liberalization may affect wages by altering the relative demand for various types of workers or by influencing discriminatory practices. Most studies investigate the latter aspect. They can be grouped in two schools of thought. Following Becker (1959), some researchers assert that globalization is likely to lead to competitive pressures that will reduce the scope for employers to discriminate, including against women. By contrast, others argue that increased competition may reduce the bargaining power of wage workers, especially female workers, if they are disproportionately employed in sectors competing internationally on the basis of cheap labor.

Consistent with the first school of thought, Oostendorp (2004) finds a negative association between openness (measured as either exports plus imports as a percentage of GDP or foreign direct investment net inflows as a percentage of GDP) and the size of the gender wage gap within occupational categories in a sample of both developed and developing countries between 1983 and 1999. He finds that the narrowing impact of openness on the occupational gender wage gap is confined to the tradable sectors; it is not discernible in the nontradable sectors. The impact is rather small, however, and the quality of the data used uncertain, thus casting doubt on the reliability of the results.[3] Moreover, Oostendorp is not able to establish whether the narrowing of the gender gap reflects a decline in men's wages or an increase in women's wages. This distinction is of some importance.

Berik's (2000) industry-level panel analysis of Taiwan (China) over the 1984–93 period finds that, after controlling for employment segregation by gender and other industry characteristics, greater export orientation is associated with larger adverse effects on men's wages than on women's wages. The period under study is marked by higher job losses for female workers than for male workers. It is possible that, as a result, women who remained in the export sector had higher skills than their male co-workers who kept their jobs but, on average, had fewer skills and earned lower wages. Lack of wage data disaggregated by skills prevents this aspect from being analyzed.

Artecona and Cunningham (2002) find that after accounting for differences in human capital characteristics, the residual gender wage gap declined in Mexico between 1987 and 1993 in concentrated industries with greater exposure to competing imports than in nonconcentrated industries. They interpret this result as evidence supporting Becker's hypothesis that discrimination tends to be reduced in more competitive environments. Their results, however, are not statistically significant. Artecona and Cunningham also find that greater exposure to trade increased the overall gender wage gap in both concentrated and nonconcentrated industries. The gender wage gap declined only in nonconcentrated industries not exposed to trade.

Using the same data set, Ghiara (1999) explores different aspects of the male–female wage differential. These findings are consistent with those of Artecona and Cunningham. Ghiara finds that the economywide wage differential between women and men fell only slightly between 1987 and 1993, with the proportion attributable to discrimination falling marginally and that attributable to endowment differences rising slightly. Analysis of female wages in two industries—tradable machinery and nontradable social services—indicates that the wage differential rose sharply in manufacturing, mainly because of changes in the human capital endowments of women and men. The human capital characteristics of female and male workers in the service industry remained equal, as did their wages. The study emphasizes differences in impact between unskilled and skilled women, concluding that while skilled women in the nontraded service sectors have become better off, unskilled women in manufacturing have become worse off.

Fleck (2001) finds that female–male wage ratios in the *maquila* sector in Mexico vary greatly across industries. The gender wage gap is wider the higher the concentration of women in an industry and the greater the industry's capital intensity. Fleck suggests that the growing number of male workers relative to female workers in the *maquila* sector over time could be caused by lack of available female labor. This seems improbable, however, because other studies document declines in female–male wages, suggesting the phenomenon is more likely to be demand driven.

Evidence from Bangladesh (Bhattarchaya 1999) and Morocco (Belghazi 1995, cited in Joekes 1999a) suggests that, in these countries, wage discrimination against women in the export textile industry was lower than in any other manufacturing sector in the early stages and declined over time more than in other sectors. In Bangladesh trends in female–male wage differentials in garments indicate a narrowing of the gap between 1983 and 1990 but a widening from 1990 to 1997. This change is attributed to a higher proportion of men than women taking up high-skilled jobs and an increase in the number of temporary workers among women (Zohir 1998; Paul-Majumder and Begun 2000). For similar reasons, a widening of the gender wage gap was simulated in Madagascar (Nicita and Razzaz 2003).

A few studies of East Asian countries explain pay discrimination as a result of the employer objective to maintain export competitiveness. These studies predict—and find—that greater openness widens the gender wage gap. Seguino (2000), for example, argues that divergent trends in the unadjusted gender wage ratio in Taiwan (China) and the Republic of Korea between 1981 and 1992 are related to differences in the nature of foreign direct investment flows in the two countries. Greater mobility of capital in Taiwan's female labor–intensive sectors left women workers more vulnerable to losses of bargaining power in wage negotiations. In Korea an environment of more restricted capital mobility encouraged firms to maintain competitiveness by other strategies, such as technological upgrading and improvement in product quality. Seguino (1997) finds that despite strong demand for women's labor, female-male wage differentials in Korea narrowed only marginally between 1975 and 1990. In principle, this could have been because of the existence of surplus female labor, although this seems unlikely in Korea, where unemployment rates have been low.

Berik, Rodgers, and Zveglich (2004) find that increases in international competition in concentrated industries in both Taiwan and Korea between 1981 and 1999 are associated with widening wage gaps between men and women. The more robust regression results are for Taiwan, where rising import shares are associated with rising wage discrimination against women workers in concentrated industries, such as textiles and electronics. In Korea a slight decline in export orientation is weakly associated with a reduction in wage discrimination against female workers in concentrated industries.

It is difficult to draw general conclusions from these studies. The gender wage gap caused by occupational segregation appears to be widening. One of the factors inhibiting the narrowing of the gap is likely to be the informalization of labor contracts through subcontracting and outsourcing (most workers in these arrangements are female). An increasing proportion of women's work in manufacturing is being shifted to the informal sector, where wages are significantly lower than in the formal sector (Balakrishnan 2002).

None of the few studies of gender and earnings in agriculture examines the wage gap between women and men. Instead, these studies explore issues of income control, making greater use of qualitative approaches and small ad hoc surveys than the other work does. A study of tomato contract farming in the Dominican Republic (Raynolds 2001) finds that expansion of NTAEs has enhanced women's ability to renegotiate household rights and obligations and helped them legitimize claims for compensation. Women who managed to claim wages for their contributions were from working-class households and involved to a significant extent in other income-earning activities. Other studies of NTAEs—in Guatemala (Katz 1995), Kenya (von Braun and Immink 1994), and Uganda (Dolan 2001)—find the opposite effects, with women losing control over income and having less of a say on household expenditures.

Being paid does not necessarily entail retaining significant control over income. Even in the manufacturing sector, there are accounts of women handing over a large proportion of their pay to other family members. A survey of more than 800 women factory workers in Pakistan finds that 48 percent of them give their income to their husbands (Hafez 1986, cited in Elson 1999). However, most of the evidence shows that women working in export-oriented industries retain some control over their earnings (Zohir 1998; Kabeer 2000; Kusago and Barham 2001).

Control depends on the type of employment, whether payment is made as a lump sum or in regular installments, and many other factors. Women are likely to have greater control if they work in factories away from male relatives than if they are home based (Kabeer 2000). It is important to consider the effect on all sources of income. Women may find that, once they are earning their own income, there is an offsetting reduction in income transfers from nonmarket sources, particularly from the fathers of their children (Katz 1995). In agriculture a key factor affecting control is whether women participate in the marketing of what they produce (Kiggundu 1996).

Greater control over income enhances women's decision-making power within households. This may have important effects on which items are bought and how what is bought is distributed among household members, with important implications for welfare. These aspects are examined in the next section.

How Does Trade Liberalization Affect Intrahousehold Dynamics?

By changing the employment opportunities and earnings patterns of women and men, trade liberalization is likely to influence the allocation of time and resources among household members. An increase in the market value of a woman's time, for example, would lead her to spend more time on market-oriented activities, while her husband might reallocate some of his time to domestic work or other nonpaid activities. More likely, she would endure a longer working day than her husband, because of strong social and cultural norms that prevent reallocation of household tasks between family members. Which food and nonfood items are purchased, the quantities of these items, and their distribution among household members will also be affected by who earns the income. Because women and men, as well as younger and older people, have different needs and preferences (for health care and nutrition, for example) reallocation of both time and consumption goods will affect their welfare differently. Trade may also affect intrahousehold dynamics through changes in public provision of social services. No study of this issue appears to have been published.

These dimensions are rarely included in analyses of trade impacts, perhaps because they are more difficult to assess than income and employment effects. Most of the studies that include analysis of nutrition, health, and time allocation effects are in agriculture, a sector in which the domestic sphere and market production appear to be more intertwined. The attention paid by these studies to women's work appears to be motivated mainly by concerns about women's role as providers of care to other family members, especially children. "Women's time is valuable not only in agricultural cultivation but also for child nutrition—care in the form of breastfeeding practices, hygiene practices, and psychosocial stimulation has been shown to be as important as food and health for children's welfare" (Paolisso and others 2002, p. 314). This emphasis is important, but women's own well-being should also be given adequate attention.

The most comprehensive study to date of the impact of cash cropping on nutrition was carried out by the International Food Policy Research Institute (IFPRI) (von Braun and Kennedy 1994), using a common research methodology in several countries undergoing agricultural commercialization: The Gambia, Guatemala, Kenya, the Philippines, Rwanda, and, with more limited coverage, Malawi, Papua New Guinea, and Zambia. Commercialization was not directly linked to international trade in all cases, but the findings nevertheless yield important general insights. The main strength of these case studies is their detailed assessments of the commercialization-production-income-consumption-nutrition chain, which come closer than most other studies to adopting a general equilibrium approach.[4] The studies are based on household-level surveys, including both participants and nonparticipants, conducted in the mid-1980s. As this valuable research is about 20 years old, it is surprising that no other studies using similar methodologies have been undertaken more recently.

Despite reallocation of land to new cash crops, staple food production per capita was maintained or even increased in all countries—a challenge to the commonly held view that agricultural export production comes at the expense of food production. Net income gains were generally smaller than gross income from the new cash crops, because of substitution within agricultural production and between agricultural and off-farm employment. These gains were still significant, however, leading to increases in overall household income. Women's direct control over income from the new cash crops was much less than that of men. In none of the studies did women play a significant role as decision makers or managers of the more commercialized crop production, even when typical "women's crops" were promoted (as in The Gambia, where rice was commercialized). In the Guatemala study (von Braun and Immink 1994), reallocation of women's labor time to the new contract for multinational exporters came at the expense of other off-farm activities, which had been a source of independently controlled income for them. In all countries for which information was available, women's income had a beneficial effect on household calorie consumption. Any tendency to spend less on food because of loss of income control by women was generally small, with the increased income from commercialization still resulting in more food being purchased.

Participation in commercialization schemes appeared to have no effect on children's health, although this result may reflect the relatively short time frame of the case studies. In Guatemala membership in the export crop–producing cooperative had a beneficial effect on children's health, but this seems to be because of a special package of health and social services funded from cooperative profits. An important finding from the Kenya study of expansion of sugar cane production (Kennedy 1994) is that increases in women's own income were associated with decreases in their body mass index. For many women energy expenditures increase as a result of the additional work involved in the increase in their income. This increase in the energy intensity of activities exceeded the concurrent increase in their caloric intake.

In her study of the impact of growing broccoli and snow peas in the central highlands of Guatemala, Katz (1995) finds a loss of control over income by females. She finds a statistically significantly greater incidence among export crop adopters of expenditures on several "male" and "joint" goods and substantially lower incidence of purchases of "female" goods, such as pots and buckets. In this case, women's labor contributions to the new male-controlled crops come not at the expense of their own income-generating activities but from sacrifices in domestic production, which may in part be compensated by increased activity of older daughters. Daughters enable their mothers to devote time to the new crops, either by relieving them of some of their domestic responsibilities or by directly contributing labor to their mothers' other income-generating endeavors. One of the many valuable contributions of this study is that of differentiating children by age and thus drawing attention to the role of older children in sharing housework.[5]

A negative impact of NTAEs on young girls' use of time is also found in a study of Uganda (Elson and Evers 1996). Extra demands on women's labor time caused by vanilla production are transferred to their daughters. Pollination by hand at critical stages in the growth cycle is often undertaken by girls at the expense of their schooling. In contrast to the results from the IFPRI studies, Elson and Evers (1996, p.12) find that NTAEs also damage children's health and nutrition: "Increasing workloads of women have led to a decline in breastfeeding and worsening child care practices and food insecurity has been intensified, as families sell food to raise cash for basic family expenses."

The evidence on this point is mixed. In their study of villages in two Ugandan districts, Kasente and others (2002) find that farmers are not compromising food security in response to NTAE incentives. In these villages, men control more than 90 percent of the income from vanilla, but the responsibility of meeting household needs, especially food, falls on women.

Paolisso and others (2002) analyse the impact on male and female time allocation patterns of commercialization of vegetables and fruits in rural Nepal.[6] Compared with nonadopters, participating households with more than one child under the age of five increase working time on vegetables and fruits at the expense of time devoted to other agricultural activities. This is true of both men and women in the household. Time spent on child care increases for women but declines for men. In households with only one preschooler, however, children receive less care from their parents, who work more, especially on vegetable crops but also on food crops. Men's leisure (defined as the sum of time spent on social activities, recreation, or inactivity) increases as a result of participation in the project, while women's leisure is unaffected. The authors suggest that "in the short run there is perhaps scope for protecting childcare time by reducing time to leisure ... At least VFC [vegetable and fruit commercialization] participation has not increased overall work time burdens" (Paolisso and others, p. 326). The study takes into account only time allocation patterns of adult (both female and male) household heads, neglecting other household members, such as older daughters, whose time contributions to their mothers' activities may have increased, as it did in the studies by Katz (1995) and Elson and Evers (1996). Moreover, energy consumption may have increased for women because they perform more strenuous tasks, negatively affecting their well-being but not necessarily translating into declines in their leisure time.

A study of the effects of employment in the flower industry on the time allocation patterns of husbands and wives in Ecuador (Newman 2001) finds that husbands of women working in the flower industry participate more in household work than either husbands of women working in other sectors or husbands of women not involved in paid employment. This positive effect on the gender distribution of household tasks appears to be stronger when men also work in the flower industry. Newman suggests that this result may arise because the gender gap in wages in the flower industry is smaller than in any other sector (a significant number of married women in the flower industry earn higher wages than their male counterparts), but this hypothesis is not tested directly. In households in which both wife and husband work in the flower industry, overall time devoted to household tasks by both partners is less than in other households (299 minutes per day, compared with 348 minutes in families in the same villages working in other sectors and 393 minutes for families in the control group). The share of men in total household work is 25 percent, compared with 17 percent for men in families working elsewhere and only 8 percent in the control group. Even in households in which both partners work in the flower industry, however, the bulk of household work is still performed by women, who spend more than three hours a day on it while men spend about one hour. Like the study of Nepal (Paolisso and others 2002), this study does not consider possible reallocation of household tasks to older children.

Other studies (Jacoby 1993; Skoufias 1993) examine how the time allocation and work of individual household members responds to the activity patterns of other members of the same household. They do not examine responses to trade liberalization opportunities, however.

Fewer studies of the manufacturing sector have explored the impact of trade liberalization on intrahousehold resource allocation. The few that have been conducted explore dimensions that are different from those addressed in the studies of agriculture, for several reasons. First, the characteristics and circumstances of women working in export-oriented manufacturing differ from those of women involved in agricultural production. A significant proportion of female workers in manufacturing are young and single and are often new migrants to cities. They have left their families of origin and not yet formed new ones. Their role in the household is mainly that of a daughter, with relatively few housework responsibilities. They have been able to leave their households partly because their households have other females who could take up their household duties. Second, the nature of the work in manufacturing is different, with fewer direct linkages with food production and consumption decisions than in agriculture. Manufacturing is often located in urban areas, where market substitutes for social and household services are more easily available. As a result, the studies of export-oriented manufacturing and household impact focus more on individual lifestyles—including women's ability to make independent choices about marriage and fertility—and less on nutrition and children's health.

Most studies of manufacturing are of Bangladesh. Hewett and Amin (2000) find that female garment workers marry and first give birth later than women of similar socioeconomic background who do not work in the garment sector. Some female garment workers even make decisions about whom to marry and how many children to have. They are more likely to have better quality housing conditions and access to modern infrastructure. Controlling for income level, women working in the garment sector have a higher propensity than other women to spend their money on jewelry, entertainment, cosmetics, and gifts. The nutritional intake of garment workers appears to be quite high, but they are more likely than other women to suffer from a range of minor health problems (Zohir 1998 reaches the same conclusions). According to Hewitt and Amin (2001), additional health indicators show that female garment workers do not suffer from major health problems and that the cause of the minor problems may be urban living rather than factory conditions.

Most studies (Zohir 1998; Hewett and Amin 2000; Kabeer 2000) appear to agree that women working in factories feel that their status has improved. Garment work positively affects self-esteem and decision making, with benefits extending to other family members. Kusago and Barham (2001) report that migrant daughters in Malaysia who send remittances home to their mothers enable their mothers to express their preferences. Younger sisters in Bangladesh benefit because some garment workers increase their say in decisions regarding their education (Zohir 1998). Some garment workers report that their husbands help them with household work (Zohir 1998); others have been able to escape domestic violence (Kabeer 1995).

Conclusions

A comprehensive assessment of the gender effects of trade reform must analyze changing patterns and conditions of work, including paid and unpaid work; gender gaps in wages; patterns of ownership and control over assets; changes in public provision of social services; and changes in consumption patterns and gender-based power relations within households. The literature has explored some of these dimensions more fully than others.

The employment effects of trade have been most favorable to women in countries that specialize in the production of labor-intensive manufactures. Less well-established property rights in land and other resources than in labor have limited the gains from trade for women in agriculture, especially in Africa. The new employment opportunities for women do not often appear to be secure or to challenge traditional gender roles in the labor market, however. There is evidence of a moderate decline in horizontal segregation, especially in some middle-income Asian countries, but vertical segregation seems to have become more pronounced.

Evidence on the impact of trade on the gender gap in wages is sparser than that on employment and does not permit any general conclusion. The component of the gender wage gap caused by employment segregation appears to be widening.

In most cases women gain greater control over their income by working in export-oriented factories, away from male relatives. Trade liberalization of agriculture, however, often causes them to lose sources of independent income. The impact on women's well-being and that of their family members appears to be more positive for women working in manufacturing than in agriculture, but this area is underresearched.

Lack of data prevents several areas from being investigated adequately. The gender effects of trade in manufacturing are better documented than the effects in other sectors, but this sector employs a relatively small number of women. Most women work in agriculture and the informal sector. Research in these sectors is growing, but very little is known. Sex-disaggregated data on household labor, earnings, and expenditures should be collected more systematically.

The studies reviewed use a variety of approaches, depending on the aspect examined, but most look at specific sectors or households in isolation, neglecting economywide effects and interactions between different dimensions. Recently, computable general equilibrium (CGE) models have been used to assess the gender effects of trade liberalization in a number of developing countries (for a review and examples, see Fontana and Rodgers 2005 and Fontana 2007). This methodology has the potential to complement other ex post empirical evaluations. It could provide the opportunity for a more integrated approach to allow consideration of net impacts and a better understanding of gains and losses from greater exposure to trade.

To serve this purpose, however, it is not sufficient for general equilibrium models to simply disaggregate variables by sex. In order to be credible and useful, such models should incorporate a range of behavioral patterns that capture the nature of unequal gender relations in the economy. For instance, the unpaid sector of reproduction and care should be modeled alongside the market sector; their interaction should be interpreted in a nonmechanical way. A model that represents gender relations adequately would be one in which the characterization of the unpaid sector highlights its essential function as sector contributing to the production, maintenance, and well-being of the labor force. Representing this sector only as a constraint to women's ability to respond to market incentives creates a distorted picture of what takes place in reality and leads to incorrect policy recommendations. Fontana and Rodgers (2005) provide a comprehensive checklist of characteristics required in a gender-aware CGE model.

Notes

Earlier versions of this article appeared as a University of Sussex Discussion Paper in Economics 101 and in the proceedings of the Inter-American Development Bank–Poverty and Economic Policies Network Trade Policy forum, held in Lima June 10–12, 2007. Marzia Fontana's e-mail address is M.Fontana@ids.ac.uk.

1. Van Steveren and others (2007) offer interesting analyses of these issues.

2. The extent of price effects from trade liberalization on the output structure may also vary. It will depend on the strength of various transmission mechanisms, including how easy it is to reallocate resources across sectors.

3. The author needs to make several adjustments to correct for inconsistencies in the ILO October Inquiry survey data used.

4. The approach taken in these studies is even better than general equilibrium modeling, because all relations are estimated empirically, not simulated.

5. This study is also valuable in highlighting factors affecting alternative choices of women for remunerated labor. For example, marketing

activities that require women to be mobile are undertaken only by older women with no young children, independent agricultural activities are undertaken only by women with sons, and so forth.

6. This study uses a combination of qualitative and quantitative methods and innovative collection techniques for time allocation data.

References

Artecona, R., and W. Cunningham. 2002. "Effects of Trade Liberalization on the Gender Wage Gap in Mexico." Gender and Development Working Paper 21, World Bank, Washington, DC.

Atthill, C., S. Thakur, M. Carr, and M. Williams. 2007. *Gender and Trade Action Guide: A Training Resource.* Commonwealth Secretariat, London.

Baden, S., and S. Joekes. 1993. "Gender Issues in the Development of the Special Economic Zones and Open Areas in the People's Republic of China." Institute of Development Studies, Brighton, United Kingdom.

Balakrishnan, R. 2002. *The Hidden Assembly Line: Gender Dynamics of Subcontracted Work in a Global Economy.* Bloomfield, CT: Kumarian Press.

Barrientos, S., and C. Dolan. 2003. "Labour Flexibility in African Horticulture." *ID21 Insights 47*, Institute of Development Studies, Brighton, United Kingdom.

Becker, G. S. 1959. *The Economics of Discrimination.* Chicago: University of Chicago Press.

Bell, E. 2002. "Gender and Economic Globalisation." Bridge Bibliography 12, Institute of Development Studies, Brighton, United Kingdom.

Beneria, L., and K. Lind. 1995. "Engendering International Trade: Concepts, Policy, and Action." Gender and Sustainable Development (GSD) Working Paper 5, Cornell University, Ithaca, NY.

Berik, G. 2000. "Mature Export-Led Growth and Gender Wage Inequality in Taiwan." *Feminist Economics* 6 (3): 1–26.

Berik, G., Y. van der Meulen Rodgers, and J. E. Zveglich. 2004. "International Trade and Gender Wage Discrimination: Evidence from East Asia." *Review of Development Economics* 8 (2): 237–54.

Bhattacharya, D. 1999. "The Post–MFA Challenges to the Bangladesh Textile and Clothing Sector." In *Trade, Sustainable Development and Gender,* 197–232. Geneva: United Nations Conference on Trade and Development.

Cagatay, N. 2001. *Trade, Gender and Poverty.* New York: United Nations Development Programme.

Carr, M., ed. 2004. *Chains of Fortune: Linking Women Producers and Workers with Global Markets.* Commonwealth Secretariat, London.

Chen, M., J. Vanek, F. Lund, and J. Heintz. 2005. *Progress of the World's Women: Women, Work and Poverty.* New York: United Nations Development Fund for Women.

Darity, W. 2007. "The Formal Structure of a Gender-Segregated Low-Income Economy." In *Feminist Economics of Trade,* ed. D. Elson, C. Grown, I. Steveren, and N. Cagatay, 78–90. London: Routledge.

Dolan, C. 2001. "The 'Good Wife': Struggles over Resources in the Kenyan Horticultural Sector." *Journal of Development Studies* 37 (3): 39–70.

El-Kogali, S., and E. Nafilova. 2002. "Does Trade Liberalization Have Gender-Differentiated Effects?" World Bank, Poverty Reduction and Economic Management Gender and Development (PRMGE) Unit, Washington DC.

Elson, D. 1999. "Labor Markets as Gendered Institutions: Equality, Efficiency and Empowerment Issues." *World Development* 27 (3): 611–27.

Elson, D., and B. Evers. 1996. "Gender-Aware Country Economic Reports: Uganda." Genecon Unit Working Paper 2, University of Manchester, United Kingdom.

Fleck, S. 2001. "A Gender Perspective on *Maquila* Employment and Wages in Mexico." In *The Economics of Gender in Mexico,* ed. E. Katz and M. Correia, 133–53. Washington, DC: World Bank.

Fontana, M. 2007. "Modelling the Effects of Trade on Women, at Work and at Home: Comparative Perspectives." In *Feminist Economics of Trade,* ed. D. Elson, C. Grown, I. Steveren, and N. Cagatay, 117–40. London: Routledge.

Fontana, M., S. Joekes, and R. Masika. 1998. *Global Trade Expansion and Liberalisation: Gender Issues and Impacts.* BRIDGE Report 42, Institute of Development Studies, Brighton, United Kingdom.

Fontana, M., and Y. Rodgers. 2005. "Gender Dimensions in the Analysis of Macro-Poverty Linkages." *ODI Development Policy Review* 23 (3): 333–49.

Gammage, S., H. Jorgensen, and E. McGill. 2002. *Framework for Gender Assessments of Trade and Investment Agreements.* Women's Edge, Washington, DC.

Gammage, S., and R. Mehra. 1999. "Trends, Countertrends, and Gaps in Women's Employment." *World Development* 27 (3): 533–50.

Ghiara, G. 1999. "Impact of Trade Liberalisation on Female Wages in Mexico." *Development Policy Review* 17 (2): 171–90.

Hewett, P., and S. Amin. 2000. *Assessing the Impact of Garment Work on Quality of Life Measures.* Population Council, New York.

ILO (International Labour Office). 2007. *Global Employment Trends for Women.* Geneva: International Labour Office.

Jacoby, H. 1993. "Shadow Wages and Peasant Family Labour Supply: An Econometric Application of the Peruvian Sierra." *Review of Economics Studies* 60 (4): 903–21.

Joekes, S. 1995. "Trade-Related Employment for Women in Industry and Services in Developing Countries." UNRISD Occasional Paper 5, United Nations Research Institute for Social Development, Geneva.

———. 1999a. "A Gender-Analytical Perspective on Trade and Sustainable Development." In *Trade, Sustainable Development and Gender*, 33–59. Geneva: United Nations Conference on Trade and Development.

———. 1999b. "Gender, Property Rights and Trade: Constraints to Africa Growth." In *Enterprise in Africa: Between Poverty and Growth*, ed. K. King and S. McGrath, 48–60. Centre of African Studies, Oxford University, Oxford.

Joekes, S., and A. Weston. 1994. *Women and the New Trade Agenda.* New York: United Nations Development Fund for Women.

Kabeer, N. 1995. "Necessary, Sufficient or Irrelevant? Women, Wages and Intra-Household Power Relations in Urban Bangladesh." IDS Working Paper 25, Institute of Development Studies, Brighton, United Kingdom.

———. 2000. *The Power to Choose: Bangladeshi Women and Labour Market Decisions in London and Dhaka.* London: Verso.

———. 2003. "The Poverty Impacts of Female Employment." *ID21 Insights* 47, Institute of Development Studies, Brighton, United Kingdom.

Kabeer, N., and Mahmud, S. 2004. "Globalization, Gender and Poverty: Bangladeshi Women Workers in Export and Local Markets." *Journal of International Development* 16 (1): 93–109.

Kanji, N., and R. Jazdowska. 1995. "Gender, Structural Adjustment and Employment in Urban Zimbabwe." *Third World Planning Review* 17 (2): 133–54.

Kasente, D., M. Lockwood, J. Vivian, and A. Whitehead. 2002. "Gender and the Expansion of Non-Traditional Agricultural Exports in Uganda." In *Shifting Burdens: Gender and Agrarian Change under Neoliberalism*, ed. S. Razavi, 35–66. United Nations Research Institute for Social Development. Sterling, VA: Kumarian Press.

Katz, E. 1995. "Gender and Trade within the Household: Observations from Rural Guatemala." *World Development* 23 (2): 327–42.

Kennedy, E. 1994. "Effects of Sugarcane Production in Southwestern Kenya on Income and Nutrition." In *Agricultural Commercialisation, Economic Development and Nutrition*, ed. J. von Braun and E. Kennedy, 252–63. Baltimore, MD: Johns Hopkins University Press for the International Food Policy Research Institute.

Kiggundu, R. 1996. "Gender and Diversification." In *Report of the Conference on Commodities: Africa and the World Market.* Amsterdam.

Kusago, T. 2000. "Why Did Rural Households Permit Their Daughters to Be Urban Factory Workers? A Case from Rural Malay Villages." *Labour and Management in Development Journal* 1 (2): 1–24, Canberra.

Kusago, T., and B. Barham. 2001. "Preference Heterogeneity, Power, and Intrahousehold Decision-Making in Rural Malaysia." *World Development* 29 (7): 1237–56.

Kusago, T., and T. Tzannatos. 1998. "Export-Processing Zones: A Review in Need of Update." HDDSP Discussion Paper 9802, World Bank, Washington, DC.

Malhotra, S., and E. de Graff. 1997. "Entry versus Success in the Labor Force: Young Women's Employment in Sri Lanka." *World Development* 25 (3): 379–94.

McCulloch, N., and M. Ota. 2002. "Export Horticulture and Poverty in Kenya." IDS Working Paper 174, Institute of Development Studies, Brighton, United Kingdom.

Mitter, S., G. Fernandez, and S. Varghese. 2004. "On the Threshold of Informalization: Women Call Centre Workers in India." In *Chains of Fortune: Linking Women Producers and Workers with Global Markets*, ed. M. Carr, 165–84. London: Commonwealth Secretariat.

Moser, C. 1989. "Gender Planning in the Third World: Meeting Practical and Strategic Gender Needs." *World Development* 17 (11): 1799–1825.

Newman, C. 2001. "Gender, Time Use and Change: Impacts of Agricultural Export Employment in Ecuador." Gender and Development Working Paper 18, World Bank, Washington, DC.

Nicita, A., and S. Razzaz. 2003. "Who Benefits and How Much? How Gender Affects Welfare Impacts of a Booming Textile Industry in Madagascar." World Bank Policy Research Working Paper 3029, Washington, DC.

Oostendorp, R. 2004. "Globalization and the Gender Wage Gap." World Bank Policy Research Working Paper 3256, Washington, DC.

Paolisso, M., K. Hallman, L. Haddad, and S. Regmi. 2002. "Does Cash Crop Adoption Detract from Childcare Provision? Evidence from Rural Nepal." *Economic Development and Cultural Change* 50 (2): 313–37.

Paul-Majumder, P., and A. Begum. 2000. "The Gender Imbalances in the Export-Oriented Garment Industry in Bangladesh." Gender and Development Working Paper 12, World Bank, Washington, DC.

Pearson, R. 1999. "'Nimble Fingers' Revisited: Reflections on Women and Third World Industrialisation in the Late Twentieth Century." In *Feminist Visions of Development*, ed. C. Jackson and R. Pearson, 171–88. London: Routledge.

Raynolds, L. 2002. "Wages for Wives: Renegotiating Gender and Production Relations in Contract Farming in the Dominican Republic." *World Development* 30 (5): 783–98.

Seguino, S. 1997. "Gender Wage Inequality and Export-Led Growth in South Korea." *Journal of Development Studies* 34 (2): 102–32.

———. 2000. "The Effects of Structural Change and Economic Liberalisation on Gender Wage Differentials in South Korea and Taiwan." *Cambridge Journal of Economics* 24 (4): 437–59.

Skoufias, E. 1993. "Labor Market Opportunities and Intrafamily Time Allocation in Rural Households in South Asia." *Journal of Development Economics* 40 (April): 277–310.

Smith, L., and Chavas, J. 1999. "Supply Response of West African Agricultural Households: Implications of Intra-Household Preference Heterogeneity." Food Consumption and Nutrition Division Discussion Paper 69, International Food Policy Research Institute, Washington, DC.

Standing, G. 1999. "Globalization through Flexible Labor: A Theme Revisited." World Development 27 (3): 583–602.

Tibaijuka, A. 1994. "The Cost of Differential Gender Roles in African Agriculture: A Case Study of Smallholder Banana-Coffee Farms in the Kagera Region, Tanzania." Journal of Agricultural Economics 45 (1): 69–81.

Tran-Nguyen, Anh-Nga, and Beviglia-Zampetti, Americo, eds. 2004 Trade and Gender: Opportunities and Challenges for Developing Countries. Geneva: United Nations Conference on Trade and Development.

Tzannatos, Z. 1999. "Women and Labour Market Changes in the Global Economy: Growth Helps, Inequalities Hurt and Public Policy Matters." World Development 27 (3): 551–69.

Udry, C. 1996. "Gender, Agricultural Productivity and the Theory of the Household." Journal of Political Economy 104 (5): 1010–45.

UN (United Nations). 1999. 1999 World Survey on the Role of Women in Development: Globalization, Gender and Work. New York: United Nations.

Valodia, I. 1996. "Work." In The Women Budget, ed. D. Budlender, 53–96. Institute for Democracy in South Africa, Cape Town.

Van Steveren, I., D. Elson, D., C. Grown, and N. Cagatay, eds. 2007. Feminist Economics of Trade. London: Routledge.

von Braun, J., and M. D. C. Immink. 1994. "Nontraditional Vegetable Crops and Food Security among Smallholder Farmers in Guatemala." In Agricultural Commercialization, Economic Development and Nutrition, ed. J. von Braun and E. Kennedy, 189–203. Baltimore, MD: Johns Hopkins University Press for the International Food Policy Research Institute.

von Braun, J., K. John, and D. Puetz. 1994. "Nutritional Effects of Commercialisation of a Woman's Crop: Irrigated Rice in the Gambia." In Agricultural Commercialisation, Economic Development and Nutrition, ed. J. Von Braun and E. Kennedy, 343–63. Baltimore, MD: Johns Hopkins University Press for the International Food Policy Research Institute.

von Braun, J., and E. Kennedy, eds. 1994. Agricultural Commercialisation, Economic Development and Nutrition. Baltimore, MD: Johns Hopkins University Press for the International Food Policy Research Institute.

Wold, B. K. 1997. Supply Response in a Gender Perspective: The Case of Structural Adjustment in Zambia. Statistics Norway, Oslo.

Wood, A. 1991. "North–South Trade and Female Labour in Manufacturing: An Asymmetry." Journal of Development Studies 27 (2): 168–89.

Wood, A., and J. Mayer. 2001. "Africa's Export Structure in a Comparative Perspective." *Cambridge Journal of Economics* 25 (3): 369–94.

Zohir, S. C. 1998. "Gender Implications of Industrial Reforms and Adjustment in the Manufacturing Sector of Bangladesh." Ph.D. diss., Department of Economics and Social Studies, University of Manchester, United Kingdom.

PART I

The Macro Approach: Social Accounting Matrices and Computable General Equilibrium Models of Trade, Gender, and Poverty

3

Oil Price Shocks, Poverty, and Gender: A Social Accounting Matrix Analysis for Kenya

Jean-Pascal Nganou, Juan Carlos Parra, and Quentin Wodon

Following pioneering work by Stone (1985), among others, social accounting matrices (SAMs) have been used as consistent accounting frameworks reconciling national income and product accounts with input-output analysis and in many cases household survey data. A SAM is primarily a data framework, but it can also be used as a model. As a database, a SAM is a double-entry square matrix recording in columns payments (or expenditures) and in rows receipts (or incomes) of transactions made by various activities, commodities, and agents in the economy. SAMs are constructed according to the same accounting principles underlying input-output tables (that is, each operation is recorded twice, so that any inflow into one account must be balanced by an outflow from a counterpart account). When SAMs are used as models—to assess the impact of trade shocks, for example—they are typically static models with fixed technical coefficients (that is, Leontief technology) and prices (as explained below). The key advantage of SAMs over input-output tables for distributional analysis is that the data from household surveys on the incomes and consumption patterns of various types of households can be directly integrated into the modeling exercise in order to conduct distributional analysis.

Most of the applications of the SAM technique have focused on the impact of exogenous quantity or demand shocks (a brief review of the literature is provided later in this chapter). The objective here is instead to use a recent SAM for Kenya to assess the potential impact of the increase in oil prices on the cost of the consumption basket of various types of households.[1] Indeed, virtually everything that can be done for quantity shocks using SAMs can also be done for price shocks, as discussed in the next section. The key advantage of the Kenya SAM is that it defines the categories of households by poverty status (ultrapoor, poor, and nonpoor); gender (male or female household head); and location (urban versus rural). This makes it feasible to take into account both poverty and gender dimensions simultaneously in assessing who will suffer most from an increase in oil prices.

The increase in oil prices is important, because many developing countries have had difficulties paying higher oil prices. This has manifested itself most visibly through higher deficits by electric utilities in countries in which a substantial part of power generation is thermal. In some countries taxes on oil products have been reduced in order to limit the impact of rising prices on consumers. But in a majority of countries, pass-throughs are in place, which means that consumers lose purchasing power, both through the higher prices paid for oil-related products and through the more general increase in producer and consumer prices that higher oil prices generate through multiplier effects. It is precisely to be able to take these multiplier effects into account that the use of a SAM model is appropriate.

Work by Semboja (1994) and Karingi and Siriwardana (2003) suggests that the Kenyan economy was already highly vulnerable to oil price shocks in the 1970s (see also Dick and others 1984; Mitra 1994). Together with Burundi, Rwanda, Tanzania, and Uganda, Kenya belongs to Africa's Great Lakes region, which borders Lake Kivu, Lake Tanganyika, and Lake Victoria. According to the U.S. Department of Energy (2004), Kenya accounted for almost 60 percent of the region's commercial energy consumption in 2001, despite the fact that its population, at 37 million people, represented only about a third of the 107 million residents of the region. Kenya's large share in the energy consumption of the region is caused by the fact that the country is richer and more urbanized than its neighbors.

Macroeconomic statistics suggest the potential for a relatively large impact of the increase in oil prices on households and the economy (Kumar 2005). In 2003, for example, net oil imports accounted for 5.6 percent of GDP; this figure rose to 6.9 percent in

2004 and an estimated 8.9 percent in 2005. The incremental cost of oil imports in 2004 over 2003 caused by the increase in prices was about $200 million (1.2 percent of GDP). Inflation was kept in check, but fuel and power prices rose at more than twice the rate of the consumer price index (CPI) between December 2004 and October 2005 (9.2 percent versus 4.4 percent for the CPI). More generally, the substantial impact of the increase in oil prices on the economy is caused by the fact that oil represents an important share of the intermediate inputs of a wide range of sectors, from electricity to transportation. In the case of electricity, while hydroelectric plants account for three-fourths of production, the rest is based in large part on oil. In 2005 the low-cost electricity that had been granted to the Kenya Power and Lighting Company (KPLC) by the Kenya Electricity Generating Company was terminated. According to news stories, the change was motivated by the need to make KPLC more attractive to foreign investors for privatization, but increasing oil prices may have added pressure to increase prices.

This chapter is organized as follows. The next section provides a general background on SAMs as a modeling tool (two annexes provide mathematical derivations for the key concepts used). The following section presents the results for Kenya. The last section summarizes the chapter's main conclusions.

Social Accounting Matrices: A Brief Review

For any economic analysis that supposes the existence of general equilibrium feedback effects, a multisectoral approach is typically preferable to a partial equilibrium framework, because interlinkages among different parts of the economy are too complex to be considered in partial equilibrium models.[2] In principle, applied general equilibrium analysis can be performed using econometric methods (Jorgenson 1984, 1998) on a system of simultaneous linear or nonlinear equations describing technology and consumption behavior of various sectors and institutions considered. But such an approach requires a considerable amount of data, not readily available for many countries, including industrial economies. To circumvent these data requirements, researchers have used static input-output and SAM-based general equilibrium models in much of the empirical work on developing economies. These models require only a single year of data (the base year). Input-output or SAM databases are transformed into models to evaluate the impact of exogenous shocks on endogenous accounts (outputs, factor payments, and institutional incomes), yielding comparative static analysis with respect to base-year values.

The use of input-output models can be traced back to seminal work by Leontief (1951, 1953), who gave impetus to the development of applied general equilibrium models. Since then, a very extensive body of literature on both input-output and SAMs has been produced; only a few contributions, focusing on SAM–based work, can be cited here.

Early work on developing countries includes that by Adelman and Taylor (1990), who use a SAM of Mexico to explore the intersectoral impacts of alternative adjustment strategies, and Dorosh (1994), who develops a semi-input-output model based on a 1987 SAM to analyze how changes in economic policies and external shocks affected poor households in Lesotho. Taylor and Adelman (1996) develop the concept of village SAMs, which they apply to India, Indonesia, Kenya, Mexico, and Senegal. Thorbecke and Jung (1996) develop a decomposition method of the fixed multiplier matrix to analyze poverty alleviation. They study the impact of sectoral growth on poverty alleviation in Indonesia, concluding that agriculture and service sectoral growth could contribute more to overall poverty reduction than industrial growth.

In a study of South Africa, Khan (1999) attempts to explore the link between sectoral growth and poverty alleviation along the same lines as Thorbecke and Jung (1996). Other lines of research by the International Food Policy Research Institute (IFPRI) include Arndt, Jenson, and Tarp (2000), who adopt the SAM multiplier approach to argue the relative importance of sectors of activity in Mozambique, and Bautista, Robinson, and El-Said (2001), who use SAM and computable general equilibrium (CGE) frameworks to analyze alternative industrial development paths for Indonesia. Although Bautista, Robinson, and El-Said (2001) recognize the limitations of the SAM multiplier analysis (which is linear and in some cases ignores supply constraints), they conduct simulations under the two frameworks and obtain the same result: agricultural demand-led industrialization yields higher increases in real GDP than two other industrial-led development paths (food processing-based and light manufacturing-based industry).

Along the lines of Defourny and Thorbecke (1984), Thorbecke (2000) provides a thorough and comprehensive presentation of the SAM as both database and model. Starting with a very descriptive presentation of the SAM, followed by arguments on the transformation of a SAM into a model through the separation between endogenous and exogenous accounts, he presents an alternative to the multiplier decomposition based on structural path analysis. He argues that although multipliers capture the global effects of injections from exogenous variables on endogenous variables, they do not clarify the structural and behavioral mechanism (or "black box") responsible for these global effects. From a policy stand-point, it is therefore important to complement knowledge of the magnitude of multipliers with structural path analysis that identi-fies the various paths along which a given injection travels or breaks down the "channels of influence" (Thorbecke 2000). Some critics argue that structural path analysis is a more micro-oriented approach, which does not reveal much about the whole system linkage (Round 1989).

Input-output, SAM, and CGE models all belong to the same fam-ily of economywide or general equilibrium models. There is a key difference between input-output and SAM models on the one hand and CGE models on the other, however. This difference can be explained intuitively through a simple algebraic representation fol-lowing Taylor and others (2002). We start with the impact of a quantity shock, because input-output models and SAMs are typi-cally used to analyze the impact of this type of shock. Let us consider the effect of a change in an exogenous variable Q_Z (the quantity of oil imported in a country, with Z denoting oil and Q denoting the quantity of oil imported) on an endogenous variable (or vector) Y (the income of a household group). Let P denote a vector of local input and output prices. Assuming for simplicity that $Y = Y(Q_Z, P)$, the impact of a change in Q_Z on Y is given by

$$(3.1) \qquad \frac{dY}{dQ_Z} = \frac{\partial Y}{\partial Q_Z} + \frac{\partial Y}{\partial P}\frac{dP}{dQ_Z}.$$

The first term on the right-hand side of equation (3.1) represents direct income effects. The second term represents the indirect (gen-eral equilibrium) effects of the exogenous shock through endogenous local prices. Taylor and others (2002) argue that the second term could be ignored if all prices are given to the local economy by out-side markets (that is, if the tradability of all goods and factors is assumed) or if perfect elasticity of supply of all goods and services is assumed. It is common practice to use input-output and SAM mul-tiplier models to estimate the effects of policy change when the trad-ability of all goods and inputs and perfect elasticity of supply are assumed. Indeed, input-output and SAM–based models are Keynesian demand-based systems based on the assumption of unconstrained resources (that is, excess capacity in all sectors) and perfectly elastic supplies (for example, unemployment/underemployment of factors of production).

An implicit assumption underlying many input-output and SAM multiplier models is that the economy is assumed to be operating below its production possibilities frontier. Put differently, one assumes the existence of excess capacity and unused resources under the SAM–based demand-driven Keynesian framework, so that any exogenous increase in demand can be satisfied by a corresponding increase in supply (Thorbecke 2000). Exogenous changes in demand are also assumed not to influence local prices.

The excess capacity assumption was relaxed in the literature in two steps. First, Lewis and Thorbecke (1992) allowed sectors with zero excess capacity in their analysis of economic linkages in the town of Kutus, Kenya. Later, Parikh and Thorbecke (1996) relaxed the assumption a bit farther by including sectors with small excess capacity while studying the impact of decentralization of industries on rural development. Other assumptions in input-output and SAM models include the linearity of so-called technological coefficients, as well as linearity on the consumption side caused by assuming unitary income elastic demand (that is, the activities in SAM models assume Leontief production functions and there is no substitution between imports and domestic production in the commodity columns [Thorbecke and Jung 1996; Arndt, Jensen, and Tarp 2000]). Another important limitation of the "traditional" SAM model is the assumption that the average expenditure propensities (technical coefficients) hold for exogenous demand shocks, implying income elasticities equal to one. A more realistic alternative, noted in Lewis and Thorbecke (1992), is to use marginal expenditure propensities, if available (this applies to a traditional quantity-based SAM model, not to the price-based model used here).

Input-output and SAM models are generally used to simulate the impact of a change in the demand block (exports, government spending) on output, factor allocation, and income distribution. However, if some goods or inputs (output, labor services) are nontradable or supplies are not perfectly elastic, the second term in equation (3.1) may not be zero. The CGE model is the appropriate tool in this case, because it adds more realism to the input-output and SAM–multiplier approach. In fact, although static, like input-output and SAM models, CGE models can address issues such as resource constraints, nonlinearities, and price effects within an economywide modeling framework.

Input-output and SAM models have traditionally been used to analyze the impact of quantity shocks. They can also be used to assess the economywide and distributional implications of price shocks. How this is done is explained below. Intuitively, if one considers the effect of a change in the price of oil, denoted by P_Z, on the same endogenous variable (or vector) $\mathbf{Y}$ as before and assumes that $\mathbf{Y} = \mathbf{Y}(P_Z, Q)$, where Q is a vector of local input and output quantities, the impact of the change in P_Z on $\mathbf{Y}$ is

$$(3.2) \qquad \frac{dY}{dP_Z} = \frac{\partial Y}{\partial P_Z} + \frac{\partial Y}{\partial Q} \frac{dQ}{dP_Z}.$$

The implication of equation (3.2) is that when using input-output and SAM models to analyze the impact of price shocks on the economy and households, it is the second term of the equation that is ignored, because all quantities are considered as given. In the case of price as well as quantity shocks, the use of SAM as an analytical tool rests less on its forecasting ability than in the study of the underlying economic structure through an analysis of its inverse multipliers and their multiplier matrix. Annex 3A shows in more detail how to transform the SAM (that is, the database) into a model (that is, a set of simultaneous equations).

Beyond the estimation of the impact of a shock, additional insights can be gained by looking at the main factors behind specific impacts. We use a decomposition analysis of the multiplier model along the lines of Pyatt and Round (1979) and Thorbecke (2000). (The derivation of the decomposition is provided in annex 3B.) Essentially, three separate effects are distinguished under this approach: transfer effects, spillover effects, and feedback effects. Transfer (or within-account) effects capture the interindustry (input-output) interactions among production activities or any interdependencies emanating from the patterns of transfers of income between households. Spillover (or open-loop/cross) effects show the impacts transmitted to other categories of endogenous accounts (for example, factor payments and household accounts) when a set of accounts (say, activities) is affected by an exogenous shock, with no reverse effects. Feedback (also called between-account or closed-loop) effects capture the full impact of a shock caused by the full circular flow (Round 1985). They capture how a shock to a sector travels outward to other sectors or endogenous accounts and then back to the point of original shock. Closed-loop effects ensure that the circular flow is completed among endogenous accounts by capturing injections that enter through one subgroup but do not return after a tour through the other subgroups (see, for example, Pyatt and Round 1979).

Oil Price Shocks in Kenya

All of the computations in this chapter were performed using SimSIP SAM, a powerful and easy to use Microsoft Excel–based application with MATLAB running in the background that can be used to conduct policy analysis under a SAM framework. SimSIP SAM was developed by Parra and Wodon (2008b); it is distributed free of charge, together with the necessary MATLAB components. The accompanying user's manual describes how to use the software and explains the theory behind the computations. The application can be used to perform various types of analysis and decompositions and to obtain detailed and graphical results for experiments.

Basic Structure of the Kenya SAM

The 2001 SAM for Kenya was provided by IFPRI (for a discussion of how the SAM was constructed, see Wobst and Schraven 2004). It includes 33 activities and commodities; agricultural and nonagricultural labor and capital; 12 categories of households; and 4 accounts for government (recurrent, indirect taxes, tariffs, and direct taxes). Of the 33 activities, 15 are agricultural: maize, other cereals, roots and tubers, pulses, sugar cane, fruits, vegetables, cut flowers, tea, coffee (green), beef and veal, milk and dairy, other livestock, fishing, and forestry and logging. Another 7 are manufacturing activities: food, textiles, leather and footwear, wood and paper, petroleum, metal products, and nonmetallic products and other chemicals. There are three industrial activities: mining; construction; and electricity, gas, and water. Eight activities belong to the service sector: trade, transport and communication; owned housing; other private services (including hotels, restaurants, and financial services); public administration; education; health; and agricultural services.

The technical coefficients of the macro SAM provide an overall macroeconomic profile of Kenya (table 3.1). Some 56 percent of the costs of production for activities are accounted for by intermediate inputs, 17.7 percent by labor payments, and 26.2 percent by payments to capital (the fact that the capital payments' shares exceeds labor's is a result of the way the SAM was constructed, with all non-wage factor payments being assigned to capital). The supply of commodities is satisfied at 72.5 percent by marketed domestic output, 8.9 percent by marketing margins, 4.8 percent by indirect taxes, and 13.8 percent by imports. Households spend 68.7 percent of their total income on final consumption, 16.8 percent on autoconsumption,[3] and 12.7 percent on taxes, saving 1.8 percent. The government spends 35.8 percent of its income on purchases of goods and services and 8.7 percent on transfers to households, saving 5.5 percent. Exports represent 75.3 percent of the rest of the world account.

Data on the sources of income and expenditures of six groups of households are disaggregated according to poverty status and the gender of the household head (table 3.2). The poorer a household group is, the larger the share of income it receives as payments to

Table 3.1 Technical Coefficients for the 2001 Kenya SAM
(percent)

Coefficient	Activities	Commodities	Labor	Capital	Households	Government	Capital account	Rest of world
Activities		72.5			16.8			
Commodities	56.0	8.9			68.7	35.8	100.0	75.3
Labor	17.7		100.0					
Capital	26.2			100.0				
Households						8.7		
Government		4.8			12.7	50.0		
Capital account					1.8	5.5		24.7
Rest of world		13.8						

Source: Authors' estimates using SimSIP SAM.
Note: All empty cells are equal to zero.

Table 3.2 Sources of Income and Expenditure, by Location, Level of Poverty, and Gender, Kenya SAM 2001 (percent)

Type of household	Source of income			Expenditure category			
	Labor	Capital	Government	Auto-consumption	Final consumption	Taxes	Savings
Rural							
Female ultrapoor	58.7	41.3	0.0	25.4	73.3	1.2	0.2
Female poor	49.7	40.1	10.2	25.4	71.7	2.6	0.4
Female nonpoor	28.2	56.4	15.4	34.3	57.2	7.5	1.1
Male ultrapoor	60.7	39.3	0.0	25.4	71.3	2.9	0.4
Male poor	51.3	45.5	3.2	27.5	66.4	5.4	0.8
Male nonpoor	33.0	63.8	3.2	22.2	59.5	16.0	2.3
Urban							
Female ultrapoor	89.6	10.4	0.0	1.3	96.6	1.9	0.3
Female poor	82.4	13.7	3.9	0.7	95.7	3.1	0.5
Female nonpoor	34.2	65.1	0.6	1.2	76.4	19.6	2.8
Male ultrapoor	74.5	25.5	0.0	3.5	92.2	3.7	0.5
Male poor	67.2	32.8	0.0	1.3	89.8	7.8	1.1
Male nonpoor	30.3	65.1	4.6	0.8	79.1	17.6	2.5

Source: Authors' estimates using SimSIP SAM.

labor and the smaller its income share from payments to capital. Government transfers account for a small share of total income, except among urban female-headed households that are poor or nonpoor. Autoconsumption accounts for a quarter of rural households' expenditures and is negligible for urban households. Ultrapoor households spend almost all of their resources on consumption (autoconsumption plus final consumption), while poor households—and especially nonpoor households—pay taxes and manage to save a very small proportion of their resources. Taxes are thus progressive, as shares of expenditures increase with the level of income, as does the share of expenditures for savings.

Impact of Increase in Oil Price

This section simulates the impact of a 25 percent increase in oil prices on the cost of living for different types of households (exogenous accounts are government, the capital account, and the rest of the world; see annex 3A for the methodology).[4] The activities most affected by the increase in the price of oil are electricity, gas, and water; mining; nonmetallic products; and agricultural services (table 3.3). As expected, these activities are those with the largest direct effects. Overall however, indirect effects account for a larger share of the total effect than direct effects. While this may lead to an overestimation of the total effects (because of the assumption that no behavioral adjustments in the economy are made), it does suggest that at least in theory, the total effects may be large. The total potential effect is indeed large, with the producer price index potentially increasing 9.5 percent following the oil price shock. This means that for every 1 percent increase in the price of oil, the producer price index rises 0.38 percent (this is thus the elasticity of the producer price index to the oil price).

The overall increase in the cost of living to households is estimated at 9.2 percent (table 3.4 and figure 3.1). The aggregate increase in the cost of living is lower than the increases for most of the household categories because of the large share of rural male nonpoor households in aggregate households expenditure (36.6 percent) together with the lower cost of living increase for this group (9.1 percent).

The results suggest that the impact of an oil price increase on household expenditure could be large. This result is not surprising given that petroleum imports represented 2.5 percent of GDP and 7.2 percent of total imports in 2001. Households spent only 2.7 percent of their total consumption on oil, but oil is used in many sectors of the economy, which means that the multiplier or indirect

Table 3.3 Impact of Exogenous Increase of 25 Percent in
the Price of Oil on Prices, by Sector, 2001 Kenya SAM
(percent)

Sector	Price change (1)	Direct effect (2)	Direct effect as share of total effect (2)/(1)	Share of aggregate value added
Electricity, gas, and water	15.1	10.3	68.5	0.9
Mining	13.3	7.7	57.5	0.2
Nonmetallic products	12.6	6.1	48.5	1.6
Oil	12.4	7.3	59.2	1.1
Agricultural services	12.1	5.1	42.4	1.1
Construction	11.2	4.4	38.9	1.8
Education	10.8	3.9	36.3	1.0
Public administration	10.5	3.5	33.2	2.9
Fishing	10.1	1.8	18.3	1.2
Forestry and logging	10.0	1.6	16.4	0.5
Wood and paper	9.7	2.6	27.2	1.1
Health	9.7	1.8	18.4	1.8
Trade	9.6	1.6	16.3	11.3
Transport	9.6	1.7	17.3	11.7
Owned housing	9.4	0.0	0.0	3.5
Vegetables	9.3	1.3	13.6	3.1
Pulses	9.2	1.2	12.5	2.8
Milk and dairy	9.2	1.0	11.2	2.3
Other livestock	9.2	1.0	11.1	2.3
Textiles	9.2	1.9	20.2	0.4
Other private services	9.2	0.8	9.0	13.0
Maize	9.1	1.4	14.9	3.4
Roots and tubers	9.1	1.0	10.5	1.9
Fruits	9.1	1.0	11.0	2.1
Tea	9.1	1.0	10.9	2.2
Coffee (green)	9.1	0.9	9.4	1.4
Beef and veal	9.1	1.0	10.6	1.9
Sugar cane	9.0	0.7	8.0	0.5
Cut flowers	9.0	0.7	7.8	0.4
Other cereals	8.9	0.1	1.6	3.0
Food	8.9	0.6	7.2	16.5
Other chemicals	8.8	1.7	19.3	0.7
Metal products	6.8	1.8	26.3	0.5
Total (producer price index)	9.5	1.5	16.0	100.0

Source: Authors' estimates using SimSIP SAM.

Table 3.4 Impact on Cost of Living of a 25 Percent Increase in Oil Prices, 2001 Kenya SAM

Category	Change in cost of living (1)	Direct effect (2)	Direct effect as share of total effect (2)/(1)	Share of petroleum in final consumption	Share of aggregate household expenditure
Individual household group					
Rural female ultrapoor	8.8	0.4	4.6	2.2	2.4
Rural female poor	8.8	0.4	4.0	2.0	1.6
Rural female nonpoor	9.0	0.2	2.6	1.6	11.7
Rural male ultrapoor	8.8	0.4	4.2	2.1	7.1
Rural male poor	8.8	0.3	3.2	1.7	5.4
Rural male nonpoor	9.1	0.4	4.2	2.5	36.6
Urban female ultrapoor	9.1	0.7	7.8	2.9	0.2
Urban female poor	9.1	0.7	7.8	3.0	1.6
Urban female nonpoor	9.4	0.5	5.2	2.5	3.2
Urban male ultrapoor	9.0	0.7	7.3	2.8	0.5
Urban male poor	9.2	0.6	6.3	2.6	5.0
Urban male nonpoor	9.7	0.7	7.4	3.7	24.7
Aggregate household group					
Rural households	9.0	0.3	3.8	2.2	64.8
Urban households	9.6	0.7	7.1	3.3	35.2
Ultrapoor households	8.8	0.4	4.5	2.2	10.2
Poor households	9.0	0.5	5.0	2.3	13.7
Nonpoor households	9.3	0.5	5.1	2.9	76.1
Female households	9.0	0.3	3.8	2.1	20.7
Male households	9.2	0.5	5.3	2.8	79.3
Total (consumer price index)	9.2	0.5	5.0	2.7	100.0

Source: Authors' estimates using SimSIP SAM.

Figure 3.1 Change in Cost of Living as a Result of a 25
Percent Increase in Oil Price, by Gender and Poverty Status,
2001 Kenya SAM

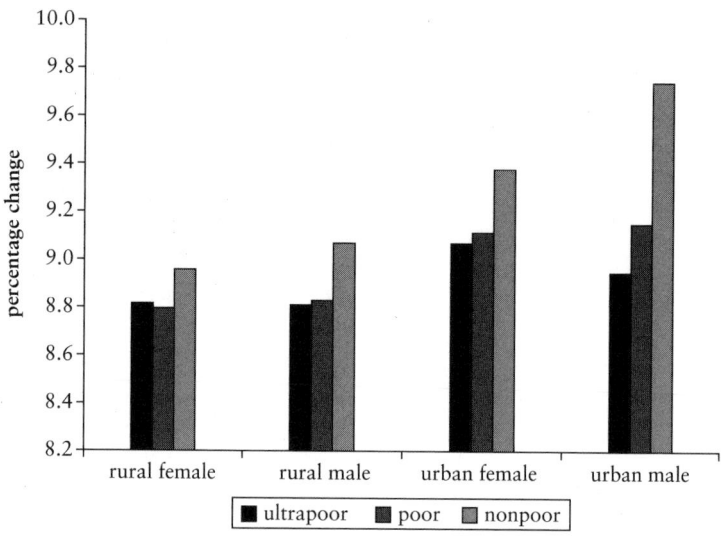

Source: Authors' estimates using SimSIP SAM.

effects are large. Indeed, oil represented 15.9 percent of all intermediate
consumption,[5] and the sector exhibits strong forward linkages, meaning that it is affected by other sectors' growth more strongly than the
average sector in the economy is. Oil exhibits strong backward linkages in the price model, which means that it can affect prices in other
sectors more than the average sector does (by construction, strong
forward linkages in the quantity-based SAM model translate into
strong backward linkages in the price-based SAM model).

Two findings stand out. First, for both rural and urban households, the richer a household is, the greater the impact an increase in
oil prices is likely to have (figure 3.2). Second, urban households tend
to be affected by increases in oil prices more than rural households.
The greater impact on richer households can be explained mainly by
their larger consumption shares for oil; electricity, gas, and water;
and education. The larger consumption share devoted to oil-related
products makes the impact of the shock greater for these households,
despite the fact that very poor households tend to devote a higher
proportion of their total income to consumption. Put differently,
these sectors are among the most severely affected by oil price

Figure 3.2 Price Changes and Contribution to Change in Cost of Living for Nonpoor and Ultrapoor Households as a Result of a 25 Percent Increase in Oil Price, 2001 Kenya SAM

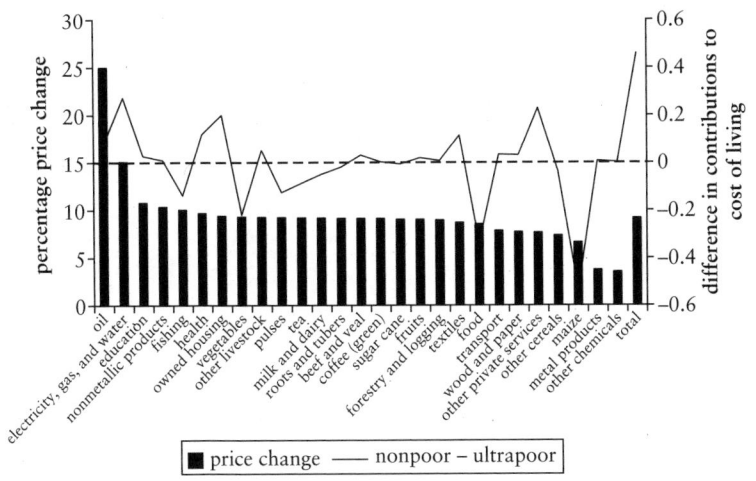

Source: Authors' estimates using SimSIP SAM.

Note: The right-hand y axis represents the impact on cost of living of nonpoor households minus the impact on cost of living of ultrapoor households. Points above the dotted horizontal line (which represents equal contributions for both types of households) indicate that an increase in the price of oil has a greater impact on the cost of living of nonpoor households than on the cost of living of ultrapoor households.

increases, and richer households tend to consume larger shares than poorer households of the goods and services these sectors produce.

Two conclusions can be drawn from analysis of the price changes in various sectors resulting from a 25 percent increase in the price of oil. First, an increase in the price of oil affects nonpoor households more than it affects ultrapoor households (a 25 percent increase in the price of oil generates a 9.3 percent increase in the cost of living among the nonpoor and an 8.8 percent among the ultrapoor) (figure 3.2). Second, the increase in the price of oil affects male-headed households slightly more than it affects female-headed households (a 25 percent increase in the price of oil generates a 9.2 percent increase in the cost living for households headed by males and a 9.0 percent increase for households headed by females) (figure 3.3). The consumption shares for oil and utilities (electricity, gas, and water) following the oil price shock (the relative prices of which rise) determine the types of households in which the shock increases the cost

Figure 3.3 Price Change and Contribution to Change in Cost of Living for Male- and Female-Headed Households as a Result of a 25 Percent Increase in Oil Prices, 2001 Kenya SAM

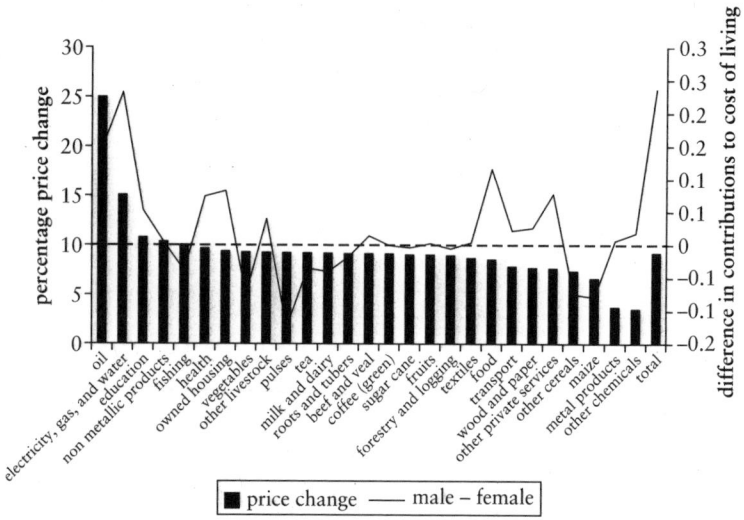

Source: Authors' estimates using SimSIP SAM.

Note: The right-hand y axis represents the impact on cost of living of male-headed households minus the impact on cost of living of female-headed households. Points above the dotted horizontal line (which represents equal contributions for both types of households) indicate that an increase in the price of oil has a greater impact on the cost of living of households headed by men than on the cost of living of households headed by women.

Table 3.5 Price Multiplier Decomposition

Household group	Multiplier (K Sh millions)	Open-loop (K Sh millions)	Closed-loop (K Sh millions)	Closed-loop/ multiplier (percent)
Rural female ultrapoor	35.3	7.6	26.1	73.9
Rural female poor	35.2	7.7	26.1	74.2
Rural female nonpoor	35.8	8.2	26.7	74.6
Rural male ultrapoor	35.2	7.7	26.1	73.9
Rural male poor	35.3	8.0	26.2	74.2
Rural male nonpoor	36.3	8.7	26.1	71.9
Urban female ultrapoor	36.3	7.2	26.3	72.4
Urban female poor	36.5	7.4	26.2	71.7
Urban female nonpoor	37.5	9.2	26.4	70.4
Urban male ultrapoor	35.8	7.4	25.8	72.1
Urban male poor	36.6	7.7	26.6	72.7
Urban male nonpoor	39.0	10.5	25.6	65.8

Source: Authors' estimates using SimSIP SAM.

Note: Figures show response to shock of 100 million Kenya shillings (K Sh).

of living more (both ultrapoor and male-headed households consume higher shares of oil and utilities).

Decomposition of the multiplier effects indicates that 65–75 percent of the final effect of an increase in the price of oil on households is explained by closed-loop (feedback) effects and 20–27 percent by open-loop (interaccount) effects (table 3.5).[6] Transfer effects are zero (households belong to the institutions group of accounts and oil belongs to the activities group), so the portion of the price change that is not explained by open- and closed-loop effects is explained by the initial shock.

Conclusion

This chapter uses a SAM–multiplier approach to examine the impact of oil price shocks on various categories of households in Kenya. It identifies which sectors of the economy would be most affected and analyzes the distributional implications of these shocks on households given the patterns of consumption observed for different categories of households.

Two findings stand out. First, the potential impact of an oil price shock is high in Kenya. For a 25 percent increase in oil price, the overall increase in the cost of living to households estimated with the SAM is 9.2 percent. This does not necessarily mean that observed inflation would increase as dramatically. Indeed, households and other economic agents tend to adjust to price changes by modifying their behavior, which tends to reduce the impacts predicted using standard SAM multipliers. Nevertheless, the results suggest that the impact of higher oil prices on household living standards and thereby on poverty could be large. Second, there are differences in impacts according to household groups. As a result of differences in consumption patterns, in both rural and urban areas richer households are likely to be more severely affected by oil price hikes than poorer households, and male-headed households are likely to be more severely affected than female-headed households.

Annex 3A: SAM Model for Impact of Price Shocks

Algebraically, a SAM is a schematic representation of the flow transactions between different sectors or institutions in an economy. The convention that is used defines the cell T_{ij} of the SAM as the value of payments from sector/institution j to sector/institution i (see table 3.1).

Some accounts in the SAM model have to be considered exogenous (that is, expenditures can be set independently of income). The choice usually depends on the nature of the simulation experiment, but government, the capital account, and the rest of the world are often candidates.

Let n be the number of endogenous accounts and $r-n$ the number of exogenous accounts. Summing down the jth column of the SAM yields

$$(3.3) \qquad Y_j = \sum_{i=1}^{n} T_{ij} + \sum_{m=n+1}^{r} W_{mj},$$

where Y_j denotes total expenditures of sector j, and W_{mj} denotes total payments to the mth exogenous account made by sector j. Let P_j denote the price of the good produced by sector j; Q_j the total output (in physical units) of sector j; and S_{ij} the amount of sector i's good (in physical units) used by sector j. Equation (3.3) can then be rewritten as

$$(3.4) \qquad P_j Q_j = \sum_{i=1}^{n} P_i S_{ij} + \sum_{m=n+1}^{r} P_m S_{mj}.$$

Dividing both sides by Q_j yields

$$(3.5) \qquad P_j = \sum_{i=1}^{n} \frac{P_i S_{ij}}{Q_j} + \sum_{m=n+1}^{r} \frac{P_m S_{mj}}{Q_j}.$$

Denote the physical technical coefficients for the endogenous accounts as $c_{ij} = s_{ij}/Q_j$ for $i=1,\ldots$ and define $b_j = \sum_{m=n+1}^{r}\left(P_m S_{mj}/Q_j\right)$ as the value of total payments to exogenous accounts per physical unit of sector j's output. Equation (3.5) can then be rewritten as

$$(3.6) \qquad P_j = \sum_{i=1}^{n} P_i c_{ij} + b_j,$$

which implies that the price of output of sector j is a weighted average of the prices of the goods sector j buys, with weights given by the physical technical coefficients plus exogenous payments per unit of sector j's output. Using matrix notation, the resulting system of price equations can be written as

$$(3.7) \qquad P = C'P + B,$$

where C' is the transpose of $C=[c_{ij}]$. The system defined in equation (3.7) can be solved (under mild conditions [see ten Raa 2005, theorem 2.1]) as

$$(3.8) \qquad P=(I-C')^{-1}B,$$

which is known as the Leontief price formation model.

At first sight, this price model does not seem to be very useful, because the physical technical coefficients are very rarely available. Instead, value technical coefficients a_{ij} can be computed by dividing each cell in T by the respective column sum. The matrix $A=[a_{ij}]$ is usually referred to as the technical coefficients matrix, where $a_{ij}=T_{ij}/\sum_{k=1}^{r}T_{kj}$. According to Blair and Miller (1985), these value-based technical coefficients can also be given a physical interpretation using "dollars worth of output" as a measure of physical quantity. Under this interpretation, because the physical measure is equivalent to the monetary measure, all prices are equal to one. In physical terms the technical coefficient a_{ij} represents the dollar's worth of output of sector i per each dollar worth of output of sector j. Equations (3.7) and (3.8) then become

$$(3.9) \qquad P=A'P+B$$

and

$$(3.10) \qquad P=(I-A')^{-1}B=M'B.$$

One of the key features of the SAM model is the constancy of the technical coefficients implied by the excess capacity assumption for all sector/institutions. This implies not only the constancy of the physical technical coefficients but also the constancy of the price ratio (for details see Moses 1974 or Miller and Blair 1985):

$$(3.11) \qquad \Delta P=(I-A')^{-1}\Delta B,$$

which means that the effect on prices of a change in the exogenous payments per unit of output (or simply a change in exogenous per unit costs) is given by the inverse (multiplier) matrix $M'=(I-A')^{-1}$. Because all prices are equal to one, the absolute change in prices/costs is exactly equal to the percentage change.

The economic interpretation of most of the prices in the model is straightforward. The prices of activities can be understood as producer prices, the prices of commodities as consumer prices, and the prices of production factors as rental payments for their use. The price of households can be understood as a cost of living index, because it is computed as a weighted average of all the goods the households buy (in and outside the household) plus tax payments. In this chapter we consider government, capital account, and the rest of the world accounts to be exogenous. Because the shock studied is an increase in the price of oil, which is usually either controlled by the government or a function of international oil prices, we also set the oil commodity account as exogenous, which means that we actually model the commodity oil as a supply-constrained commodity.

Annex 3B: Block Decomposition of the Multiplier Matrix

Cell m_{ji} of the multiplier matrix M' in equation (3.10) quantifies the effect of a unitary change in sector i's cost in the price of sector j.[7] To decompose the matrix M', for any $n \times n$ matrix, the nonsingular matrix $\tilde{A}$ equation (3.9) can be rewritten as

(3.12) $$P = (A' - \tilde{A})\,P + \tilde{A}P + B$$

(3.13) $$P = A^*P + (I - \tilde{A})^{-1}B,$$

where

(3.14) $$A^* = (I - \tilde{A})^{-1}(A' - \tilde{A}).^8$$

Multiplying equation (3.13) through by A^* yields

(3.15) $$A^*P = A^{*2}P + A^*(I - \tilde{A})^{-1}B.$$

From equation (3.13), we have an expression for A^*P; replacing it on the left-hand side yields

(3.16) $$P = A^{*2}P + A^*(I - \tilde{A})^{-1}B.$$

Multiplying equation (3.16) through by A^{*2} and replacing the expression for $A^{*2}P$ from (3.15) yields

(3.17) $$P = (I - A^{*3})^{-1}\,(I + A^* + A^{*2})\,(I - \tilde{A})^{-1}B.$$

Notice that we just decomposed multiplicatively the multiplier matrix M' from (3.10) into three different matrices. Define

(3.18) $$M_1 = (I - \tilde{A})^{-1},\ M2 = (I + A^* + A^{*2}),\ \text{and}\ M_3 = (I - A^{*3})^{-1}.$$

Then $M = M_3 M_2 M_1$. It is also possible to present the decomposition in an additive way, as follows:

(3.19) $$M = I + \frac{(M_1 - I)}{TR} + \frac{(M_2 - I)M_1}{OL} + \frac{(M_3 - I)M_2 M_1}{CL},$$

where the first term (the identity matrix) is the initial unitary injection. The matrix M_1 captures the net effect of a group of accounts on itself through direct transfers, the matrix M_2 captures all net effects between partitions, and the matrix M_3 captures the net effect of circular income multipliers among endogenous accounts. The terms in the additive decomposition labeled TR (for transfer effects), OL for (open-loop effects), and CL (for closed-loop effects) have broadly the same interpretation as the corresponding multiplicative effects (the matrices M_i).

The $n \times n$ matrix $\tilde{A}$ (partition of A') was chosen as follows:

$$\tilde{A} = \begin{pmatrix} A'_{11} & 0 & 0 \\ 0 & 0 & 0 \\ 0 & 0 & A'_{33} \end{pmatrix},$$

where the first row and column correspond to the activities/commodities group, the second to the production factors, and the third to enterprises/households. Using the definition of A^* from (3.14),

$$A^* = (I - \tilde{A})^{-1}(A' - \tilde{A})$$

(3.20)

$$= \begin{pmatrix} (I - A'_{11})^{-1} & 0 & 0 \\ 0 & I & 0 \\ 0 & 0 & (I - A'_{33})^{-1} \end{pmatrix} \begin{pmatrix} 0 & A'_{21} & 0 \\ 0 & 0 & A'_{32} \\ A'_{13} & 0 & 0 \end{pmatrix}$$

$$= \begin{pmatrix} 0 & A^*_{12} & 0 \\ 0 & 0 & A^*_{23} \\ A^*_{31} & 0 & 0 \end{pmatrix}, \quad \begin{cases} A^*_{12} = (I - A'_{11})^{-1} A'_{21} \\ A^*_{23} = A'_{32} \\ A^*_{31} = (I - A'_{33})^{-1} A'_{13} \end{cases}.$$

Using the expression for A^* and the definitions in (3.18) yields

(3.21) $$M_1 = \begin{pmatrix} (I - A'_{11})^{-1} & 0 & 0 \\ 0 & I & 0 \\ 0 & 0 & (I - A'_{33})^{-1} \end{pmatrix}$$

(3.22) $$M_2 = \begin{pmatrix} I & A^*_{12} & A^*_{12}A^*_{23} \\ A^*_{23}A^*_{31} & I & A^*_{23} \\ A^*_{31} & A^*_{31}A^*_{12} & I \end{pmatrix}$$

$$(3.23) \quad M_3 = \begin{pmatrix} \left(I - A_{12}^* A_{23}^* A_{31}^*\right)^{-1} & 0 & 0 \\ 0 & \left(I - A_{23}^* A_{31}^* A_{12}^*\right)^{-1} & 0 \\ 0 & 0 & \left(I - A_{31}^* A_{12}^* A_{23}^*\right) \end{pmatrix}.$$

We now provide expressions for the matrices TR, OL, and CL defined in equation (3.19):

$$(3.24) \quad TR = \begin{pmatrix} \left(I - A_{11}'\right)^{-1} - I & 0 & 0 \\ 0 & 0 & 0 \\ 0 & 0 & \left(I - A_{33}'\right)^{-1} - I \end{pmatrix}$$

$$(3.25) \quad OL = \begin{pmatrix} 0 & A_{12}^* & A_{12}^* A_{23}^* \left[\left(I - A_{33}'\right)^{-1} - I\right] \\ A_{23}^* A_{31}^* \left[\left(I - A_{11}'\right)^{-1} - I\right] & 0 & A_{23}^* \left[\left(I - A_{33}'\right)^{-1} - I\right] \\ A_{31}^* \left[\left(I - A_{11}'\right)^{-1} - I\right] & A_{31}^* A_{12}^* & 0 \end{pmatrix}$$

(3.26)

$$CL = \begin{pmatrix} M_{3,11}^* \left(I - A_{11}'\right)^{-1} & M_{3,11}^* A_{12}^* & M_{3,11}^* A_{12}^* A_{23}^* \left(I - A_{33}'\right)^{-1} \\ M_{3,22}^* A_{23}^* A_{31}^* \left(I - A_{11}'\right)^{-1} & M_{3,22}^* & M_{3,22}^* A_{23}^* \left(I - A_{33}'\right)^{-1} \\ M_{3,33}^* A_{31}^* \left(I - A_{11}'\right)^{-1} & M_{3,33}^* A_{31}^* A_{12}^* & M_{3,33}^* \left(I - A_{33}'\right)^{-1} \end{pmatrix},$$

$$\text{where} \begin{cases} M_{3,11}^* = \left(I - A_{12}^* A_{23}^* A_{31}^*\right)^{-1} - I \\ M_{3,22}^* = \left(I - A_{23}^* A_{31}^* A_{12}^*\right)^{-1} - I \\ M_{3,33}^* = \left(I - A_{31}^* A_{12}^* A_{23}^*\right)^{-1} - I. \end{cases}$$

We now interpret and describe some features of the matrices TR, OL, and CL defined in equation (3.19). TR, which quantifies the net effect (with respect to the initial unitary shock) of groups of accounts into themselves (intra), is a block diagonal matrix with an identity matrix in the second block on the diagonal, a consequence of the absence of transfers among production factors. OL, which captures the net direct effect (with respect to the matrix M_1) between (inter) accounts, has zeros along the diagonal. The matrix that captures the net closed-loop effects (with respect to the product M_2M_1), CL, has no special structure.

Because the price of oil is assumed to be given by the international market, oil is modeled as a fixed-price sector (the equivalent of a supply-constrained sector in the value model). This means that the price of the sector can be increased from its current level only exogenously. Following the notation used by Lewis and Thorbecke (1992) after adapting it to the price model, we show that the final effects on prices, given an exogenous price shock, are given by

$$(3.27) \quad d\begin{bmatrix} p_{nc} \\ b_c \end{bmatrix} = \left[\begin{array}{c|c} (I-C'_{nc}) & 0 \\ \hline -R' & -I \end{array} \right]^{-1} \left[\begin{array}{c|c} I & Q' \\ \hline 0 & -(I-C'_c) \end{array} \right] d\begin{bmatrix} b_{nc} \\ p_c \end{bmatrix} = M'_m d\begin{bmatrix} b_{nc} \\ p_c \end{bmatrix}$$

where p_{nc} is a vector of prices of unconstrained sectors; b_c is a vector of endogenous costs for fixed-price sectors; C_{nc} is a matrix of expenditure propensities among unconstrained sectors (using average expenditure propensities [technical coefficients]); R is a matrix of expenditure propensities of unconstrained sectors on fixed-price sectors; Q is a matrix of expenditure propensities of fixed-price sectors on unconstrained sectors; C_c is a matrix of expenditure propensities among fixed-price sectors; b_{nc} is a vector of exogenous costs for unconstrained sectors; p_c is a vector of exogenous prices of fixed-price sectors; I is the conformable identity matrix; 0 is the null matrix; M_m is the mixed multiplier matrix; and the prime symbol (′) denotes the transpose of a matrix.

Using the formula for the inverse of partitioned matrices, we can rewrite the effect of the shock on the unconstrained sectors as

$$(3.28) \quad d\begin{bmatrix} p_{nc} \\ b_c \end{bmatrix} = \left[\begin{array}{c|c} (I-C'_{nc})^{-1} & (I-C'_{nc})^{-1}Q' \\ \hline -R'(I-C'_{nc}) & -R'(I-C'_{nc})Q' + (I-C'_{nc}) \end{array} \right] d\begin{bmatrix} b_{nc} \\ p_c \end{bmatrix}$$

$$= M'_m d\begin{bmatrix} b_{nc} \\ p_c \end{bmatrix}.$$

In the case in which only a single sector is shocked, the shock vector becomes $d[0/p_c]$, where dp_c is the size of the shock. From equation (3.28), we know that

$$(3.29) \qquad dp_{nc} = 0.25(I-C'_{nc})^{-1}Q',$$

where $\left(I - C'_{nc}\right)^{-1}$ is an inverse matrix computed using the matrix of expenditure propensities after deleting the column and row corresponding to the fixed-price sector (oil in this case) and Q is a vector of oil expenditure propensities for unconstrained sectors. Under mild conditions (see Ten Raa 2005, theorem 2.1), the inverse of equation (3.29) exists and can be decomposed as explained in equation (3.19). In this case the open-loop effect of the ith term of dp_{nc} is the dot product of the ith row of the open-loop matrix derived from the inverse matrix $\left(I - C'_{nc}\right)^{-1}$ and the vector of expenditure propensities Q. The same is true for the transfer and closed-loop effects.

Notes

This chapter was prepared at the Development Dialogue on Values and Ethics in the Human Development Vice Presidency at the World Bank for a research project on trade, gender, and poverty organized by the World Bank's Development Prospects Group. Comments from Ataman Aksoy and Erik Thorbecke, an anonymous reviewer, the editors of this volume, and participants at the World Bank workshop titled "Gender Aspects of the Trade and Poverty Nexus: A Macro-Micro Approach" are gratefully acknowledged. This work was funded by the Belgian Poverty Reduction Partnership as part of a broader program of work on social accounting matrices. Quentin Wodon is the corresponding author; his e-mail address is qwodon@worldbank.org.

1. See Roland-Holst and Sancho (1995) for an application of the SAM price model to the U.S. economy.

2. This review draws on Nganou (2005).

3. *Autoconsumption* is the nonmarketed production of goods and services consumed by the household.

4. The choice of the level of the increase in prices (25 percent) corresponds to the actual oil price increase at the time this chapter was first drafted. The figure is irrelevant, however, because the model is linear (meaning that the effects of a shock of 50 percent would simply be twice as large as the effect for a 25 percent shock).

5. The comparable figures were 5.6 percent in Lesotho in 2000, 1.1 percent in Tanzania in 2001, 4.1 percent in South Africa in 2000, and 11.1 percent in Uganda in 1999, according to SAMs for these countries.

6. See annex 3.2 for the decomposition formulas with flexible- and fixed-priced sectors (following Parra and Wodon 2008a).

7. This section is adapted from Parra and Wodon (2008a), who provide expressions for the block decomposition of the multiplier matrix under price constraints.

8. For details on computation, see Pyatt and Round (1979).

References

Adelman, I., and J. Edward Taylor. 1990. "A Structural Adjustment with a Human Face Possible? The Case of Mexico." *Journal of Development Studies* 26 (3): 387–407.

Arndt, C., H. Jensen, and F. Tarp. 2000. "Structural Characteristics of the Economy of Mozambique: A SAM–Based Analysis." *Review of Development Economics* 4 (3): 292–306.

Bautista, R., S. Robinson, and Moataz El-Said. 2001. "Alternative Industrial Development Paths for Indonesia: SAM and CGE Analyses." In *Restructuring Asian Economics for the New Millennium*, vol. 9B, ed. J. Behrman, M. Dutta, S. L. Husted, P. Sumalee, C. Suthiphand, and P. Wiboonchutikula, 773–90. Amsterdam: Elsevier Science/North Holland.

Defourny, J., and E. Thorbecke. 1984. "Structural Path Analysis and Multiplier Decomposition within a Social Accounting Matrix Framework." *Economic Journal* 94 (373): 111–36.

Dorosh, Paul A. 1994. "Adjustment, External Shocks, and Poverty in Lesotho: A Multiplier Analysis." Working Paper 71, Cornell Food and Nutrition Program, Ithaca, NY.

Dick, H., S. Gupta, D. Vincent, and H. Voigt. 1984. "The Effect of Oil Price Increases on Four Oil-Poor Developing Countries: A Comparative Analysis." *Energy Economics* 6 (1): 59–70.

Jorgenson, Dale. 1984. "Econometric Methods for Applied General Equilibrium Analysis." In *Applied General Equilibrium Analysis*, ed. H. E. Scarf and J. B. Shoven, 139–203. New York: Cambridge University Press.

———, ed. 1998. *Growth Volume 2: Energy, the Environment, and Economic Growth*. Cambridge, MA: MIT Press.

Karingi, S. N., and M. Siriwardana. 2003. "A CGE Model Analysis of Effects of Adjustment to Terms of Trade Shocks on Agriculture and Income Distribution in Kenya." *Journal of Developing Areas* 37 (1): 87–108.

Khan, H. A. 1999. "Sectoral Growth and Poverty: A Multiplier Decomposition Analysis for South Africa." *World Development* 27 (3): 521–30.

Kumar, P. 2005. *Oil Price Increase and the Kenyan Economy*. World Bank, AFTP2, Washington, DC.

Leontief, Wassily. 1951. *The Structure of the American Economy 1919–1939*, 2nd ed. New York: Oxford University Press.

———. 1953. *Studies in the Structure of the American Economy*. New York: Oxford University Press.

Lewis, B., and E. Thorbecke. 1992. "District-Level Economic Linkages in Kenya: Evidence Based on a Small Regional Social Accounting Matrix." *World Development* 20 (6): 881–97.

Miller, R., and P. Blair. 1985. *Input-Output Analysis: Foundations and Extensions*. Upper Saddle River, NJ: Prentice Hall.

Mitra, P. K. 1994. *Adjustment in Oil-Importing Developing Countries: A Comparative Economic Analysis.* Cambridge: Cambridge University Press.

Moses, L. 1974. "Output and Prices in Interindustry Models." *Papers of the Regional Science Association* 32 (1): 7–18.

Nganou, Jean-Pascal Nguessa. 2005. *A Multisectoral Analysis of Growth Prospects for Lesotho: SAM-Multiplier Decomposition and Computable General Equilibrium Perspectives.* Ph.D. thesis, Department of Economics, American University, Washington, DC.

Parikh, A., and E. Thorbecke. 1996. "Impact of Rural Industrialization on Village Life and Economy: A Social Accounting Matrix Approach." *Economic Development and Cultural Change* 44 (2): 351–77.

Parra, J. C., and Q. Wodon. 2008a. "Decomposition of SAM Multipliers under Supply Constraints: Derivation and Application to Oil Price Shocks in Senegal." World Bank, Development Dialogue on Values and Ethics, Washington, DC.

———. 2008b. "SimSIP SAM: Policy Analysis under a SAM Framework." World Bank, Development Dialogue on Values and Ethics, Washington, DC.

Pyatt, G., and J. Round. 1979. "Accounting and Fixed Price Multipliers in a Social Accounting Matrix Framework." *Economic Journal* 89 (356): 850–73.

Roland-Holst, D., and F. Sancho. 1995. "Modeling Prices in a SAM Structure." *Review of Economics and Statistics* 77 (2): 361–71.

Round, Jeffery I. 1985. "Decomposing Multipliers for Economic Systems Involving Regional and World Trade." *Economic Journal* 95 (378): 383–99.

———. 1989. "Decomposition of Input-Output and Economy-Wide Multipliers in a Regional Setting." In *Frontiers of Input-Output Analysis*, ed. Ronald E. Miller, Karen R. Polenske, and Adam Z. Rose, 103–118. Oxford: Oxford University Press.

Semboja, H. 1994. "The Effects of Energy Taxes on the Kenyan Economy: A CGE Analysis." *Energy Economics* 16 (3): 205–15.

Stone, J. R. N. 1985. "The Disaggregation of the Household Sector in the National Accounts." In *Social Accounting Matrices: A Basis for Planning*, ed. G. Pyatt and J. I. Round, 145–85. Washington, DC: World Bank.

Taylor, J. Edward, and I. Adelman. 1996. *Village Economies.* New York: Cambridge University Press.

Taylor, J. Edward, Antonio Yunez-Naude, George A. Dyer, Micki Stewart, and Sergio Ardila. 2002. "The Economics of 'Eco-Tourism': A Galapagos Island Economywide Perspective." *Economic Development and Cultural Change* 51 (4): 977–97.

Ten Raa, Thijs. 2005. *The Economics of Input-Output Analysis*. Cambridge: Cambridge University Press.

Thorbecke, Erik. 2000. "The Use of Social Accounting Matrices in Modeling." Paper prepared for the 26th General Conference of the International Association for Research in Income and Wealth, Cracow, Poland, August 27–September 2.

Thorbecke, Erik, and Hong-Sang Jung. 1996. "A Multiplier Decomposition Method to Analyze Poverty Alleviation." *Journal of Development Economics* 48 (2): 279–300.

U.S. Department of Energy. 2004. *Country Analysis Brief: Great Lakes Region*. Energy Information Administration, Washington, DC.

Wobst, P., and B. Schraven. 2004. "The 2001 Social Accounting Matrix (SAM) for Kenya." International Food Policy Research Institute, Washington, DC.

4

Exports and Labor Income by Gender: A Social Accounting Matrix Analysis for Senegal

Ismael Fofana, Juan Carlos Parra, and Quentin Wodon

Raising the incomes of women can help reduce poverty in both the short run (by providing more resources to households) and the long run (by increasing investments in the human capital of children). Substantial research on gender disparities in labor incomes in developing countries has been conducted using microeconomic household survey data. These studies do not necessarily provide insights on how broad structural shifts in an economy can differentially affect opportunities for work and income generation for men and women, however.

This chapter uses a recent Social Accounting Matrix (SAM) for Senegal to assess how growth in various sectors of the economy, especially exports from tourism, affects the incomes of women and men, both directly and indirectly through initial and multiplier effects. It finds that a tourism export boom could increase not only the level of income of Senegalese women but also their share of total labor income in the economy. The differential impact on labor income shares from growth in various sectors is not necessarily as large as one might expect, however. This suggests that broad policies to encourage the development of specific sectors may not be sufficient to fundamentally affect gender labor income shares.

Why should we be interested in gender disparities in labor income shares and more generally labor market conditions? In sub-Saharan Africa such disparities can have important implications for poverty reduction. At least three different aspects of poverty can be related to the decisions made by various household members in terms of their allocation of time and their prospects for labor income.

First, traditional consumption-based poverty is directly related to the earnings of household members as well as to household size. Both factors depend in part on who is working in the household and how much various household members earn.

Second, the issue of relative power within the households (for example, whether the household head or the spouse makes key decisions, either separately or jointly) also depends on the earnings of various household members. It can have important long-term effects on children. Typically, the less women are engaged in income-generating activities, the less influence they have on household decision making and the less the household invests in the human capital of children, which may in turn reduce the likelihood that their children will avoid poverty in the future (Hoddinott and Haddad 1995; for evidence on Senegal, see chapter 7 of this volume).

Third, time poverty (working more hours than desirable) is an important welfare measure. It is the direct result of the decisions made within the household regarding the allocation of both domestic and productive work. For example, women tend to work much less in the labor market, but this is more than compensated by long hours spent on domestic work, so that they tend to be more time poor than men (that is, a larger share of women than men work long hours) (Blackden and Wodon 2006).

In a microeconomic setting, standard regression analysis techniques can be applied to household survey data to measure the likelihood of labor force participation as well as the time spent on various household activities by different household members. The same techniques can be used to see how expected levels of earnings for women compare with the expected values for men. Differences between men and women can then be analyzed using alternative decomposition methods to assess what drives differences in earnings and what remains unexplained.[1] Access to basic infrastructure services, such as electricity and water, is important, because such access has a direct impact on the time allocation of household members, especially in Africa, as well as on the productivity of labor.

While standard microeconomic techniques can help shed light on gender disparities, they do not typically provide insights on how broad structural shifts in the economy affect opportunities for work for men and women differently. This chapter uses a recent

SAM for Senegal to assess how demand shocks in various sectors of the economy are likely to affect the incomes of women and men differently.

Since the 1994 devaluation of the CFA franc, the performance of the Senegalese economy has been good, both in comparison with other countries in the subregion and from an historical perspective. As a result, poverty reduction has been substantial. According to estimates by Ndoye and others (2008), the share of the population living in poverty declined from 67.9 percent in 1994/95 to 50.8 percent in 2005/06, the latest year for which household survey data are available.[2] Despite the decline, concerns remain that the poor may not have benefited as much from growth as they could have. The real average growth rate reached almost 5 percent over this period, and fiscal and external balances were maintained. Growth slowed after 2006, however, and has been uneven in various sectors of the economy. Growth has been achieved mainly in trade, telecommunications, agriculture (with ups and downs), construction, and real estate activities.

One of the sectors that has traditionally been important for exports in Senegal is tourism, which has grown in recent years. Given the high labor intensity of this sector and the fact that it employs many women, one might expect that growth of the sector would contribute to a larger income share for women over time. However, beyond the direct impact of tourism on female income shares is the indirect impact of growth in the tourism sector on labor income through the multiplier effect tourism has on the rest of the economy. Analysis of this type can easily be conducted using a SAM approach.

The rest of this chapter is organized as follows. The next section provides a brief description of the structure of a standard SAM, as well as some details on the construction of the 2004 Senegal SAM used for the analysis, with a focus on the steps that were taken to disaggregate the labor shares of different sectors in the SAM by gender. The following section presents the results of the simulations. The last section summarizes the chapter's main conclusions.

Basic Structure of a Social Accounting Matrix

SAMs have been used fairly extensively to model the impact of shocks on an economy. (For a brief literature review of SAMs, see chapter 3.) Intuitively, the SAM model is a static comprehensive model that assumes that all agents and accounts in the SAM behave according to their expenditure propensities (what one agent or account in the

economy buys from another agent or account), and that these propensities are unaffected by shocks simulated in the model (that is,
there are no behavioral responses or changes following a shock). The
general equilibrium nature of the SAM model comes from the fact
that the model takes into account multiplier effects. If production in
one account or sector is increased, that sector must buy inputs from
other accounts, which in turn must purchase additional inputs, and
so on. All these spillover effects from an initial shock are taken into
account in the SAM model, which reveals the overall impact on the
economy of a shock after the economy has reached a new equilibrium
following the shock.[3]

The core of the SAM model is the technical coefficients matrix
containing the expenditure propensities for every account in the
matrix. The equilibrium character of the model is given by the fact
that, at a solution, there are no forces suggesting additional changes.
In the simplest form of the model, no resource constraint is specified
because it is assumed that any additional production required is
feasible, so that all resources (factors) required to undertake additional production are available (this assumption can be relaxed).

The simplicity of the SAM model is both its main weakness and
strength. This simplicity is a weakness because no behavioral response
is taken into account, and the model cannot be used to simulate at
the same time price and quantity shocks (when a price shock is simulated, quantities are held constant, and when a quantity shock is
simulated, prices are held constant). But simplicity is also a strength,
because the model is easy to understand and its results can be easily
replicated. More complicated models, such as computable general
equilibrium (CGE) models, can take into account behavioral
responses, but their results depend on many assumptions which are
not always easy to assess for the external reader. Obviously, strong
assumptions are implicit in the SAM model, but they are transparent
and easier to comprehend. SAM models are probably especially helpful in low-income countries where data are limited.

Another potentially important advantage of the SAM model is the
possibility of analyzing the structure of the economy and quantifying the strength of the linkages between the different accounts. The
final effect of any shock can be easily decomposed in several ways
to shed light on the economic links between accounts and their
intensity. This type of decomposition analysis is much more difficult
to do with a CGE given the more complex nature of such models.

In technical terms, SAMs are numerical arrays representing the
circular flow of income in an economy between sectors or activities,
as well as between sectors, the government, households, and the rest
of the world. Each cell in a SAM, denoted by SAM_{ij}, reflects payments

from an account j to another account i. When using a SAM for simulations, some accounts have to be set as endogenous (which means that they can react to a shock in the economy) and the rest of the accounts are set as exogenous (no change in the account following a shock). It is customary to set the government, capital, and rest of the world accounts as exogenous, but this choice depends on the nature of the analysis. Mathematically, the structure of simulations can be presented using a simple representation of a SAM (table 4.1).

The core of the SAM analysis is the multiplier model. Assume there are n endogenous accounts. Let A_{nxn} denote the matrix of technical coefficients, that is, the matrix resulting from dividing every cell T_{ij} in T_{nxn} by the respective column sum Y_j. Let Y_{nx1}, N_{nx1}, and X_{nx1} denote column vectors with the sums of total expenditures for the endogenous accounts, the endogenous component of those expenditures, and the exogenous component, respectively. Then by construction, the following two equations hold: $Y = N + X$ and $N = AY$. Combining these equations yields

$$(4.1) \qquad\qquad Y = AY + X,$$

which can be rewritten as

$$(4.2) \qquad\qquad Y = (I - A)^{-1} X = MX,$$

where I is the $n \times n$ identity matrix. The matrix $M = (I - A)^{-1}$ is known as the accounting multiplier matrix, the Leontief inverse matrix, or simply the inverse matrix. Each cell m_{ij} of M quantifies the change in total income of account i as a result of a unitary increase in the exogenous component of account j. This change takes into account all the interactions in the economy that follow from an initial shock, so that SAMs are general equilibrium models.

As already mentioned, when using SAMs for simulations of standard demand shocks (for example, an increase in the demand of tourism from the rest of the world), it is important to realize that a number of assumptions are implicit in the framework. The two main assumptions are that all prices remain fixed, as do all expenditure propensities, whether one considers productive activities or

Table 4.1 Schematic Social Accounting Matrix

Income/expenditure	Endogenous accounts	Exogenous accounts	Total
Endogenous accounts	T	X	Y
Exogenous accounts	L	W	Y_x
Total	·	Y'	Y'_x

Source: Adapted from Defourney and Thorbecke 1984.

commodities purchased by households. Thus a SAM is essentially a picture at one point in time of the economy and of the relations between different sectors as well as institutions or groups of agents. When using the SAM for simulations, we assume that the structural relations observed in the economy do not change, which is to say that there are no behavioral adjustments by agents following a shock. This is a strong assumption, which implies that the analysis obtained from a SAM is often tentative and indicative only, and may lead to an overestimation of the impact of a shock.

Characteristics of the 2004 Senegal SAM

This section provides a basic description of key features of the Senegal SAM. It begins with the activities identified in the SAM and then focuses on how the SAM labor accounts have been disaggregated by gender, which is the feature of the SAM then used to assess the impact of various shocks on labor income by gender.

Activities

The Senegal SAM used here is based on an input-output table for 2004. The SAM includes 35 activities and commodities and 8 production factors, including 6 labor income accounts disaggregated by urban versus rural location, gender, and education (literate versus illiterate workers in urban areas). There are two capital accounts, one for households and the self-employed and one for firms and government. Households are defined according to their geographic location (Dakar, other urban households, and rural households).

Commerce is by far the largest contributor to value added, accounting for almost 17 percent of the total (table 4.2). This sector is followed by public administration, with almost 7 percent, and by a group of industries, including real estate, financial services, telecommunications, and agriculture, with contributions of about 5–6 percent of total value added. Other industries—such as construction, transport, livestock and hunting, and meat and fish processing—each account for about 4–5 percent.

Senegal's main imports are machinery and equipment, metallic products, transport materials, mining, food, and petroleum, which together accounted for 82 percent of cif imports in 2004. The country relies on imports for 90 percent of its demand for machinery and equipment and transport materials; 70–80 percent of its demand for chemical products, mining, and metallic products; and 30–40 percent of its demand for rubber products, food (excluding cereals, meat, and

Table 4.2 Sectoral Analysis for the 2004 Senegal SAM

Sector	Production (Q) US$ millions	Production (Q) Percentage of total	Value added at factor costs US$ millions	Value added at factor costs Percentage of total	Imports (M) US$ millions	Imports (M) Percentage of total	Exports (X) US$ millions	Exports (X) Percentage of total	M/Q	X/XS	Import taxes	Local taxes
Commerce	1,979	15.2	1,292	16.9	0	0.0	0	0.0	0.00	0.00		1.4
Public administration	727	5.6	529	6.9	0	0.0	0	0.0	0.00	0.00		0.1
Real state	476	3.7	442	5.8	0	0.0	0	0.0	0.00	0.00		7.1
Financial services	817	6.3	417	5.5	121	4.0	118	5.8	0.15	0.14	12.8	6.1
Agriculture	441	3.4	382	5.0	135	4.5	8	0.4	0.24	0.02	23.4	-24.3
Telecommunications	573	4.4	363	4.8	26	0.9	96	4.7	0.05	0.17	4.2	6.6
Construction	1,253	9.6	327	4.3	0	0.0	0	0.0	0.00	0.00		0.2
Livestock and hunting	362	2.8	297	3.9	1	0.0	3	0.1	0.00	0.01	17.3	8.9
Transport	608	4.7	298	3.9	52	1.7	91	4.4	0.09	0.15	15.6	6.4
Education	293	2.3	259	3.4	6	0.2	0	0.0	0.02	0.00	32.2	7.2
Meat and fish processing	478	3.7	243	3.2	32	1.1	154	7.5	0.09	0.32	25.9	5
Industrial agriculture	251	1.9	192	2.5	22	0.7	8	0.4	0.08	0.03	16	78.9
Utilities	377	2.9	167	2.2	0	0.0	0	0.0	0.00	0.00		7.7
Chemical products	404	3.1	151	2.0	322	10.6	302	14.8	0.76	0.75	17.9	-73.7
Other private services	217	1.7	144	1.9	0	0.0	56	2.8	0.00	0.26	32.2	5.7
Fishing	258	2.0	141	1.8	12	0.4	91	4.5	0.06	0.35	1.8	3.5
Textiles	261	2.0	107	1.4	75	2.5	32	1.6	0.25	0.12	21.1	6.7
Health	153	1.2	105	1.4	0	0.0	0	0.0	0.00	0.00	32.2	7.2

(Continued on the following page)

Table 4.2 (Continued)

	Production (Q) US$ millions	Production (Q) Percentage of total	Value added at factor costs US$ millions	Value added at factor costs Percentage of total	Imports (M) US$ millions	Imports (M) Percentage of total	Exports (X) US$ millions	Exports (X) Percentage of total	M/Q	X/XS	Import taxes	Local taxes
Mining	168	1.3	88	1.2	386	12.7	105	5.1	0.72	0.26	2.3	35.4
Food	469	3.6	92	1.2	288	9.5	75	3.7	0.42	0.16	29.8	4.8
Other manufacturing	153	1.2	89	1.2	31	1.0	8	0.4	0.18	0.05	25.5	8.1
Grains and cereals	541	4.2	83	1.1	224	7.4	6	0.3	0.29	0.01	28.8	5.9
Tourism	330	2.5	74	1.0	*0	0.0	249	12.2	0.00	0.75		2.5
Forestry	92	0.7	59	0.8	9	0.3	2	0.1	0.10	0.02	14.4	43.9
Glass and pottery	199	1.5	64	0.8	65	2.1	32	1.6	0.28	0.16	18	34.7
Metallic products	137	1.1	57	0.7	194	6.4	42	2.1	0.67	0.31	15.8	−45.9
Wood products	94	0.7	43	0.6	63	2.1	51	2.5	0.15	0.04	4.7	5.2
Paper products	129	1.0	44	0.6	72	2.4	15	0.8	0.31	0.00	14.4	8.7
Beverages	73	0.6	29	0.4	19	0.6	2	0.1	0.21	0.02	30.1	6.9
Petroleum	453	3.5	34	0.4	265	8.7	459	22.5	0.03	0.44	1.1	13.9
Rubber products	90	0.7	30	0.4	54	1.8	21	1.0	0.44	0.23	19.1	6.3
Tobacco	64	0.5	12	0.2	0	0.0	12	0.6	0.01	0.18	27	6.2
Leather products	27	0.2	15	0.2	13	0.4	3	0.2	0.35	0.13	31.9	6.3
Machinery and equipment	34	0.3	8	0.1	385	12.7	0	0.0	0.92	0.00	17	3.2
Transport materials	13	0.1	4	0.1	162	5.3	0	0.0	0.93	0.00	20.3	0.3
Total	12,992	100.0	7,634	100.0	3,037	100.0	2 039	100.0	0.19	0.13	16.1	3.3

Source: Authors, using SimSIP SAM.

Note: M/Q is the import share within sector production; X/XS is the export share of production.

fish), leather products, and paper products. Petroleum represents 23 percent of total fob exports. Chemical products and tourism ("hotels and restaurants" in the national accounts) are also important commodities sold to nonresidents, with chemical products representing 15 percent and tourism 12 percent of total exports. Meat and fish processing, mining, fishery, financial services, telecommunications, and transport are also important export sectors. Tourism and chemical products are the most export-oriented industries, exporting three-quarters of their production. Petroleum, fishing, meat and fish processing, and metallic products are also export oriented.

Gender Disaggregation for Labor Income

Gender-disaggregated SAM accounts are needed to analyze the impact of exogenous shocks on labor income shares by gender. This section explains how the labor income component of the Senegal SAM was disaggregated for each activity by using data from the 1994/1995 and 2001/02 nationally representative household surveys (Enquête Sénégalaise Auprès des Ménages [ESAM]) and establishing a correspondence between the SAM activities and the sectors of occupation listed by household members in the surveys. Both surveys identify the sector of activity of workers; data on earnings are available only in the first survey. It was therefore necessary to impute earnings in the second survey. Both the levels of earnings and the share of workers in different sectors by gender were then used to estimate the labor income shares accruing to women in each sector of the SAM.

The estimates of the earnings by gender in the SAM are based on two sources of data. The first is the distribution of employment by gender and sector in the ESAM II survey. According to that survey, there were 1.57 million women and 1.92 million men working in Senegal in 2002. Agriculture was the principal activity for both men (64 percent of all male workers) and women (63 percent of all female workers) (table 4.3 and figures 4.1 and 4.2). It was followed by commerce, with 19 percent of male and female workers. The shares of workers in these two sectors increased between 1995 and 2002, at the expense of activities such as construction, transport, other manufacturing, fishing, and (somewhat surprisingly) public administration. In absolute terms all sectors except public administration (where female employment fell 26 percent) witnessed an increase in male and female employment. Male employment increased at a rapid annual rate in construction (10 percent) and other manufacturing (9 percent). Female employment witnessed a significant increase in activities that have not traditionally been female intensive, such as construction

Table 4.3 Female and Male Employment in Senegal,
by Sector, 2002

Sector	Number of workers		Share of total (percent)		
	Female	Male	Female	Male	intensity
Agriculture	996,856	1,077,828	63.3	64.4	0.9
Commerce	294,681	181,482	18.7	18.6	1.6
Other private services	163,404	135,110	10.4	8.6	1.2
Public administration	38,944	102,833	2.5	3.4	0.4
Food processing	28,521	31,631	1.8	1.8	0.9
Fishing	13,816	56,826	0.9	0.9	0.2
Other manufacturing	13,506	79,460	0.9	0.8	0.2
Tourism	11,531	6,517	0.7	0.7	1.8
Transport	5,027	94,391	0.3	0.3	0.1
Construction	3,049	122,149	0.2	0.2	0.0
Financial services	2,137	4,112	0.1	0.1	0.5
Electricity, gas, and water	1,905	15,638	0.1	0.1	0.1
Mining	725	9,616	0.0	0.0	0.1
All	1,574,101	1,917,593	100.0	100.0	0.8

Source: Authors, based on data from ESAM 1995 and ESAM 2002.

(29 percent) and mining (25 percent). (The ratio of female to male employment in these industries nevertheless remains small.) Female employment in other private services rose by 24 percent over the period. This sector is the most female intensive after tourism and commerce. Overall, the ratio of female to male employment remained at roughly 0.8 between 1995 and 2002. Activities with a large share of female workers include private and social services (tourism, as well as commerce and other private services); food-processing activities; and agriculture. Manufacturing industries (including construction, transport, and mining) are less female intensive.

To compute labor income shares by gender, we also need data on earnings. Gender differences in earnings in Africa are large, as the data from the 1995 ESAM survey indicate (table 4.4). Because the 2002 ESAM II survey did not include wage or income data, we used the wage data from the ESAM I survey (indexed by inflation between 1995 and 2002) combined with the labor employment shares of the ESAM II survey to construct labor earnings in the SAM. This information was then used to estimate male and female income shares for the SAM.

Nationally, only one-third of total labor income accrues to female workers. This share is larger in the primary sector (43 percent) and much smaller in the secondary sector (12 percent) (table 4.5). In urban areas men and women are involved primarily in services, and differences in total labor incomes by gender are smaller than they

Figure 4.1 Shares of Male and Female Workers in Senegal, by Sector, 2002

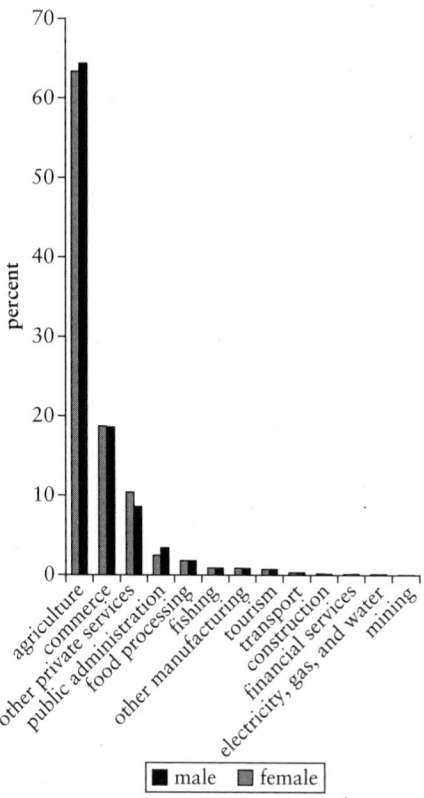

Source: Authors, based on ESAM 2002 data.

are in rural areas. In rural areas agriculture is the main activity, and differences in labor incomes are larger. The largest share of labor income accrues to men in mining, construction, other manufacturing, and transport and telecommunications.

The next step in computing gender-disaggregated labor income data for the SAM consists of mapping the industrial sectors observed in the ESAM surveys with the sectors as defined in the SAM (table 4.6). Overall, tourism is the most female-intensive labor activity, with 55.9 percent of total payments to labor going to female workers. Shares of labor income for women are 52.7 percent in commerce and 49.2 percent in agriculture. Petroleum is the most important export product, representing 22.5 percent of total exports, followed by chemical products (14.8 percent) and hotels and restaurants (12.2 percent). These three sectors also

Figure 4.2 Ratio of Female to Male Workers in Senegal, by Sector, 1995 and 2002

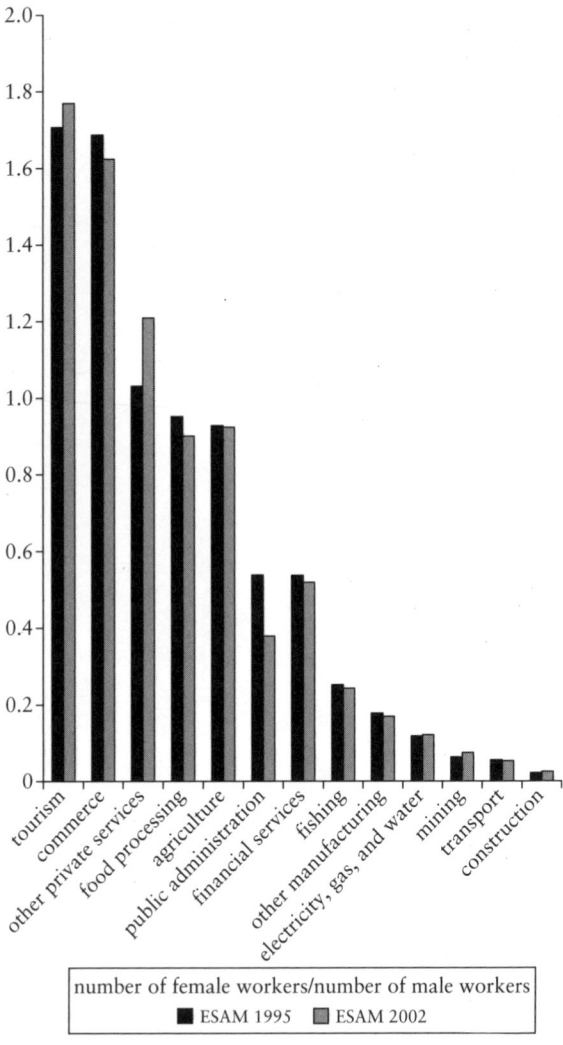

number of female workers/number of male workers
■ ESAM 1995   ■ ESAM 2002

Source: Authors, based on ESAM 1995 and 2002 data.

exhibit high export propensities (55.7 percent for petroleum, 51.4 percent for chemical products, and 19.9 percent for hotels and restaurants). One might expect that tourism would have the largest potential among export sectors for increasing the share of total income earned by women. In fact, the effect also depends on multiplier effects, as shown in the next section.

Table 4.4 Average Monthly Earnings by Females and
Males in Senegal, 1995

(CFA francs)

Item	Female	Male	Female/male ratio
Sector			
Transport	193,548	137,617	1.41
Commerce	70,441	83,511	0.84
Electricity, gas, and water	173,288	224,461	0.77
Fishing	85,575	122,900	0.70
Other manufacturing	56,889	96,613	0.59
Financial services	135,404	231,140	0.59
Food processing	56,753	110,513	0.51
Public administration	130,883	269,087	0.49
Construction	23,000	63,094	0.36
Other private services	85,173	267,473	0.32
Tourism	25,906	88,579	0.29
Agriculture	7,964	32,483	0.25
Mining	0	140,387	0.00
Type of employment			
Self-employed workers	5,591	10,809	0.52
Salary and wage workers	44,306	124,151	0.36
Family helpers	3,574	17,602	0.20
Individuals in training	28,777	30,702	0.94
All	86,690	166,892	0.52

Source: Authors, based on data from ESAM 1995.

Sectoral Growth and Impact on Labor Income Shares by Gender

We start by presenting the labor income multipliers following a unitary exogenous demand shock for specific sectors of the economy (table 4.7).[4] Because male workers as a group earn much more than women—because of both the larger number of male workers and the higher average wage for male workers—the multiplier impacts are larger for male than for female workers. For example, after multiplier effects are taken into account, an additional CFAF 1,000 million of exports in tourism generates an increase of CFAF 654.6 million in male labor income and CFAF 367.7 million in female labor income (CFAF = Communauté Financière Africaine franc). Exports of other private services (entertainment, gambling, betting, and personal services, among others) have the greatest impact on labor income among the four export sectors, with CFAF 1,313 million of additional labor income per CFAF 1,000 million of additional exports. Agriculture experiences

Table 4.5 Labor Income Shares and Labor Intensity of
Females and Males in Senegal, by Sector, 2002

(percent)

Indicator	Share			Intensity	
	Female	*Male*	*All*	*Female*	*Male*
Senegal	100.0	100.0	100.0	32.2	67.8
Primary sector	31.3	20.1	23.7	42.5	57.5
Secondary sector	6.4	22.7	17.5	11.7	88.3
Tertiary sector	62.4	57.2	58.9	34.1	65.9
Urban areas	100.0	100.0	100.0	41.9	58.1
Primary sector	84.0	62.7	71.7	49.2	50.8
Secondary sector	0.8	9.8	6.1	5.7	94.3
Tertiary sector	15.2	27.4	22.3	28.6	71.4
Rural areas	100.0	100.0	100.0	28.6	71.4
Primary sector	3.1	7.4	6.2	14.2	85.8
Secondary sector	9.4	26.5	21.6	12.4	87.6
Tertiary sector	87.6	66.0	72.2	34.7	65.3
Sector of activity	100.0	100.0	100.0	32.2	67.8
Agriculture	29.8	14.6	19.5	49.2	50.8
Fishing and hunting	1.5	4.2	3.3	14.4	85.6
Mining	0.0	1.3	0.9	0.0	100.0
Food industry	2.7	7.7	6.1	14.1	85.9
Other industries	3.3	8.5	6.8	15.7	84.3
Electricity, gas, and water	0.3	1.2	0.9	9.4	90.6
Construction	0.1	5.3	3.6	1.0	99.0
Commerce	29.3	12.5	17.9	52.7	47.3
Tourism	1.9	0.7	1.1	55.9	44.1
Transport and telecommunications	1.1	11.6	8.3	4.4	95.6
Financial services	13.6	9.6	10.9	40.2	59.8
Public administration	6.9	10.1	9.0	24.4	75.6
Other private services	9.6	12.7	11.7	26.3	73.7

Source: Authors, based on ESAM 1995 and ESAM 2002 data.

the largest increase in labor income for female workers as a multiple
of the corresponding increase for male workers (1.6). The increase in
labor income primarily favors illiterate male workers. The impact is
also greater among urban than rural workers.

Although the share of labor income initially obtained by female
workers exceeds 50 percent for tourism (see table 4.6), the final effect
of an exogenous demand shock in that sector is much greater for male
workers. This is caused in large part by the multiplier effects and the
fact that for most other sectors, the male labor income share is higher
than the share obtained by women. Because male labor income is high

Table 4.6 Female Labor Income Share and Labor Intensity in Senegal SAM, by Sector, 2004

(percent)

Sector	Female labor income share	Female labor intensity
Tourism	55.9	10.7
Commerce	52.7	28.9
Agriculture	49.2	63.7
Industrial agriculture	49.2	49.7
Livestock and hunting	49.2	51.3
Forestry	49.2	36.0
Financial services	40.2	24.1
Real state	40.2	31.8
Health	28.6	43.9
Other private services	28.6	44.9
Public administration	24.4	39.8
Education	24.4	72.0
Textiles	15.7	29.6
Leather products	15.7	19.8
Wood products	15.7	20.2
Paper products	15.7	8.8
Petroleum	15.7	1.7
Chemical products	15.7	9.8
Rubber products	15.7	4.0
Glass and pottery	15.7	5.2
Metallic products	15.7	6.2
Machinery and equipment	15.7	7.3
Transport materials	15.7	12.1
Other manufacturing	15.7	20.5
Fishing	14.4	40.9
Meat and fish processing	14.1	20.3
Grains and cereals	14.1	7.7
Food	14.1	10.0
Beverages	14.1	8.4
Tobacco	14.1	5.8
Electricity, gas, and water	9.4	7.6
Transport	4.4	18.2
Telecommunications	4.4	26.7
Construction	1.0	9.3
Mining	0.0	16.8

Source: Authors, based on ESAM 1995 and ESAM 2002 data.

Table 4.7 Effect of Exogenous Demand Shock of CFAF 1,000 Million on Labor in Senegal, by Sector and Population Segment, 2004

(CFA francs, millions)

Population segment	Tourism	Petroleum	Agriculture	Financial services	Other private services	Transport	Construction
Rural							
Male	171.0	62.3	296.8	128.5	187.2	142.8	129.8
	(0.63)	(0.23)	(1.09)	(0.47)	(0.69)	(0.52)	(0.48)
Female	139.9	45.4	261.6	93.4	120.6	91.1	83.0
	(0.71)	(0.23)	(1.32)	(0.47)	(0.61)	(0.46)	(0.42)
Total	310.9	107.7	558.4	221.9	307.9	233.9	212.8
	(0.66)	(0.23)	(1.19)	(0.47)	(0.65)	(0.50)	(0.45)
Urban							
Male illiterate	360.8	167.8	283.0	444.3	568.1	374.4	343.5
	(0.53)	(0.24)	(0.41)	(0.65)	(0.83)	(0.55)	(0.50)
Female illiterate	147.3	58.1	104.3	206.3	221.3	122.5	117.2
	(0.61)	(0.24)	(0.43)	(0.85)	(0.91)	(0.50)	(0.48)
Male literate	122.8	57.3	100.2	105.6	133.8	153.6	130.2
	(0.52)	(0.24)	(0.42)	(0.45)	(0.57)	(0.65)	(0.55)
Female literate	80.6	33.8	64.5	63.0	81.9	64.7	55.7
	(0.64)	(0.27)	(0.51)	(0.50)	(0.65)	(0.51)	(0.44)
Total	711.4	317.0	551.9	819.1	1,005.0	715.1	646.7
	(0.55)	(0.25)	(0.43)	(0.63)	(0.78)	(0.55)	(0.50)
Gender							
Male	654.6	287.4	680.0	678.3	889.1	670.7	603.5
	(0.55)	(0.24)	(0.57)	(0.57)	(0.74)	(0.56)	(0.50)
Female	367.7	137.3	430.3	362.7	423.8	278.3	255.9
	(0.65)	(0.24)	(0.76)	(0.64)	(0.75)	(0.49)	(0.45)

Source: Authors, using SimSIP SAM.

Note: All multipliers have been multiplied by 1,000 for ease of exposition. Figures in parentheses represent percentage changes.

in other sectors that respond to the initial shock in the tourism sector, the total gains in income are larger for males than for females even when the sector that is shocked initially is female intensive.

Indirect effects represent a large proportion of the total multiplier effect (table 4.8). In tourism they account for 73.1 percent of the total effect for male workers and 63.9 percent of the total effect for female workers (indirect effects are defined here as closed-loop effects divided by total effects; see the annex for details). For two other sectors, agriculture and financial services, the indirect effects are greater for female workers. This is not observed for the other sectors in the table, mainly because the initial labor income shares for females in those sectors is smaller than it is in tourism, agriculture, and financial services.

While the increase in labor income from an initial shock is larger for male than female workers in all seven sectors examined, the proportion of total labor income that goes to female workers increases in five of the seven sectors (transport and construction are the exceptions). Expressing the changes in labor income caused by an increase in exports in percentage terms rather than values thus yields a different picture (see table 4.7). In rural areas the proportional increase in labor income is larger for female than male workers in tourism, petroleum, agriculture, and financial services. In urban areas the proportional gain is larger among literate workers in these sectors as well as in other private services. The transport and construction sectors benefit male workers more than female workers, regardless of location and education.

In order to compare the percentage increases in labor income by gender in the seven sectors in tables 4.7 and 4.8 with other sectors, we simulate an increase in the demand for each of the sectors in the SAM equal to 1 percent of aggregate exports (CFAF 11,217 million) and estimate the resulting increase in labor income in percentage terms (figure 4.3). (The size of this shock is arbitrary; it was chosen as a percentage of aggregate exports to give an idea of the importance of the shock relative to macroeconomic aggregates.) Education generates the greatest growth in male labor income, with an increase in total male income of 1.0 percent. Manufacturing activities for machinery and equipment generate, on average, the smallest percentage increases in male labor income (almost 0.2 percent, partially explained by their low labor intensities). The effect on labor income is related in part to the labor intensity of different activities, as well as to the gender shares of labor income in the various sectors, but the multiplier effects of the various sectors also play a role. Commerce exhibits the highest elasticity on labor income (0.7). Agriculture, grains and cereals, and food also have high elasticities (greater than 0.4).

Table 4.8 Share of Total Multiplier Effect Caused by Indirect Effects in Senegal, by Sector and Population Segment, 2004
(percent)

Population segment	Tourism	Petroleum	Agriculture	Financial services	Other private services	Transport	Construction
Rural							
Male	70.2	91.6	45.0	94.0	73.7	80.8	82.2
Female	64.2	94.5	39.4	96.2	85.2	94.4	96.1
Urban							
Male illiterate	74.4	76.4	93.3	62.0	55.2	70.5	70.4
Female illiterate	64.8	78.5	89.5	47.7	50.4	76.7	73.5
Male literate	73.1	74.3	90.4	87.0	78.2	57.1	61.9
Female literate	61.6	69.4	79.4	80.3	70.6	74.7	79.5
Gender							
Male	73.1	79.3	71.8	72.0	62.5	69.6	71.1
Female	63.9	81.6	57.5	65.9	64.2	82.0	82.1

Source: Authors, using SimSIP SAM.

Figure 4.3 Impact of a 1 Percent Change in Aggregate Exports on Male Labor and Labor Elasticity in Senegal, by Sector

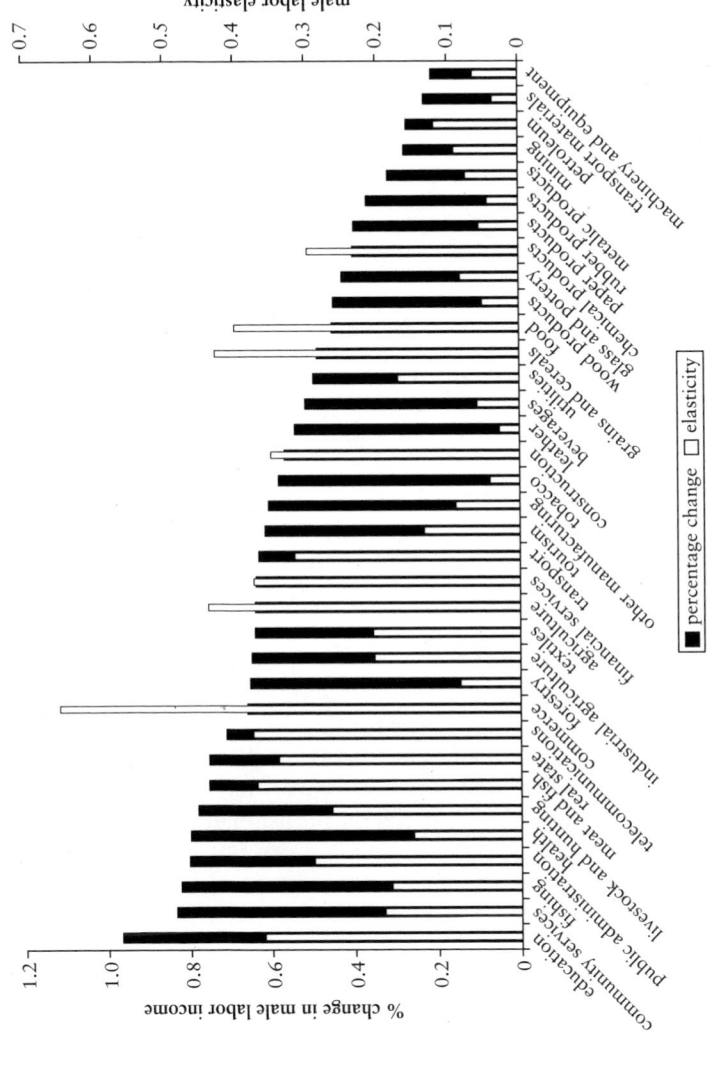

Source: Authors, using SimSIP SAM.

Note: The bar denoting elasticity is narrower (white) and is superimposed on the wider (black) bar denoting percentage change.

The procedure described above is used to look at the impact of shocks on female labor income (figure 4.4). The livestock and hunting sector experiences the strongest growth in female labor income (1.0 percent) when all sectors face the same shock equal to 1 percent of aggregate exports. As it does for male labor income, commerce has by far the highest elasticity on female labor income (0.8).

Both male and female labor incomes exhibit a very high elasticity to demand shocks in commerce, with a moderate impact on labor income. In contrast, labor income for both genders exhibits very low elasticity to demand shocks in forestry, tobacco, and leather. The use of the elasticity corrects for the "size bias" that is present in simulations when using the same shock for all sectors—that is, the fact that the shock may be too large for some sectors and too small for others. In this case commerce is the largest sector in the Senegalese economy, and forestry, tobacco, and leather are among the smallest.

The percentage change in labor income for female and male workers reveals that tourism ranks only fifth among the sectors that benefit female workers, after livestock and hunting, agriculture, commerce, industrial agriculture, and forestry (figure 4.5). (Sectors with bars above the horizontal line benefit female workers more than male workers in percentage terms.)

Many different factors contribute to these rankings and to the overall impact on labor income. One factor is the labor intensity of the sector. Another is the labor income shares by gender for each sector. A third is the multiplier effects, which depend in large part on the backward and forward linkages of the various sectors with the rest of the economy. Even if indirect effects matter, however, the original labor income shares in each sector (direct effect) apparently play an important role, because the sectors that have the largest pro-female labor impacts tend to be those with the largest income shares going to women (primary and service-oriented sectors).

Differences are also computed for rural and urban workers (figure 4.6). Sectors with bars above the horizontal line benefit rural workers more than urban workers. Once again tourism ranks fifth, after livestock and hunting, agriculture, industrial agriculture, forestry, and grains and cereals.

Computation of the percentage increases in labor income for illiterate and literate workers in urban areas resulting from a 1 percent increase in total exports reveals that fishing is by far the sector with the largest difference (that is, the sector that generates the largest relative benefit to illiterate workers): an exogenous increase in demand equal to 1 percent of aggregate exports would increase labor income for illiterate workers by 0.4 percent more than the increase in labor income for literate workers (figure 4.7). Public

Figure 4.4 Impact of a 1 Percent Change in Aggregate Exports on Female Labor and Labor Elasticity in Senegal, by Sector

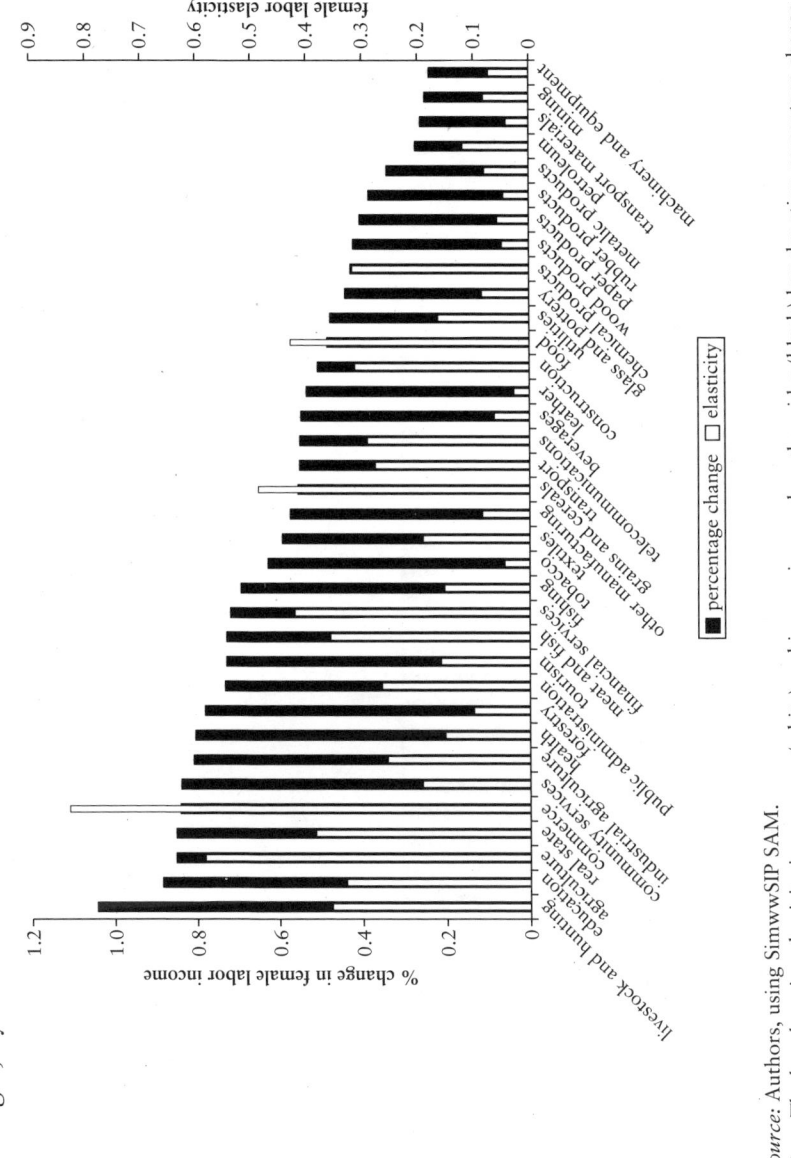

Source: Authors, using SimwwSIP SAM.
Note: The bar denoting elasticity is narrower (white) and is superimposed on the wider (black) bar denoting percentage change.

Figure 4.5 Relative Impact of a 1 Percent Change in Aggregate Exports on Labor Income of Males and Females in Senegal, by Sector

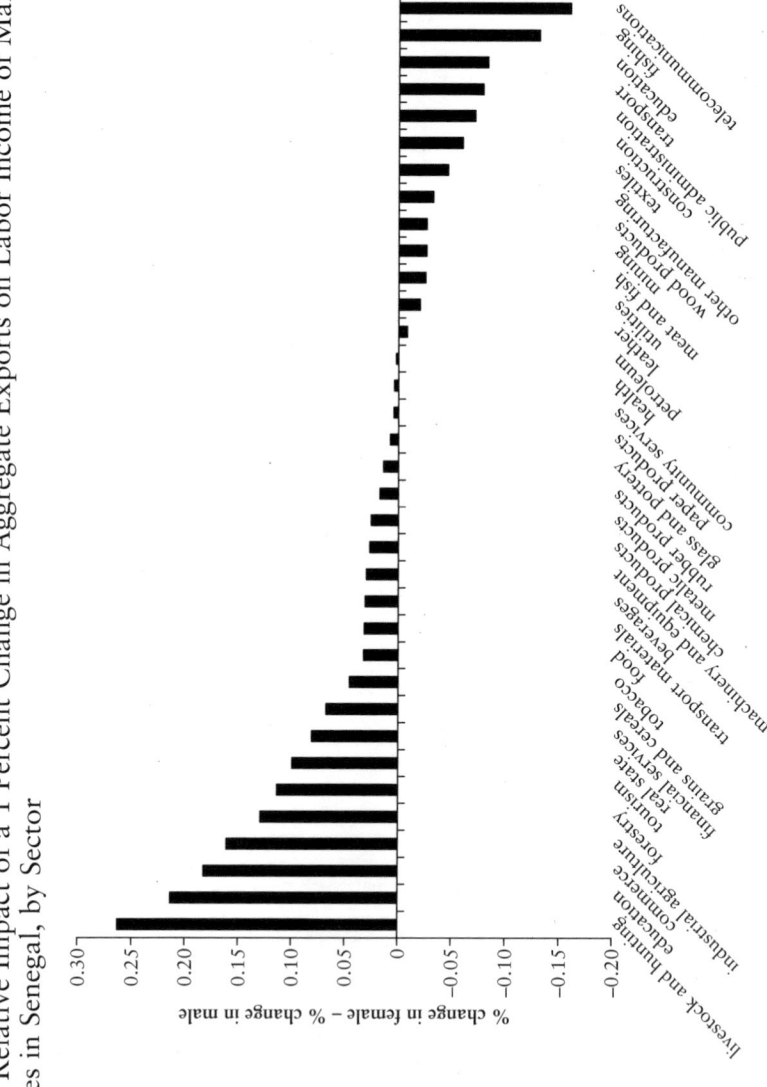

Source: Authors, using SimSIP SAM.

Note: The y-axis label in full is percentage change in female labor income minus the percentage change in male labor income.

Figure 4.6 Relative Impact of a 1 Percent Change in Aggregate Exports on Labor Income of Rural and Urban Workers in Senegal, by Sector

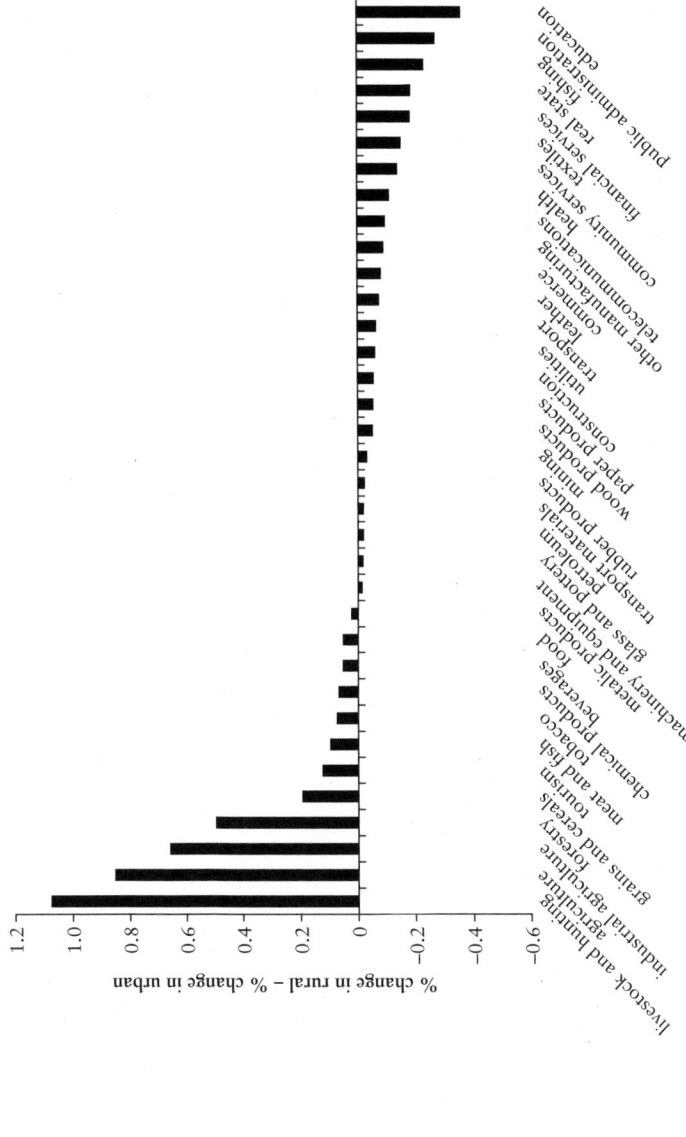

Source: Authors, using SimSIP SAM.
Note: The y-axis label in full is percentage change in labor income of rural workers minus the percentage change in labor income of urban workers.

Figure 4.7 Relative Impact of a 1 Percent Change in Aggregate Exports on Labor Income of Illiterate and Literate Workers in Senegal, by Sector

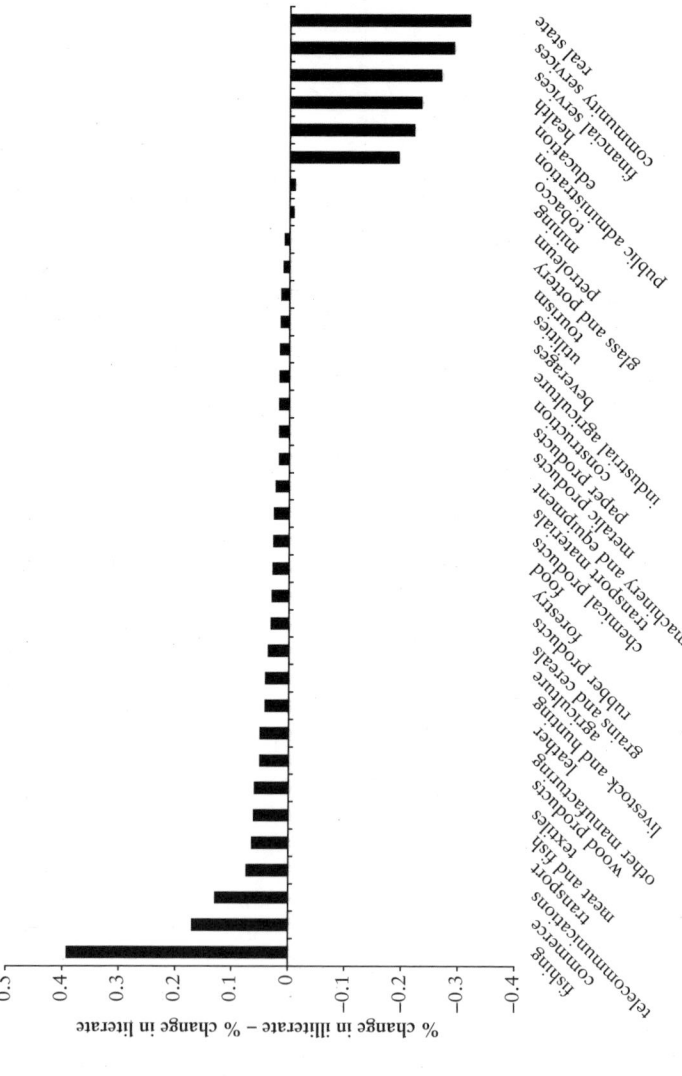

Source: Authors, using SimSIP SAM.

Note: The y-axis label in full is percentage change in labor income of illiterate workers minus the percentage change in labor income of illiterate workers.

administration, education, health, financial services, other private services, and real estate would contribute relatively more to the increase of literate workers' labor income. In all of these sectors, small shares of labor income are going to illiterate workers.

To sum up, in certain sectors (livestock and hunting, agriculture, industrial agriculture, forestry, tourism, grains and cereals, food, beverages, chemical products, and metallic products), an exogenous increase in aggregate exports benefits female workers more than male workers, workers in rural areas more than workers in urban areas, and illiterate workers more than literate workers. In other sectors (public administration and education), the same shock has a greater effect on male workers, workers in urban areas, and literate workers.

Conclusion

Increasing labor income for women and reducing gender disparities in labor income can reduce poverty. In addition to the direct impact from higher household income, research shows that a larger labor income share for women tends to shift consumption choices toward human capital for children.

This chapter uses simple macro-micro simulation techniques to assess how changes in the production of various exports affect labor income shares. It finds that over time, an expansion in tourism exports equal to 1 percent of aggregate exports would increase the income share of women from 32.2 to 32.4 percent. The impact on female labor income of an expansion in tourism is smaller than that of some other sectors, such as agriculture and financial services. Among export-oriented sectors, however, tourism is the sector in which women stand to gain the most from an increase in demand. The direct impact of tourism expansion on female labor incomes is important, because this sector has a large share of female workers; the indirect impact through multiplier effects is also important, with almost two-thirds of the labor income gains caused by indirect effects. At the same time, the differential impact on labor income shares from demand shocks in various sectors with high initial labor shares is not necessarily as large as one might expect, because multiplier effects typically reduce the initial direct effects observed within sectors. This suggests that broad policies to encourage the development of specific sectors of the economy may not be sufficient to fundamentally affect gender labor income shares and thereby gender differences in income.

Annex: Block Decomposition of the Multiplier Matrix

This annex describes the same technique of matrix block decomposition as that presented in annex 3B of chapter 3. However, this annex applies this decomposition technique to a quantity model with fixed prices, whereas annex 3B applies it to a price model with fixed quantities. Furthermore, this annex describes the decomposition of the multiplier matrix M, but annex 3B describes that of its transpose M'.

Cell m_{ji} of the multiplier matrix M quantifies the change in total income of account i as a result of a unitary increase in the exogenous component of sector j. In order to decompose the matrix M^4, for any matrix $n \times n$ nonsingular matrix, we can rewrite equation (4.2) as

$$(4.3) \qquad Y = (A - \tilde{A})Y + \tilde{A}Y + X$$

$$(4.4) \qquad Y = A^*Y + (I + \tilde{A})^{-1}X,$$

where

$$(4.5) \qquad A^* = (I - \tilde{A})^{-1}(A - \tilde{A}).$$

Multiplying equation (4.4) through by A^* yields

$$(4.6) \qquad A^*Y = A^{*2}Y + A^*(I - \tilde{A})^{-1}X.$$

From equation (4.4) we have an expression for A^*Y. Replacing it on the left-hand side yields

$$(4.7) \qquad Y = A^{*2}Y + (I + A^*)(I - \tilde{A})^{-1}X.$$

Multiplying equation (4.4) through by A^{*2} and replacing the expression for $A^{*2}Y$ from equation (4.6) yields

$$(4.8) \qquad Y = (I + A^{*3})^{-1}(I + A^* + A^{*2})(I - \tilde{A})^{-1}X.$$

Notice that we just decomposed multiplicatively the multiplier matrix M from equation (4.2) into three different matrices. Define

$$(4.9) \quad M_1 = (I - \tilde{A})^{-1}, \ M_2 = (I + A^* + A^{*2}), \text{ and } M_3 = (I - A^{*3})^{-1}.$$

Then $M = M_3 M_2 M_1$. It is also possible to present the decomposition in an additive way:

$$(4.10) \quad M = I + \frac{(M_1 - I)}{TR} + \frac{(M_2 - I)M_1}{OL} + \frac{(M_3 - I)M_2 M_1}{CL},$$

where the first term (the identity matrix) is the initial unitary injection, matrix M_1 captures the net effect of a group of accounts on itself through direct transfers, matrix M_2 captures all net effects between partitions, and matrix M_3 captures the net effect of circular income multipliers among endogenous accounts. The terms in the additive decomposition (labeled *TR* for transfer effects, *OL* for open-loop effects, and *CL* for closed-loop effects) have broadly the same interpretation as the corresponding multiplicative effects (the matrices M_i).

The $n \times n$ matrix A^* (partition of A) was chosen as follows, considering that the first row (and column) corresponds to the activities/commodities group, the second to the production factors, and the third to enterprises/households:

$$\tilde{A} = \begin{pmatrix} A_{11} & 0 & 0 \\ 0 & 0 & 0 \\ 0 & 0 & A_{33} \end{pmatrix}.$$

Using the definition of A^* from equation (4.5) yields

$$A^* = \left(I - \tilde{A}\right)^{-1}\left(A - \tilde{A}\right) = \begin{pmatrix} \left(I - A_{11}\right)^{-1} & 0 & 0 \\ 0 & I & 0 \\ 0 & 0 & \left(I - A_{33}\right)^{-1} \end{pmatrix} \begin{pmatrix} 0 & 0 & A_{13} \\ A_{21} & 0 & 0 \\ 0 & A_{32} & 0 \end{pmatrix}$$

(4.11)

$$= \begin{pmatrix} 0 & 0 & A^*_{13} \\ A^*_{21} & 0 & 0 \\ 0 & A^*_{32} & 0 \end{pmatrix}, \quad \begin{cases} A^*_{13} = \left(I - A_{11}\right)^{-1} A_{13} \\ A^*_{21} = A_{21} \\ A^*_{32} = \left(I - A_{33}\right)^{-1} A_{32} \end{cases}.$$

Using the expression for A^* and the definitions in equation (4.9) yields

(4.12) $$M_1 = \begin{pmatrix} \left(I - A_{11}\right)^{-1} & 0 & 0 \\ 0 & I & 0 \\ 0 & 0 & \left(I - A_{33}\right)^{-1} \end{pmatrix}$$

(4.13) $$M_2 = \begin{pmatrix} I & A^*_{13}A^*_{32} & A^*_{13} \\ A^*_{21} & I & A^*_{21}A^*_{13} \\ A^*_{32}A^*_{21} & A^*_{32} & I \end{pmatrix}$$

$$(4.14) \quad M_3 = \begin{pmatrix} \left(I - A_{13}^* A_{32}^* A_{21}^*\right)^{-1} & 0 & 0 \\ 0 & \left(I - A_{21}^* A_{13}^* A_{32}^*\right)^{-1} & 0 \\ 0 & 0 & \left(I - A_{32}^* A_{21}^* A_{13}^*\right) \end{pmatrix}.$$

We can provide expressions for the matrices TR, OL, and CL defined in equation (4.10):

$$(4.15) \quad TR = \begin{pmatrix} (I - A_{11})^{-1} - I & 0 & 0 \\ 0 & 0 & 0 \\ 0 & 0 & (I - A_{33})^{-1} - I \end{pmatrix}$$

$$(4.16) \quad OL = \begin{pmatrix} 0 & A_{13}^* A_{32}^* & A_{13}^*(I - A_{33})^{-1} \\ A_{21}^*(I - A_{11})^{-1} & 0 & A_{21}^* A_{13}^*(I - A_{33})^{-1} \\ A_{32}^* A_{21}^*(I - A_{11})^{-1} & A_{32}^* & 0 \end{pmatrix}$$

$$(4.17) \quad CL = \begin{pmatrix} C_{132}(I - A_{11})^{-1} & C_{132} A_{13}^* A_{32}^* & C_{132} A_{13}^*(I - A_{33})^{-1} \\ C_{132} A_{21}^*(I - A_{11})^{-1} & C_{132} & C_{132} A_{21}^* A_{13}^*(I - A_{33})^{-1} \\ C_{132} A_{32}^* A_{21}^*(I - A_{11})^{-1} & C_{132} A_{32}^* & C_{132}(I - A_{33})^{-1} \end{pmatrix},$$

$$\text{where} \begin{cases} C_{132} = (I - A_{13}^* A_{32}^* A_{21}^*)^{-1} - I \\ C_{213} = (I - A_{21}^* A_{13}^* A_{32}^*)^{-1} - I \\ C_{321} = (I - A_{32}^* A_{21}^* A_{13}^*)^{-1} - I. \end{cases}$$

We now interpret and describe some features of the matrices TR, OL, and CL defined in equation (4.10). TR, which quantifies the net effect (net with respect to the initial unitary effect of a shock to an account on itself) of groups of accounts into themselves (intra), is a block diagonal matrix with a zero block in the second block on the diagonal, a consequence of the absence of transfers among production factors. OL, which captures the net direct effect (net with respect to the matrix M_1) between (inter) accounts, has zeros along the diagonal. CL, the matrix that captures the net closed-loop effects (net with respect to the product $M_2 M_1$), has no special structure.

Notes

This chapter was prepared at the Development Dialogue on Values and Ethics in the Human Development Vice Presidency at the World Bank for a research project on trade, gender, and poverty organized by the World Bank's Development Prospects Group. Comments from Ataman Aksoy and Erik Thorbecke, an anonymous reviewer, the editors of this volume, and participants at the World Bank workshop "Gender Aspects of the Trade and Poverty Nexus: A Macro-Micro Approach" are gratefully acknowledged. This work was funded by the Belgian Poverty Reduction Partnership as part of a broader program of work on social accounting matrices. Quentin Wodon is the corresponding author; his e-mail is qwodon@worldbank.org.

1. Despite consensus on the existence of gender disparities in African labor markets, assessing their nature and extent remains a challenge. Databases provide incomplete and limited information on the relative situations of men and women, use very diverse methodologies and definitions of employment and earnings, and focus mostly on urban areas (see, for instance, Appleton, Hoddinott, and Krishnan 1999; Brilleau, Roubaud, and Torelli 2004). Drawing on a meta-analysis of studies on the gender pay gap, Weichselbaumer and Winter-Ebmer (2005) find that only about 3 percent of empirical studies conducted on the topic since the 1960s draw on African data.

2. In 2005–06, the poverty line computed following the cost of basic needs method was CFAF 924 per person per day in Dakar, CFAF 662 in other urban areas, and CFAF 561 in rural areas (CFAF = Communauté Financière Africaine franc).

3. Thorbecke and Jung (1996) suggest that an important limitation of the "traditional" SAM model is the assumption that the average expenditure propensities (technical coefficients) hold for exogenous demand shocks, implying income elasticities equal to one. A more realistic alternative, mentioned in Lewis and Thorbecke (1992), is to use marginal expenditure propensities, if available.

4. As in chapter 3, all of the computations in this section were performed using SimSIP SAM; see pages 59–60 for more details.

5. For details on computation, see Pyatt and Round (1979).

References

Appleton, S., J. Hoddinott, and P. Krishnan. 1999. "The Gender Wage Gap in Three African Countries." *Economic Development and Cultural Change* 47 (2): 289–312.

Blackden C. M., and Q. Wodon. 2006. "Gender, Time Use and Poverty in Sub-Saharan Africa." World Bank Working Paper 73, Washington, DC.

Brilleau A., F. Roubaud, and C. Torelli. 2004. "Employment, Unemployment and Activity Conditions in the Principal Towns in Seven UEMOA Countries: First Results of the 1-2-3 Survey, Phase 1 2001–2002." Document de Travail DT-2004–06, Développement, Institutions et Analyses de Long Terme (DIAL), Paris.

Bussolo, M., R. De Hoyos, and Q. Wodon. 2008. "Higher Prices of Export Crops, Intra-Household Inequality and Human Capital Accumulation in Senegal." World Bank, Washington, DC.

Defourney, J., and E. Thorbecke. 1984. "Structural Path Analysis and Multiplier Decomposition within a Social Accounting Matrix Framework." *Economic Journal* 94 (373): 111–36.

Hoddinott J., and L. Haddad. 1995. "Does Female Income Share Influence Household Expenditures ? Evidence from the Côte d'Ivoire." *Oxford Bulletin of Economics and Statistics* 57 (1): 77–96.

Lewis, B., and E. Thorbecke. 1992. "District-Level Economic Linkages in Kenya: Evidence Based on a Small Regional Social Accounting Matrix." *World Development* 20 (6): 881–97.

Ndoye, D., F. Adoho, P. Backiny-Yetna, M. Fall, P. Thiecouta Ndiane, and Q. Wodon. 2008. *Tendances et déterminants de la pauvreté au Sénégal de 1994 à 2006.* World Bank, Washington, DC.

Parra, J. C., and Q. Wodon. 2008. "SimSIP SAM: Policy Analysis under a SAM Framework." World Bank, Development Dialogue on Values and Ethics, Washington, DC.

Pyatt, G., and J. Round. 1979. "Accounting and Fixed Price Multipliers in a Social Accounting Matrix Framework." *Economic Journal* 89 (356): 850–73.

Thorbecke, E., and H.-S. Jung. 1996. "A Multiplier Decomposition Method to Analyze Poverty Alleviation." *Journal of Development Economics* 48 (2): 279–300.

Weichselbaumer, D., and R. Winter-Ebmer. 2005. "A Meta-Analysis of the International Gender Wage Gap." *Journal of Economic Surveys* 19 (3): 479–511.

5

Trade, Growth, and Gender in Developing Countries: A Comparison of Ghana, Honduras, Senegal, and Uganda

*John Cockburn, Bernard Decaluwé,
Ismael Fofana, and Véronique Robichaud*

Developing countries are deeply engaged in trade negotiations at the bilateral, regional, and international levels. As imports, exports, and tariff duties all occupy important parts of their economies, far-reaching impacts on production, labor, and capital markets; household incomes; and, perhaps most important, economic growth will indubitably ensue. Because men and women occupy very different roles in these economies, particularly in terms of the import and export orientation of the sectors in which they work, they will be affected very differently.

Most empirical studies find relatively small welfare and poverty impacts of trade liberalization. This result is not surprising, as a static framework is generally used in which welfare gains and poverty impacts result solely from the short-term reallocation of resources. This chapter contributes to this literature by integrating the growth effects of trade liberalization and the resulting long-run impacts on welfare and poverty. The literature tries to draw general conclusions regarding whether growth and trade liberalization are good for the poor and whether liberalization increases growth. This chapter digs deeper to show that these relations depend on the nature of the trade liberalization policies and the characteristics of the economy in which they are adopted.

The analysis is based on a systematic review of the empirical literature on the impacts of trade on growth through increased productivity, efficiency, and foreign direct investment (FDI) (Martens 2008a, 2008b). A dynamic economywide model is then used to run trade policy simulations, focusing particularly on the gender differences in the direct and growth effects of trade liberalization.

We apply our framework to the specific case of a complete removal of import tariffs in three African countries (Ghana, Senegal, and Uganda) and one Central American country (Honduras). All four countries have been members of the World Trade Organization (WTO) since 1995. They are all also members of regional trade blocs: the Economic Community of West African States (ECOWAS) (Ghana and Senegal), the West African Economic and Monetary Union (UEMOA) (Senegal), the Common Market for Eastern and Southern Africa (COMESA) (Uganda), and the Central America Free Trade Agreement (CAFTA) (Honduras). All four countries are engaged in negotiations with major trade partners (Honduras with the United States; Ghana, Senegal, and Uganda with the European Union through Economic Partnership Agreements), as well as in unilateral trade reforms.

Research suggests that trade may favor women in industrial and semi-industrial economies, because women are more active in export-oriented sectors such as garments and light manufacturing. In contrast, in agricultural economies—and in agricultural sectors in (semi-) industrial economies—trade favors men, who are more likely to be engaged in the production of cash crops for export than women, who tend focus on import-competing food crops.

We contribute to this literature by introducing the growth effects from increased openness, which increase productivity, particularly in the import-competing sectors and, to a slightly lesser degree, the export-oriented sectors. Productivity gains translate into a reduction in the demand for labor, as less labor is required for a given level of production, in these sectors. To the extent that these sectors are more intensive in female workers than other sectors, the growth effects of trade will favor men. These differences typically manifest themselves in terms of the gender wage gap, labor market participation, adjustments in the time devoted to domestic work and leisure, bargaining power, and the intrahousehold allocation of resources. The focus here is on the wage channel.

The chapter is organized as follows. The first section presents a short review of the literature on the links between trade, growth, gender, and poverty. The second section describes the salient characteristics of the model. The third section presents the results of simulations of the impacts of complete trade liberalization in the four countries. The last section summarizes the chapter's main conclusions.

Literature Review

This chapter touches on a number of emerging and important strands of literature: the gender impacts of trade liberalization and growth, the impacts of trade on growth and poverty, and the impacts of growth on poverty. Several excellent reviews of this literature have been published. This section briefly summarizes their findings.

Impact of Growth on Poverty

Analysis of growth-poverty links consists primarily of ex post econometric analysis. Although the poverty impacts are likely to vary considerably depending on the motors of growth, this literature tends to treat growth as a monolithic phenomenon. Dollar and Kraay (2001), for example, find that growth is good for the poor. Bhalla (2002) and Sala-i-Martin (2002) find that data from household surveys underestimate poverty reduction; other researchers (for example, Wade 2004) argue that the estimates published by the World Bank are overly optimistic.

Impact of Trade on Growth and Poverty

In their exhaustive reviews of the empirical evidence, Winters (2004) and Winters, McCulloch, and McKay (2004) highlight ongoing disagreement. In a study of the 1990s trade liberalization experience in seven African and Asian countries, Cockburn, Decaluwé, and Robichaud (2007) show that the transmission channels vary significantly across countries according to their initial tariff structure, the initial structure of their international trade, sectoral factor intensities, and household income sources and consumption patterns. Given our interest in trade-related motors of growth, we focus the discussion on two important mechanisms through which trade liberalization may accelerate growth: the productivity and efficiency channel and the foreign investment channel.

An extensive body of literature indicates that openness to international trade creates a more competitive environment and stimulates the diffusion of new technologies, innovation, the adoption of new methods of production, and an increase in the availability of imported inputs.[1] All of these factors are expected to lead to productivity and efficiency gains. In what might be called the "new new" trade theory, it is argued that in the presence of firm heterogeneity, increased trade will lead to a rationalization of output toward the most productive firms.[2]

Considerable evidence suggests that increased openness also directly favors FDI.[3] The standard Hecksher-Ohlin model argues that trade and foreign investment are substitutes that should lead to an international equalization of factor returns. However, this relation can be inversed when the hypotheses underlying the Hecksher-Ohlin model are not respected (because of differential production functions, economies of scale, market imperfections, factor distortions, impediments to trade, or factor intensity reversals) (see Markusen and Svensson 1985; Wong 1986; Markusen and Melvin 1988; de Melo and Grether 1997). Empirical evidence indicates that trade and foreign investment are indeed complements (see, for example, Asiedu 2002; Onyeiwu and Shrestha 2004; and Kandiero and Chitiga 2006). While there is evidence that the relation is two-way, the balance sways in favor of the causality running from trade to foreign investment. Evidence in favor of a separate impact on foreign investment of variations in the relative returns to capital was found to be scant (see, for example, Agarwal 1980 and Lizondo 1990). This channel is nevertheless tested.

Gender Impacts of Trade and Growth

Chapter 2 of this volume provides a full review of the literature on the gender impacts of trade liberalization. It outlines the main points that are germane to our analysis and discusses the gender impacts of trade-driven growth.

Female participation in the labor market has risen markedly over the past decade, corresponding to a period of liberalization in most developing countries. Studies show that the feminization of work is greater in industrial sectors and in semi-industrial economies, where export industries employ more women, than in agricultural sectors and economies.[4] In semi-industrial economies, liberalization reduces the gap between men and women in terms of wage rates, labor market participation, and income distribution.

In agricultural economies trade liberalization may be more likely to benefit men more than women (Gladwin 1991; Fontana, Joekes, and Masika 1998). In most African countries, female work constitutes the base of agricultural food production, which is generally import competing and concentrated in small plots. In these economies trade liberalization tends to favor male workers and owners of large landholdings, which are more conducive to cash crops for export; it adversely affects female workers involved in food crop production, who face increased import competition (Fontana, Joekes, and Masika 1998). In economies with large export-oriented mining sectors, which generally employ a very large proportion of male workers, trade liberalization is also likely to favor males.

While these results may hold broadly, trade liberalization creates both winners and losers among men and women in all countries. The distribution of gains from trade is closely related to factor endowments, particularly labor skills, sectoral factor intensities, and mobility. In general, when export opportunities emerge, men benefit more than women, because women face difficulties accessing loans, assets, new technologies, and education. Becker (1959) argues that trade liberalization creates competitive pressures that force employers to reduce gender discrimination. Even where women experience an increase in income, although their negotiating power within the household may increase, their welfare may not necessarily improve. The increase in household income may be accompanied by a reduction in the services they previously rendered through their domestic work. But if increased labor market participation does not lead to a reduction in female domestic work, it will necessarily lead to a decline in their leisure time, which can also have deleterious effects on their welfare.

The growth effects of trade outlined above may also have differential gender effects. First, if capital is more complementary to skilled labor than to unskilled labor, capital accumulation increases the relative demand for skilled labor, which is primarily male. Second, greater openness can simultaneously attract investment and increase productivity. Whereas increased investment should increase labor demand to women's benefit, increased productivity will have the opposite effect, by reducing the amount of labor required for a given output. The relative strength of these channels will determine the net effect, as discussed below.

Trade Policy in Ghana, Honduras, Senegal, and Uganda

Senegal is a member of UEMOA; Ghana and Senegal are members of ECOWAS. Both institutions aim to create a free trade area among member states. The trade liberalization process accelerated in both countries after 1994, notably in preparation for the adoption of a common external tariff (CET) in 2000.

Ghana adopted a flexible exchange rate regime in 1991, after decades of economic reforms. The trade liberalization process that began in the early 1990s involved the abolition of import licensing, the removal of quantitative restrictions, cuts in tariff, and the simplification of the tariff system into four tariff rates, ranging from 5 percent to 30 percent (EC 2004). The elimination of constraints to international trade remains an important issue on Ghana's policy agenda, as presented in the Ghanaian Poverty Reduction Strategy II.

Senegal has progressively eliminated quotas, which have been replaced by a surtax on basic goods. Tariff rates were brought below 30 percent following the Uruguay Round. Both Ghana and Senegal benefit from preferential access to the European and North American markets. In 2003 ECOWAS and UEMOA began negotiating economic partnership agreements with the European Union.

Uganda is party to many bilateral and regional trade agreements, notably COMESA. It has implemented significant unilateral trade liberalization since the mid-1990s in an attempt to eliminate its trade deficit by increasing export earnings (Blake, McKay, and Morrissey 2001). Uganda has converted many nontariff restrictions (including quotas and import bans) into tariff equivalents. The 1995 five-rate system of tariffs (0, 10, 20, 30, and 60 percent) was reduced to a three-rate system (0, 7, and 15 percent) in 2001 (Morrisey, Rudaheranwa, and Moller 2003). With an average tariff of 12 percent, Uganda has the lowest tariffs in the COMESA region, where the average rate is 33 percent.

Since the early 1990s, Honduras has carried out a series of trade reforms aiming at increasing liberalization. It applies no import quotas and subjects only a few products to licensing requirements. Although Honduras reduced its tariffs to an unweighted average of 6 percent in early 2003, tariffs still show escalation, and the maximum rates of 40–55 percent are still applied to certain products. It is widely considered the most open economy in Central America and among the most open economies in the world. Honduras has preferential access to the U.S. market, by far its main trading partner, through the Caribbean Basin Initiative, and it recently ratified CAFTA.

Methodology: A Gender-Disaggregated Dynamic Economywide Model

Dynamic computable general equilibrium (CGE) models can be classified as intertemporal or sequential (recursive). Intertemporal dynamic models are based on optimal growth theory, which assumes that economic agents have perfect foresight. In a number of circumstances, particularly in developing countries, this assumption is unlikely to hold. For this reason we believe that it is more appropriate to develop a sequential dynamic CGE model. In this kind of dynamics, agents have myopic behavior. A sequential dynamic model is basically a series of static CGE models that are linked between periods by behavioral equations for endogenous variables and by updating procedures for exogenous variables. Capital stock is updated endogenously with a capital accumulation equation; population (and total labor supply) are updated exogenously between periods. It is also possible to add updating mechanisms for other variables, such as public expenditure, transfers, technological change, or debt accumulation.

This section describes the static and dynamic aspects of the model. It focuses on the new characteristics of the model and those most relevant to the gender-trade-growth nexus. Equation numbers in the main text refer to the full model specification, provided in the chapter annex.

Activities

On the production side, we assume that in each sector there is a representative firm that generates value added by combining labor and capital. We adopt a nested structure for production. Sectoral output $XS_{i,t}$ is a Leontief function of value added $VA_{i,t}$ and total intermediate consumption $CI_{i,t}$. (For definitions of the subscripts, such as sector *i*, see the chapter annex.) Value added is represented by a constant elasticity of substitution (CES) function of unskilled labor $LNQ_{i,t}$ and a composite factor $KLQ_{i,t}$, which is in itself a CES function of capital $KD_{i,j}$ and skilled labor $LQ_{i,t}$. We assume that substitutability is lower between capital and skilled labor than between the composite capital factor and unskilled workers. The basic intuition is that, for a given technology, any increase in capital intensity requires an almost proportionate increase in skilled labor. In this way capital accumulation is "skilled biased," increasing the demand for skilled versus unskilled labor. The lack of skilled labor could be one of the factors limiting the growth process:

(5.1) $$XS_{i,t} = VA_{i,t}/v_i$$

(5.2) $$CI_{i,t} = io_{i,t} \cdot XS_{i,t}$$

(5.4) $$VA_{i,t} = A_i^{VA} \cdot \theta_{i,t} \cdot \left(\alpha_i^{VA} \cdot LNQ_{i,t}^{-\rho_i^{VA}} + \left(1 - \alpha_i^{VA}\right) \cdot KLQ_{i,t}^{-\rho_i^{VA}} \right)^{-1/\rho_i^{VA}}$$

$$(5.9) \quad KLQ_{i,t} = A_i^{KL} \cdot \left(\alpha_i^{KL} \cdot LQ_{i,t}^{-\rho_i^{KL}} + \left(1 - \alpha_i^{KL}\right) \cdot KD_{i,t}^{-\rho_i^{KL}} \right)^{-1/\rho_i^{KL}}.$$

All variables have a sector index i and a time index t, as the model is solved recursively over the entire period of analysis.

Labor

We adopt a nested structure for the composition of the different types of labor. Among skilled workers ($LQ_{i,t}$), we assume imperfect substitutability between urban ($LDT_{UNQ,i,t}$) and rural workers ($LDT_{RNQ,i,t}$). The same assumption is adopted for unskilled workers ($LNQ_{i,t}$), which we assume to be composed of imperfectly substitutable urban ($LDT_{UQ,i,t}$) and rural workers ($LDT_{RQ,i,t}$):

$$(5.7)$$
$$LNQ_{i,t} = A_i^{LNQ} \cdot \left(\alpha_i^{LNQ} \cdot LDT_{UNQ,i,t}^{-\rho_i^{LNQ}} + \left(1 - \alpha_i^{LNQ}\right) \cdot LDT_{RNQ,i,t}^{-\rho_i^{LNQ}} \right)^{-1/\rho_i^{LNQ}}$$

$$(5.11) \quad LQ_{i,t} = A_i^{LQ} \cdot \left(\alpha_i^{LQ} \cdot LDT_{UQ,i,t}^{-\rho_i^{LQ}} + \left(1 - \alpha_i^{LQ}\right) \cdot LDT_{RQ,i,t}^{-\rho_i^{LQ}} \right)^{-1/\rho_i^{LQ}}.$$

Among skilled and unskilled rural and urban workers, we assume that male ($MLDT_{l,i,t}$) and female ($FLDT_{l,i,t}$) workers are also imperfect substitutes:

$$(5.13)$$
$$LDT_{l,i,t} = A_{l,i}^{LG} \cdot \left(\alpha_{l,i}^{LG} \cdot FLDT_{l,i,t}^{-\rho_{l,i}^{LG}} + \left(1 - \alpha_i^{LG}\right) \cdot MLDT_{l,i,t}^{-\rho_i^{LG}} \right)^{-1/\rho_{l,i}^{LG}}.$$

From these equations, we derive the demand equations for each of the factors of production (see equations 5.6, 5.8, 5.10, 5.12, 5.13, and 5.14 in the annex).

The market equilibrium conditions determine factor and product prices (see equations 5.37, 5.38, 5.39, 5.40, 5.41, and 5.42 in the annex). In particular, we assume that all labor markets clear:

$$(5.63) \qquad\qquad \sum_h MLS_{h,l,t} = \sum_i MLDT_{l,i,t}$$

$$(5.64) \qquad\qquad \sum_h FLS_{h,l,t} = \sum_i FLDT_{l,i,t},$$

where $FLS_{b,l,t}$ ($MLS_{b,l,t}$) is the household endowment in female (male) labor of type L. Total male and female labor supply are assumed to increase at the exogenous population growth rate.

Data constraints prevented us from breaking down rural workers by skill level in Senegal. In Uganda, a rural/urban disaggregation was impossible, although the skill disaggregation breaks out "elementary workers," who are even less skilled than unskilled workers.

Some limits of the current analysis merit discussion. First, we assume that the unemployment rate and labor market participation rates are fixed. Consequently, the main gender impact of trade liberalization occurs through wage effects. While this is a serious limitation—to be addressed in future research—it is not likely to change the results qualitatively, because labor demand is driving all of these effects. Where trade liberalization is found to be pro-female, for example, one would expect to see an increase in female labor market participation and a decrease in their unemployment rates, both of which would moderate female wage gains. These effects would also likely boost growth effects, however. We do not explore the impact of changes in female income shares on their bargaining power and the resulting intrahousehold allocation of resources. Other gender impacts of trade identified in the literature—including reduced gender wage discrimination in the face of increased competition (Becker 1959) and skilled- (or gender-) biased technological progress—also merit exploration in future research.

Households and Government

Households earn their income ($YH_{b,t}$) from the remuneration of their production factors: female and male labor income and their share of the total returns to capital. They also receive dividends ($DIV_{b,t}$), government transfers ($TG_{b,t}$), and remittances from abroad ($TROW\_H_{b,t}$):

$$
\begin{aligned}
YH_{b,t} = \sum_l \left(wf_{l,t} \cdot FLS_{b,l,t} + wm_{l,t} \cdot MLS_{b,l,t}' \right) \\
+ \left(\frac{KH_{b,t}}{KS_t} \right) \cdot \sum_i r_{i,t} \cdot KD_{i,t} \\
+ PINDEX_t \cdot TG_{b,t} + DIV_{b,t} + e_t \cdot TROW\_H_{b,t},
\end{aligned}
$$

(5.16)

where $wf_{l,t}$ ($wm_{l,t}$) is the wage rate for female (male) workers of type L and $r_{i,t}$ is the sectoral rate of the returns to capital. Thus the distributional impacts of trade and growth channel in part through their impacts on factor returns and the relative endowments of each household category in these factors.

Household demand for goods and services is derived from a Cobb-Douglas utility function after deduction of savings and direct taxes to the government (see equations 5.17, 5.31, and 5.33 in the annex). Household savings and capital accumulation are discussed below in the "Motors of Growth" section.

The only "nontraditional" aspect of our modeling of government is the assumption that the government deficit (surplus) is a constant share of *GDP*:

$$(5.25) \qquad SG_t = \frac{SG^0}{GDP^0} \cdot GDP_t.$$

Dynamics

In every period, sectoral capital stocks $(KD_{i,\,t+1})$ are updated with a capital accumulation equation involving the rate of depreciation (δ) and investment by sector of destination $IND_{i,\,t}$. This equation describes the law of motion for the sectoral capital stock. It assumes that stocks are measured at the beginning of the period and that flows are measured at the end of the period. New investments are allocated across sectors through an investment demand function that is similar to that in Bourguignon, Branson, and de Melo (1989) and Jung and Thorbecke (2003).[5] The capital accumulation rate—the ratio of investment to capital stock—is increasing with respect to the ratio of the rate of return to capital $r_{i,\,t}$ and its user cost U_t. The user cost is equal to the dual price of investment (PK_t) multiplied by the sum of the depreciation rate and the interest rate (ir). The elasticity of the rate of investment with respect to the ratio of return to capital and its user cost is assumed to be equal to 2. The sum of investments by sector of destination is equal to total investment (IT), which is, in turn, determined by total savings:

$$(5.68) \qquad KD_{i,t+1} = KD_{i,t}\left(1-\delta\right) + IND_{i,t}$$

$$(5.35) \qquad \frac{IND_{i,t}}{KD_{i,t}} = \phi_i \left[\frac{r_{i,t}}{U_t}\right]^{\sigma_i^K}$$

$$(5.53) \qquad U_t = PK_t \cdot (ir_t + \delta)$$

$$(5.67) \qquad IT_i = PK_t \cdot \sum_i IND_{i,t}.$$

All interagent transfers in the model increase at the exogenous population growth rate. The exogenous dynamic updating of the model includes variables such as transfers and volumes such as government expenditures or minimum household consumption that is indexed to relevant price indices (see equations 5.73–5.82 in the annex). The model is formulated as a static model that is solved recursively over a 15-year time horizon.[6] The model is homogenous in prices, and the exchange rate is the numeraire in each period.

Motors of Growth

As discussed above, trade liberalization can affect growth in various ways. The model presented here builds in the most important of these motors of growth. We first highlight two "traditional" mechanisms found in most standard CGE models: a reduction in the price of capital goods and a redistribution of income across households with differential savings rates. We then outline three additional mechanisms, two of which—the productivity/efficiency and the foreign direct investment mechanisms—draw heavily on the econometric literature on the trade–growth link.

PRICES OF CAPITAL GOODS

The most immediate motor of growth in our model is the reduction in the cost of imported investment goods and, through import competition, their domestically produced counterparts. This reduces the investment good price index and, consequently, increases total investments (equation 5.67) and capital accumulation (equation 5.68), where the investment good price index is given by

$$(5.52) \qquad PK_t = \prod_i \left(\frac{PC_{i,t}}{\mu_i} \right)^{\mu_i}.$$

DIFFERENTIAL HOUSEHOLD SAVINGS RATES

A second channel stems from differences in the marginal propensities to save across household categories. A shock that leads to a redistribution of income toward households with high savings rates will increase capital accumulation and growth at the expense of current consumption; the opposite is true if redistribution favors big spenders.

In addition to these "standard" motors of growth, we introduce a number of other motors of growth that appear prominently in the econometric literature on growth. Each is described below.

TECHNOLOGICAL PROGRESS AND EFFICIENCY

The impacts of increased openness on technological progress and productive efficiency at the sectoral level are captured by a parameter $(\theta_{i,t})$ in the value added function. This function is in turn a function of the change in the degree of openness of the sector relative to the base year (superscript 0). We measure the degree of openness as the sum of sectoral imports $(IM_{m,t})$ and exports $(EX_{x,t})$ as a percentage of sectoral output $(XS_{i,t})$:[7]

$$(5.5)\quad \theta_{i,t} = \left[\frac{(IM_{i,t} + EX_{i,t})/VA_{i,t}}{(IM_i^0 + EX_i^0)/VA_i^0}\right]^{\sigma^{PT}} \quad or \quad \theta_{i,t} = 1 \quad if \quad EX_i^0 = IM_i^0 = 0.$$

Based on a review of the empirical literature commissioned in the context of this study, the elasticity of productivity with respect to openness is about 0.34–0.74 (see Martens 2008a).[8] We adopt an elasticity of 0.5.

The empirical literature usually focuses solely on import penetration ratios, often restricted to imports from developed countries, as the principal channel of influence of trade on productivity. Other formulations are also possible (and will be the subject of further research).

FOREIGN INVESTMENT

For several reasons, we assume that trade liberalization creates an environment that favors the investment of foreign savings in Senegal. First, foreign investors are more attracted by an open economic environment, captured by including an economywide openness index in the determination of the current account balance, which is equal to foreign savings invested in Senegal.[11] Second, to the extent that trade liberalization increases the returns to capital, it will further encourage foreign investment:

$$(5.61)\quad CAB_t = \frac{CAB^0}{GDP^0} \times \left[\frac{rmoy_t/PINDEX_t}{rmoy^0/PINDEX^0}\right]^{\sigma^{FSR}}$$

$$\times \left[\frac{(IM_t + EX_t)/GDP_t}{(IM^0 + EX^0)/GDP^0}\right]^{\sigma^{FSO}} GDP_t.$$

As a percentage of GDP (the sum of sectoral value added), the current account deficit will increase with respect to its base value if the average rate of return on capital ($rmoy_t/PINDEX_t$) or the economywide degree of openness (($IM+EX)/GDP$) increases (see equations 5.50 and 5.51 in the annex). Based on a review of the empirical literature commissioned for this study (see Martens 2008b), we adopt an estimate of 0.04 for the elasticity of substitution of foreign investment with respect to openness and an estimate of 0.5 with respect to the rate of return to capital.

Several other formulations could be considered. First, the above relation could be restricted to FDI alone, assuming that all other elements of the capital and financial accounts of the balance of payments are, for example, a fixed proportion of GDP. Second, it is likely that FDI (or all net foreign capital inflows) are, at least to some extent, sector specific. It is possible to apply the above equations at the sectoral level, where FDI in a given sector depends on the sectoral returns to capital and the sectoral openness index.

Endogenous Household Savings Rates

In static CGE models, the savings behavior of households is generally very simple. The savings rate is a simple parameter measuring either the average or the marginal savings rates of each household category.[10] We enrich this framework by assuming that household savings rates are sensitive to changes in the real rate of return to capital. We define the following equation:

$$(5.18) \qquad SH_{b,t} = \psi_b \cdot \left[\frac{rmoy_t/PINDEX_t}{rmoy^0/PINDEX^0} \right]^{\sigma_b^{HS}} \cdot YDH_{b,t}.$$

Over time, the relative capital endowments of each representative household change according to its savings. Households with a higher savings rate will have a more rapidly growing capital stock and will consequently earn a growing share of total capital income generated in the economy. In particular, after depreciation the capital stock belonging to household b will increase according to its savings:

$$(5.69) \qquad KH_{b,t+1} = KH_{b,t}(1-\delta) + \left(\frac{SH_{b,t}}{PK_t} \right),$$

where PK_t is the investment price index. All other agents accumulate capital in the same way:

$$(5.70) \qquad \text{Firms: } KF_{t+1} = KF_t(1-\delta) + \left[\frac{SF_t}{PK_t} \right]$$

(5.72)   Rest of world: $KROW_{t+1} = KROW_t \, (1-\delta) + \left(\dfrac{CAB_t}{PK_t} \right)$

(5.71)   Government: $KG_{t+1} = KG_t \, (1-\delta) + \left[\dfrac{SG_t}{PK_t} \right]$

and all agents receive a share of total returns to capital equal to their share in the capital stock.

Structure of the Social Accounting Matrices

The analysis is based on social accounting matrices (SAMs) for 2004 for Ghana, Honduras, and Senegal and for 2005 for Uganda (table 5.1). There is little disaggregation of industries or commodities in the SAMS for Ghana (13 accounts) or Honduras (18 accounts); in contrast, the SAMs for Senegal (35 accounts) and Uganda (50 accounts)

Table 5.1 Summary of Base SAMs in Ghana, Honduras, Senegal, and Uganda

Country	Year	Source	Industry/ products	Institutional sectors	Tax accounts
Ghana	2004	GSS and IFPRI (2006)	13 (5 primary, 1 manufacturing, 7 services)	5 (urban and rural representative household group)	4 (direct, sales, import, and export)
Honduras	2004	Cuesta (2004)	18 (8 primary, 6 manufacturing, 4 services)	7 (one representative household group)	5 (direct, production, sales, import, and value added)
Senegal	2004	Fofana and Cabral (2007)	35 (6 primary, 17 manufacturing, 12 services)	One representative household group, firms, government, rest of world	5 (direct, production, sales, subsidy, and import)
Uganda	2005	Zhu and Thurlow (2007)	30 (11 primary, 6 manufacturing, 13 services)	Urban/rural representative household groups, firms, government, rest of world	3 tax accounts (direct, sales, and import)

Source: Authors.

are much more disaggregated. The level of disaggregation for other accounts, such as productive factors, institutional units, and types of taxes, is more uniform across countries.

Simulation Results

This section begins by presenting the policy simulation scenarios. It then examines the immediate import response; the resulting effects on sectoral output, gender-specific factor markets, and household income; and the effects on growth.

Simulation Scenario

We simulate the complete elimination of import tariffs. While this is extreme and not likely to be observed in reality, it yields an order of magnitude of the type of effects. Tariffs are eliminated in the first year of simulations rather than gradually over time, as one would expect in an actual implementation. While this will modify the transition path and overstate the first-year impacts, it will have little impact on the long-term effects. More realistic scenarios could be developed in the analysis of specific trade agreements or trade policy reforms.

This scenario represents a case of unilateral trade liberalization. In the case of bilateral, regional, or multilateral trade agreements, one would also want to capture changes in tariffs applied by trade partners and changes in world prices as they are reflected in import and export prices. These changes could have quite different impacts. A rise in world food prices following the removal of agricultural subsidies in major developing countries, for example, would lead to an increase in import prices for countries that import food and an increase in export prices for those that export food.

In all simulations the public deficit remains constant as a share of gross national product (GDP) through the introduction of an endogenous uniform sales tax. When tariffs are eliminated, this compensatory tax increases by between 1 (Honduras) and 2 (Ghana and Senegal) percentage points throughout the 15-year simulation period.

We focus first on the short-term (first-year) effects. All results are expressed as variations with respect to the values observed in the "business-as-usual" (no trade liberalization) scenario. For ease of exposition, we focus solely on the three main sectors—primary, industrial, and services—although the actual models are much more disaggregated than this.[11]

Import Response

Industry is initially much more protected than the primary sector in Senegal and Uganda; in contrast, the primary sector is slightly more protected than industry in Ghana and Honduras (table 5.2).[12] There are no tariffs on the limited amount of service imports in all countries.

The four countries differ substantially in several other important ways. While Ghana's GDP (or value added) is almost equally shared by the primary, industry, and service sectors, in the other three countries GDP is heavily concentrated in the service sector, with much lower primary value added.[13] In all four countries, the majority of imports are industrial, with this share particularly high in Ghana, Senegal, and Uganda. The share of primary imports is particularly low in Ghana and Uganda.

The contrasts in the export structures are more dramatic. Ghana's exports are dominated by (and export intensities are highest in) the primary sector, in particular cocoa (35 percent), mining (20 percent), and forestry (10 percent). In contrast, more than half of Honduras' exports are services.[14] Honduras also has high export shares and intensities in agriculture, especially coffee and shellfish. In Senegal more than half of all exports are from the industrial sector, primarily petroleum products and phosphates, with a strong showing by tourism (15 percent of all exports). Uganda's export composition is similar to that of Senegal, with a higher share of primary exports.

Given the initial tariff structure, it is the industrial sectors in Senegal and Uganda that face the strongest first-year import competition— falling import prices and the ensuing increase in import volumes— following the elimination of import tariffs (table 5.3). The detailed sectoral results (not shown) indicate that most of this import competition occurs in industries, such as food processing, that require large quantities of inputs from the primary sector. In all four countries, the service sector is relatively unaffected, whereas the primary sectors— and in Ghana and Honduras, the industrial sectors—face moderate increases in import competition.

Output Response

The simulation results indicate that the elimination of import tariffs leads to a short-term (first-year) expansion in output and GDP (value added) in all four countries, with Senegal posting the largest gains (2.4 percent in output and 2.1 percent in GDP) and Honduras the smallest (1.4 percent in output and 0.9 percent in GDP). This result is driven mainly by the productivity/efficiency gains from increased

Table 5.2 Initial Sectoral Shares, Ratios, and Tariffs in Ghana, Honduras, Senegal, and Uganda (percent)

| | Sectoral shares | | | Ratios | | | |
Country	Value added	Imports	Exports	Imports/ consumption	Exports/ output	Value added/ output	Initial tariff
Ghana							
Primary	34.1	4.3	70.4	6.8	39.2	63.2	8.2
Industrial	33.6	80.4	9.4	66.6	10.5	41.2	7.3
Services	32.3	15.3	20.3	17.3	14.7	44.0	0.0
Total	100.0	100.0	100.0	38.2	24.6	50.1	6.2
Honduras							
Primary	12.5	21.6	31.8	35.3	31.2	19.7	6.7
Industrial	27.9	54.8	17.5	37.9	12.9	37.0	5.7
Services	59.6	23.6	50.7	25.4	31.8	68.6	0.0
Total	100.0	100.0	100.0	33.6	25.2	46.3	4.6
Senegal							
Primary	15.7	19.3	9.3	26.2	8.5	64.5	7.1
Industrial	25.7	72.9	54.5	44.4	18.6	26.2	16.7
Services	58.6	7.7	36.3	8.4	18.1	57.8	0.0
Total	100.0	100.0	100.0	30.9	18.1	45.8	13.6
Uganda							
Primary	25.6	4.3	22.6	3.7	8.6	77.6	5.2
Industrial	25.7	73.9	44.7	38.9	13.1	38.5	25.2
Services	48.7	21.9	32.7	12.7	8.2	56.5	0.0
Total	100.0	100.0	100.0	23.0	9.9	54.1	18.8

Source: Authors' calculations based on SAMs cited in table 5.1.

127

Table 5.3 Trade and Production Responses to Trade Liberalization in Ghana, Honduras, Senegal, and Uganda, by Sector

(percentage change)

Item	First year, 2004 (2005 in Uganda)					Last year, 2019 (2020 in Uganda)				
	Imports	Domestic sales	Exports	Output	Value added	Imports	Domestic sales	Exports	Output	Value added
Volume										
Ghana										
Primary	7.1	0.6	4.3	2.1	1.9	10.5	0.9	8.4	4.0	3.7
Industrial	4.0	0.3	12.5	1.2	0.9	5.7	-0.1	8.1	0.6	0.7
Services	-0.8	0.7	5.0	1.1	0.7	0.4	1.4	4.8	1.8	1.3
Total	3.5	0.6	5.2	1.5	1.3	5.2	0.8	7.6	2.3	2.2
Honduras										
Primary	5.0	-0.7	11.7	3.1	1.3	7.0	-0.4	26.2	8.7	3.6
Industrial	6.2	0.1	7.4	0.9	0.7	10.0	0.7	7.9	1.5	1.2
Services	-1.4	0.4	2.4	0.9	0.9	1.6	1.3	1.6	1.3	1.3
Total	4.2	0.0	6.2	1.4	0.9	7.5	0.7	11.0	3.1	1.5
Senegal										
Primary	5.4	1.8	9.6	2.5	2.3	8.4	2.6	18.1	4.3	3.6
Industrial	13.2	0.0	13.8	2.3	3.0	16.3	0.5	19.8	4.2	5.5
Services	-1.8	1.2	12.3	2.5	1.7	0.3	2.8	15.4	4.4	3.4
Total	10.7	0.8	13.2	2.4	2.1	13.7	1.8	18.2	4.3	3.9

Uganda										
Primary	6.6	2.6	14.3	3.6	3.7	5.7	3.7	26.0	5.7	5.5
Industrial	9.3	2.2	16.1	3.5	3.1	11.5	3.5	15.4	4.4	3.8
Services	-0.9	0.4	6.5	0.7	0.7	-0.3	2.2	11.5	2.7	2.7
Total	7.6	1.4	12.4	2.1	2.0	9.4	2.9	16.4	3.8	3.6
Price										
Ghana										
Primary	-5.8	-2.4	0.0	-2.6	-3.2	-5.8	-1.2	0.0	-1.8	-2.2
Industrial	-5.1	-2.5	0.0	-3.8	-4.4	-5.2	-1.4	0.0	-2.9	-2.7
Services	1.9	0.3	0.0	-1.4	-1.1	1.9	0.9	0.0	-0.9	0.0
Total	-4.2	-1.2	0.0	-2.4	-2.7	-4.2	-0.4	0.0	-1.7	-1.6
Honduras										
Primary	-4.9	-1.8	0.0	-2.2	-5.1	-4.9	-1.1	0.0	-1.6	-4.1
Industrial	-4.0	-1.7	0.0	-2.8	-3.6	-4.0	-0.8	0.0	-2.0	-2.2
Services	1.5	0.5	0.0	-0.7	-0.5	1.5	1.6	0.0	0.1	0.5
Total	-3.0	-0.9	0.0	-1.8	-1.8	-3.0	0.1	0.0	-1.0	-0.7
Senegal										
Primary	-4.8	-6.2	0.0	-7.4	-9.1	-4.4	-3.2	0.0	-4.7	-5.9
Industrial	-13.2	-4.6	0.0	-5.5	-7.1	-12.9	-2.3	0.0	-3.6	-4.3
Services	1.8	-0.8	0.0	-2.5	-1.8	1.8	1.5	0.0	-0.5	0.5
Total	-10.5	-3.2	0.0	-4.5	-4.4	-10.3	-0.8	0.0	-2.4	-1.8
Uganda										
Primary	-4.2	-3.5	0.0	-4.1	-4.3	-4.3	-2.1	0.0	-2.8	-2.3
Industrial	-9.2	-4.1	0.0	-4.4	-1.6	-9.3	-3.3	0.0	-3.7	-0.7
Services	1.2	-0.7	0.0	-1.8	-1.8	1.1	-0.4	0.0	-1.4	-1.4
Total	-7.4	-2.4	0.0	-3.1	-2.4	-7.4	-1.7	0.0	-2.4	-1.5

Source: Authors' calculations.
Note: Import and domestic sale prices include the compensatory sales tax; output and value added prices are net of sales tax.

openness, as we assume that any increase in capital stock in the first year becomes productive only as of the second year. (We return to this point in more detail below.) Trade liberalization also leads to a first-year expansion in exports, because we assume that foreign savings (the current account deficit) is fixed and thus the increase in imports following tariff cuts leads to a real devaluation.[15]

Despite the differences in import responses, it is the primary sector that posts the largest output increases in the first year in all four countries. In Ghana and Honduras, where the contrast with the other sectors is most dramatic, primary sector expansion is powered primarily by export growth as a result of the devaluation of the real exchange rate. Indeed, the primary sector is export intensive in both countries, with exports representing 31.2 percent of output in Honduras and 39.2 percent of output in Ghana. In contrast, expansion of the primary sector in Senegal and Uganda is motored by growth in local sales, which face a much smaller increase in import competition than the highly protected industrial sector. In all countries but particularly in Ghana and Uganda, import penetration rates are lower in the primary sector than in industry, which protects this sector more from import competition following tariff cuts. In Ghana and Uganda (but not Honduras and Senegal), the service sectors experience the smallest increases in output and value added, despite the fact that they face no increase in import competition. As a result, the main impact of tariff cuts is a general equilibrium reduction in production costs in the service sector, which translates into a small to moderate rise in output and small output price reductions.

Given that we are interested in the gender-specific wage and poverty effects of trade liberalization and growth, it is price changes, particularly changes in value added prices, that are the determining factor. In this regard, we note that in the first year, output prices fall more in the agricultural and industrial sectors than in the service sector, as the agricultural and industrial sectors are forced to cut their prices on the domestic market in the face of increased import competition. With the exception of Uganda, this dichotomy is accentuated when value added prices are considered, as input cost savings are smaller for the industrial and agricultural sectors. There is less divergence between the evolution of value added prices in the agricultural and industrial sectors, although, except in Ghana, valued added prices fall more in the primary sector. This has important distributive and gender implications, as shown below.

In conclusion, the primary sector benefits the most from trade liberalization in all four countries. In Ghana and Honduras, where the contrast is greatest, this is caused primarily by the greater export orientation of the sector; in Senegal and Uganda, it reflects the fact that the primary sector is much less affected by import competition, given its much lower initial tariff rates. More important for the factor return analysis presented below, value added prices fall more in the primary sector in all countries but Ghana. It is this divergence in the behavior of value added prices that drives the impacts on factor returns.

Gender-Specific Factor Market Impacts

How do the sectoral output effects of trade liberalization map into the first-year variations in gender-specific factor returns? The labor categories are slightly different in each country (table 5.4). In Ghana and Honduras, labor is distinguished by gender, location, and skill level. In Senegal rural labor is not broken down by skill level. In Uganda labor is decomposed by gender and skill level only, although a third category of worker ("elementary" workers) is distinguished.[16] The increase in the consumer price index ranges from 1.4 percent (in Honduras) to 7.5 percent (in Senegal). As a result, although factor returns fall, relative to consumer prices many of them actually increase.

In the short term, trade liberalization increases the average gender wage gap in all three African countries, because female wages fall more than male wages. In contrast, in Honduras there is no significant difference in the evolution of average male and female wage rates. The causes of these divergences are multiple and vary across countries. They include greater participation of rural men in export-oriented cocoa production in Ghana and greater participation of rural women in the inward-oriented agricultural sector and of urban men in the outward-oriented industrial export sector in Senegal.[17]

This gender bias in wage variation is slightly greater for unskilled workers, except rural Honduran workers. Among urban workers in Senegal, for example, the wages of unskilled workers fall by 4.0 percent for females and 3.9 for males. In contrast, among skilled workers, wages fall less among females (2.1 percent) than among males (2.2 percent).

Trade liberalization reduces rural wages relative to urban wages, except among Honduran female workers. In particular, in rural Senegal wages fall 5.2 percent among males and 5.3 percent among females; in urban areas wages fall 4.0 percent among males and 4.1 percent among females. These results reflect the larger reductions in primary sector value added prices noted in the preceding section. No rural–urban labor market analysis is possible in Uganda because the required data are not available.

Table 5.4 Factor Market and Household Income Effects of Trade Liberalization in Ghana, Honduras, Senegal, and Uganda
(percentage change)

| | Initial share in total income | | | Change in rates of returns to factors | | Change in income by source | | | | | |
| | | | | First period | Last Period | First period | | | Last period | | |
Item	Urban	Rural	All	All	All	Urban	Rural	All	Urban	Rural	All
Ghana											
Male labor											
Rural											
Unskilled	0.0	26.5	12.8	-1.7	0.1	0.0	-0.5	-0.2	0.0	0.0	0.0
Skilled	0.0	25.5	12.3	-1.8	1.2	0.0	-0.5	-0.2	0.0	0.3	0.2
Total				-1.8	0.6						
Urban											
Unskilled	6.0	0.0	3.1	-1.6	0.1	-0.1	0.0	-0.1	0.0	0.0	0.0
Skilled	23.1	0.0	12.0	-1.6	1.4	-0.4	0.0	-0.2	0.4	0.0	0.2
Total				-1.6	1.1						
Total male				-1.7	0.8						
Female labor											
Rural											
Unskilled	0.0	10.8	5.2	-2.0	-0.2	0.0	-0.2	-0.1	0.0	0.0	0.0
Skilled	0.0	3.7	1.8	-1.8	1.0	0.0	-0.1	0.0	0.0	0.0	0.0
Total				-2.0	0.1						

Urban											
Unskilled	7.5	0.0	3.9	−1.9	−0.1	−0.1	0.0	−0.1	0.0	0.0	0.0
Skilled	9.3	0.0	4.8	−1.8	1.2	−0.2	0.0	−0.1	0.1	0.0	0.1
Total				−1.9	0.6						
Total female				−1.9	0.4						
Capital	28.9	24.8	26.9	−1.0	−1.4	−0.3	−0.3	−0.3	0.0	0.0	0.0
Nonfactor income	25.2	8.6	17.2	−0.6	−0.4	−0.1	−0.1	−0.1	−0.1	−0.1	−0.1
Total household income	100.0	100.0	100.0			−1.2	−1.6	−1.4	0.3	0.3	0.3
Consumer price index						−2.4	−2.6	−2.5	−1.6	−1.8	−1.7
Relative income						1.3	1.1	1.2	2.0	2.1	2.0
Change in capital endowment						0.0	0.0	0.0	1.1	1.2	1.2
Honduras											
Male labor											
Rural											
Unskilled			9.0	−2.0	−0.1			−0.2			0.0
Skilled			2.4	−1.2	0.9			0.0			0.0
Total				−1.9	0.1						
Urban											
Unskilled			12.0	−1.1	0.4			−0.1			0.1
Skilled			18.6	−0.9	1.4			−0.2			0.3
Total				−1.0	1.0						
Total male				−1.2	0.7						

(Continued on the following page)

Table 5.4 (Continued)

Item	Initial share in total income			Change in rates of returns to factors		Change in income by source					
				First period	Last Period	First period			Last period		
	Urban	Rural	All	All	All	Urban	Rural	All	Urban	Rural	All
Female labor											
Rural											
Unskilled			2.6	-0.7	0.5			0.0			0.0
Skilled			1.1	-1.0	1.4			0.0			0.0
Total				-0.8	0.8						
Urban											
Unskilled			5.6	-1.4	0.1			-0.1			0.0
Skilled			12.0	-1.1	1.3			-0.1			0.2
Total				-1.2	0.9						
Total female				-1.1	0.9						
Capital			18.3	0.0	-0.9			0.0			0.1
Nonfactor income			18.4	-0.1	0.0			0.0			0.0
Total household income			100.0	-0.7	1.1			-0.7			0.7
Consumer price index								-1.4			-0.6
Relative income								0.7			1.3
Change in capital endowment								0.0			1.1

Senegal

Male labor					
Rural	12.1	-5.2	-2.3	-0.6	-0.3
Urban					
Unskilled	7.0	-2.2	-1.2	-0.4	-0.1
Skilled	9.3	-3.9	3.9	-0.2	0.3
Total		-3.2	1.0		
Total male		-4.0	-0.4		
Female labor					
Rural	4.5	-5.3	-2.4	-0.2	-0.1
Urban					
Unskilled	2.3	-2.1	-1.4	-0.2	-0.1
Skilled	5.7	-4.0	4.1	0.0	0.1
Total		-3.5	0.2		
Total female		-4.1	-0.8		
Capital	29.7	-3.1	-3.0	-0.9	-0.3
Nonfactor income	29.5	-5.0	-4.3	-1.4	-1.4
Total household income	-4.0			-4.0	-2.0
Consumer price index				-7.5	-6.7
Relative income				3.8	5
Change in capital endowment				0.0	1.4

(Continued on the following page)

Table 5.4 (Continued)

Item	Initial share in total income			Change in rates of returns to factors		Change in income by source					
				First period	Last Period	First period			Last period		
	Urban	Rural	All	All	All	Urban	Rural	All	Urban	Rural	All
Uganda											
Male labor											
Elementary	5.6	3.5	4.3	0.3	1.1	0.0	0.0	0.0	0.1	0.0	0.0
Unskilled	6.3	16.6	13.0	0.1	0.7	0.0	0.0	0.0	0.0	0.1	0.1
Skilled	13.8	7.1	9.5	-0.2	3.2	0.0	0.0	0.0	0.4	0.2	0.3
Total male				0.0	1.7						
Female labor											
Elementary	1.8	0.7	1.1	-2.0	-0.5	0.0	0.0	0.0	0.0	0.0	0.0
Unskilled	2.4	6.9	5.3	-1.3	0.4	0.0	-0.1	-0.1	0.0	0.0	0.0
Skilled	8.3	3.3	5.0	0.1	3.7	0.0	0.0	0.0	0.3	0.1	0.2
Total female				-0.8	1.7						
Capital	48.7	48.6	48.6	-0.7	-2.4	-0.3	-0.3	-0.3	1.0	1.0	1.0
Nonfactor income	13.1	13.3	13.2	0.0	0.0	0.0	0.0	0.0	0.0	0.0	0.0
Total household income	100.0	100.0	100.0			-0.4	-0.4	-0.4	1.9	1.5	1.6
Consumer price index						-4.1	-4.2	-4.2	-2.7	-2.9	-2.9
Relative income						3.9	4.0	4.0	4.7	4.5	4.6
Change in capital endowment						0.0	0.0	0.0	4.6	4.5	4.5

Source: Authors' calculations.

In summary, trade liberalization accentuates gender, skill, and rural–urban wage gaps, because male workers, skilled workers, and urban workers are better able to take advantage of expanding export opportunities and less exposed to increased import competition. Average returns to capital generally vary less than average wage rates, except in Uganda. This is caused primarily by the high share of capital income from the export-oriented mining industry and the nontradable construction sectors.

Household Income

Changes in household income must be considered in a context in which trade liberalization also leads to a reduction in consumer prices. In this case, even though incomes fall, purchasing power may increase if consumer prices fall even more. In Ghana and Senegal, rural and urban households are distinguished in the analysis below; data constraints did not allow such households to be distinguished in Honduras and Senegal. Consumer price reductions may vary between rural and urban households according to their consumption patterns (see table 5.4).

Household incomes fall roughly 1 percent in the first year, except in Senegal, where initial tariff rates are high and household incomes fall 4 percent. Given the changes in factor returns discussed in the previous section, the impacts of trade liberalization on the income of the different categories of households depends on their factor endowments as well as their nonfactor income shares. In Ghana rural households experience the largest average reductions in incomes; in Uganda there is no significant difference in the short-term impact on the incomes of rural and urban households. The antirural bias of the impact on rural households in Ghana and, implicitly, Senegal can be traced primarily to the fact that the wages of rural workers (both male and female) fall more than those of their urban counterparts.[18] This explains a large share of the difference in total income changes, especially in Ghana. In Senegal households are also more reliant on nonfactor income, in particular interhousehold and government transfers, which are indexed to the falling consumer price index.[19]

While the price cuts emanating from trade liberalization lead to a fall in household income, they also imply a decline in the cost of living. In all four countries, average consumer prices fall significantly more—between 1.4 percent in Honduras and 7.5 percent in Senegal—than household incomes. This results in an increase in the average purchasing power (relative income) of households that ranges from 0.7 percent in Honduras to 4.0 percent in Uganda.

Consumer price reductions are also slightly larger for rural households than urban households in Uganda and Ghana, where these two categories of households are distinguished. The difference is caused by the fact that urban households consume relatively more services, for which prices fall least.

Combining the income and consumer price effects, we find that the net effect (relative income) is positive for all countries, although the rural–urban bias varies from country to country. In Ghana, greater consumer price savings for rural households are insufficient to offset their greater income losses; as a result, their relative income increases less than that of their urban counterparts. In Senegal, rural rather than urban households benefit more. While the decline in the relative wages of rural workers would initially lead one to believe that rural households lose the most from trade liberalization, this decline is compensated for by larger consumer price savings, given that such households consume more goods from the initially protected agricultural and agroindustrial sectors, whereas urban households, particularly in Dakar, consume more services, for which prices fall only moderately. In Uganda, where household incomes vary in the same proportion, the larger reduction in consumer prices for rural households allows them to emerge as slightly bigger winners from trade liberalization.

Growth Effects

Few applied general equilibrium studies have integrated the engines of growth modeled here. These channels are important.

After an initial burst in the first year, trade liberalization continues to contribute to a gradual increase in GDP relative to business as usual over the rest of the simulation period (table 5.5). As the countries with the highest initial tariff rates, Senegal and Uganda benefit most from their elimination, with increases in GDP that reach 3.9 in Senegal and 3.8 percent in Uganda by the last year of simulations.

In all countries, growth is spurred by increases in productivity/efficiency and investment. Productivity gains are the results of increased openness, which raises competition and leads to technology transfers. Increased investment is the result of a drop in the cost of capital goods and, driven by a rise in the returns to capital (relative to the price index) and openness, increased household and foreign savings.

In all countries, more than half of the increase in GDP is obtained in the first year of simulations. This reflects the fact that liberalization . is not phased in and that the increases in the relative returns to capital and openness—and the reduction in the cost of capital goods—are

Table 5.5 Average Increase in Growth in Ghana, Honduras, Senegal, and Uganda as a Result of Trade Liberalization

(percentage change)

Country/ year	Change in GDP relative to business as usual					Change in average under full scenario		
	Full	NoPE	NoFS	NoHS	NoPK	RRC	Open	PK
Ghana								
1	1.3	0.0	1.3	1.3	1.3	1.6	2.8	–2.6
2	1.4	0.0	1.4	1.4	1.3	1.4	2.9	–2.5
3	1.5	0.1	1.5	1.4	1.3	1.2	3.0	–2.5
4	1.6	0.1	1.5	1.5	1.4	1.1	3.1	–2.5
5	1.6	0.1	1.6	1.6	1.4	1.0	3.2	–2.4
6	1.7	0.2	1.7	1.6	1.4	0.9	3.3	–2.4
7	1.8	0.2	1.8	1.7	1.5	0.8	3.4	–2.4
8	1.9	0.2	1.8	1.7	1.5	0.7	3.4	–2.4
9	1.9	0.2	1.9	1.8	1.5	0.6	3.5	–2.4
10	2.0	0.3	1.9	1.8	1.6	0.6	3.6	–2.4
11	2.0	0.3	2.0	1.8	1.6	0.5	3.6	–2.3
12	2.1	0.3	2.0	1.8	1.6	0.5	3.7	–2.3
13	2.1	0.3	2.1	1.8	1.6	0.4	3.7	–2.3
14	2.2	0.3	2.1	1.9	1.6	0.4	3.7	–2.3
15	2.2	0.3	2.2	1.9	1.7	0.4	3.8	–2.3
Honduras								
1	0.9	0.0	0.9	0.9	0.9	1.4	4.0	–2.2
2	1.0	0.0	1.0	1.0	0.9	1.1	4.6	–2.2
3	1.0	0.0	1.0	1.0	1.0	0.9	4.7	–2.1
4	1.1	0.1	1.1	1.1	1.0	0.7	4.9	–2.1
5	1.1	0.1	1.1	1.1	1.0	0.5	5.1	–2.1
6	1.2	0.1	1.2	1.1	1.0	0.4	5.3	–2.1
7	1.2	0.1	1.2	1.2	1.1	0.3	5.5	–2.0
8	1.3	0.1	1.2	1.2	1.1	0.2	5.7	–2.0
9	1.3	0.1	1.3	1.3	1.1	0.1	6.0	–2.0
10	1.3	0.1	1.3	1.3	1.1	0.0	6.2	–2.0
11	1.4	0.1	1.4	1.3	1.2	–0.1	6.4	–1.9
12	1.4	0.1	1.4	1.4	1.2	–0.2	6.6	–1.9
13	1.4	0.2	1.4	1.4	1.2	–0.2	6.8	–1.9
14	1.5	0.2	1.5	1.4	1.2	–0.2	7.0	–1.9
15	1.5	0.2	1.5	1.5	1.2	–0.3	7.2	–1.9
Senegal								
1	2.1	0.1	2.1	2.1	2.1	4.8	9.2	–4.5
2	2.3	0.2	2.2	2.2	2.1	4.7	9.4	–4.5
3	2.4	0.2	2.4	2.3	2.1	4.6	9.5	–4.5
4	2.6	0.3	2.5	2.5	2.1	4.5	9.7	–4.5
5	2.8	0.3	2.6	2.6	2.1	4.5	9.8	–4.5
6	2.9	0.4	2.7	2.7	2.1	4.4	10.0	–4.5

(*Continued on the following page*)

Table 5.5 (Continued)

Country/ year	Change in GDP relative to business as usual					Change in average under full scenario		
	Full	NoPE	NoFS	NoHS	NoPK	RRC	Open	PK
Senegal continued								
7	3.1	0.4	2.8	2.8	2.1	4.3	10.1	−4.5
8	3.2	0.4	2.9	2.9	2.1	4.3	10.2	−4.4
9	3.3	0.5	3.0	2.9	2.1	4.2	10.4	−4.4
10	3.4	0.5	3.1	3.0	2.1	4.2	10.5	−4.4
11	3.5	0.5	3.1	3.1	2.1	4.1	10.6	−4.4
12	3.6	0.6	3.2	3.2	2.1	4.1	10.7	−4.3
13	3.7	0.6	3.3	3.2	2.1	4.0	10.8	−4.3
14	3.8	0.6	3.3	3.3	2.0	4.0	10.9	−4.3
15	3.9	0.6	3.4	3.3	2.0	3.9	10.9	−4.2
Uganda								
1	2.0	0.0	2.0	2.0	2.0	3.6	2.0	−2.3
2	2.2	0.1	2.2	2.1	2.1	3.2	1.9	−2.8
3	2.4	0.2	2.3	2.2	2.2	2.9	1.8	−3.1
4	2.5	0.3	2.5	2.3	2.2	2.6	1.7	−3.4
5	2.7	0.4	2.7	2.4	2.3	2.3	1.7	−3.7
6	2.9	0.5	2.9	2.5	2.3	2.1	1.6	−3.9
7	3.0	0.6	3.0	2.6	2.4	1.8	1.5	−4.1
8	3.2	0.7	3.2	2.7	2.4	1.5	1.4	−4.3
9	3.3	0.8	3.3	2.8	2.4	1.3	1.3	−4.4
10	3.4	0.9	3.4	2.9	2.4	1.0	1.2	−4.5
11	3.5	1.0	3.5	3.0	2.4	0.7	1.1	−4.7
12	3.6	1.1	3.6	3.1	2.4	0.5	1.0	−4.8
13	3.7	1.2	3.7	3.1	2.4	0.2	0.9	−4.9
14	3.8	1.3	3.7	3.2	2.3	−0.1	0.8	−4.9
15	3.8	1.4	3.8	3.2	2.3	−0.3	0.7	−5.0

Source: Authors' calculations.

Note: Core simulation (all growth channels). Full = core simulation (all growth channels); NoPE = no openness–productivity/efficiency channel; NoFS = no capital returns/openness–foreign savings channel; NoHS = no capital returns–household savings channel; NoPK = no liberalization–capital good price effect; RRC = returns to capital deflated by economywide value added price index; Open = openness ratio; PK = capital good price.

achieved primarily immediately after liberalization. Indeed, the gains in relative returns to capital relative to business as usual fall after the first year in all four countries. Openness continues to increase after the first year in all countries except Uganda, albeit only modestly. Savings in terms of the price of capital goods declines after the first year in Ghana, Honduras, and Senegal; in Uganda they increase further.

Consequently, the long-term effects are not very different from the short-term effects. Increases in long-term output (see table 5.3) are strongest in the sectors in which openness increases most, as a result of the resulting productivity/efficient gains and the long-term investment this attracts. In all countries but Senegal, these are the primary sectors, as a result of much stronger export responses (Honduras and Uganda) or increased import competition (Ghana). Increased investment also raises the relative demand for skilled labor, which is complementary to capital in the production process. As a result, skilled wages rise dramatically in the long term (see table 5.4).

In order to distinguish the relative importance of these different growth motors, we rerun the simulations, canceling one of the channels each time. To examine the impact of the productivity/efficiency channel, for example, we set the elasticity of productivity with respect to openness equal to zero in equation 5.5. The simulation results indicate that the increase in GDP following liberalization would be much smaller in the absence of this channel. In contrast, removing the foreign savings channel has almost no impact on the GDP gains, and removing the household savings channel has only very limited impact. These results are not surprising, as real returns to capital rise only marginally in the long term and actually fall slightly in Honduras and foreign savings represent only a small share (less than 20 percent) of total savings in all four countries. [20] Removing the capital good price channel has a more substantial impact, especially in the long term, albeit much weaker than the productivity/ efficiency channel.

In the full simulation scenario, female wage rates fall relative to male wage rates, except in Honduras, where they rise only marginally (table 5.6). The strongest impact is in Uganda, where relative female wage rates fall almost 1 percent. While the causes vary from country to country, all share the common basis that female workers participate less in the export-oriented sectors and more in the import-competing sectors.

After the various growth channels are canceled, only the productivity/efficiency channel has a substantial effect on the gender wage gap. The productivity gains imply that output can be maintained— and even increased—with lower levels of factor inputs, including labor. In all countries but Ghana this channel operates to the detriment of female workers, as the gender wage gap evolves more favorably in its absence. Indeed, female workers derive a larger share of their wages from sectors in which openness increases most under trade liberalization, as a result of either high initial tariff rates or a strong export response. Rural female workers in Senegal, for

Table 5.6 Average Increase in Female Wage Gap in Ghana, Honduras, Senegal, and Uganda as a Result of Trade Liberalization

Country/ category	Full		NoPE		NoFS		NoHS		NoPK	
	First year	Last year	First year	Last year	First year	Last year	First year	Last year	First year	Last year
Ghana										
Rural	0.2	0.5	0.3	0.6	0.2	0.5	0.2	0.4	0.2	0.4
Unskilled	0.3	0.3	0.5	0.6	0.3	0.3	0.3	0.3	0.3	0.4
Skilled	0	0.1	0.1	0.4	0	0.1	0	0.1	0	0.2
Urban	0.2	0.5	0.2	0.4	0.2	0.5	0.2	0.4	0.2	0.3
Unskilled	0.3	0.2	0.5	0.3	0.3	0.2	0.3	0.2	0.3	0.2
Skilled	0.2	0.2	0.1	0.2	0.2	0.2	0.2	0.1	0.2	0.2
All	0.2	0.4	0.3	0.5	0.2	0.4	0.2	0.3	0.2	0.3
Honduras										
Rural	-1.1	-0.7	-0.8	-0.3	-1.1	-0.7	-1.1	-0.7	-1.1	-0.6
Unskilled	-1.3	-0.6	-1	-0.2	-1.3	-0.6	-1.4	-0.7	-1.3	-0.5
Skilled	-0.2	-0.5	-0.2	-0.4	-0.3	-0.5	-0.2	-0.6	-0.2	-0.5
Urban	0.2	0.1	0	-0.1	0.2	0.1	0.1	0.1	0.2	0.2
Unskilled	0.3	0.3	0	0.1	0.3	0.3	0.2	0.3	0.3	0.3
Skilled	0.2	0.1	0	0	0.1	0.1	0.1	0.1	0.2	0.1
All	-0.1	-0.2	-0.2	-0.2	-0.1	-0.2	-0.2	-0.1	-0.1	0

Senegal										
Rural	-0.1	-0.1	-0.3	-0.2	-0.2	-0.2	-0.2	-0.1	-0.1	-0.1
Urban	-0.3	-0.8	-0.4	-0.5	-0.3	-0.6	-0.3	-0.6	-0.3	-0.1
Unskilled	-0.1	-0.2	-0.3	-0.4	-0.1	-0.1	-0.1	-0.1	-0.1	-0.1
Skilled	0.1	0.2	0.1	0.0	0.1	0.2	0.1	0.2	0.1	0.3
All	-0.1	-0.4	-0.2	-0.3	-0.1	-0.2	-0.1	-0.2	-0.1	0.0
Uganda										
Elementary[a]	2.3	1.6	-0.2	-0.1	2.4	1.6	1.5	1.5	2.3	1.6
Unskilled	1.4	0.3	-0.1	-0.1	1.4	0.3	0.7	0.4	1.4	0.3
Skilled	-0.3	-0.5	0	-0.2	-0.2	-0.5	-0.3	-0.4	-0.3	-0.4
All	0.8	0	0	-0.3	0.8	0	0.3	0	0.8	0.1

Source: Authors' calculations.

Note: Core simulation (all growth channels). Full = core simulation (all growth channels); NoPE = no openness–productivity/efficiency channel; NoFS= no capital returns/openness–foreign savings channel; NoHS = no capital returns–household savings channel; NoPK = no liberalization–capital good price effect.

a. Elementary refers to jobs that require less skill than "unskilled" jobs.

example, derive almost 51 percent of their wages from the agricultural subsectors, which are initially much more protected than the other primary sectors and thus experience substantial increases in both exports and imports following trade liberalization. In contrast, their male counterparts rely more on the practically nontradable construction and service sectors.

This gender bias in the productivity effect is far from monolithic. Among urban workers in Senegal, for example, unskilled female workers suffer most, because they are overwhelmingly employed in the trading sector, where almost no productivity gains occur as a result of increased openness. Their male counterparts rely more heavily on income from sectors in which openness and productivity increase most. In Ghana and Honduras, the situation is reversed, with female workers suffering most from the impacts of productivity gains in urban areas and males suffering most in rural areas.

Unskilled workers are generally affected more than skilled workers. The direction of this impact varies from country to country, however, and between rural and urban areas within countries.

Conclusion

The originality of the analysis presented in this chapter is twofold. First, it distinguishes between male and female workers—and in most cases by skill category and area (rural versus urban)—in order to bring out important gender differences in the impacts of trade liberalization. Second, it explicitly models the principal dynamic impacts of trade liberalization, which are widely held to outweigh the more traditional resource allocation effects, and traces their differential effects on male and female workers. A sequential dynamic CGE model—the only tool that allows analysis of the multiple and interconnected mechanisms set in motion by a substantial trade policy reform—is constructed for each country.

Further extensions to the modeling framework, better data, and more realistic trade policy scenarios for specific trade reforms are required before any policy lessons can be drawn. The analysis does suggest a number of important conclusions, however.

First, trade liberalization deepens existing gender wage gaps in all three African countries, especially among unskilled workers, and has a small but negative impact on the gender wage gap in Honduras. This results reflects the fact that the African countries are more agricultural and female workers are more involved in import-competing activities, such as food crops, whereas male workers are better able to take advantage of expanding export opportunities. In contrast, female workers are relatively more involved in export activities in the semi-industrial Honduran economy. Related to this is an increase in the wage premium to urban and skilled workers. To the extent that the poor are more likely to be female, rural, and unskilled, these results raise concerns that trade liberalization may hurt the most vulnerable or disproportionately benefit the least vulnerable.

Second, the dynamic gains from trade drive the growth effects, primarily by the productivity/efficiency gains from increased openness, although a fall in capital good prices also makes a substantial contribution. Increased household and foreign savings—resulting from an increase in the returns to capital and, in the case of foreign savings, increased openness—play only a negligible role.

Third, the productivity/efficiency gains from greater openness generally increase the gender wage gap. This can be traced to the fact that female workers derive a larger share of their wages from the sectors in which openness increases most following trade liberalization. These productivity gains reduce the relative demand for female labor and thus their relative wage. These impacts vary substantially between and within countries (rural versus urban), however, underscoring the importance of country-level analysis.

Annex: The Model

Production Equations

1. $XS_{i,t} = VA_{i,t} / v_i$

2. $CI_{i,t} = io_{i,t} \cdot XS_{i,t}$

3. $DI_{i,j,t} = aij_{i,j} \cdot CI_{j,t}$

4. $VA_{i,t} = A_i^{VA} \cdot \theta_{i,t} \cdot \left(\alpha_i^{VA} \cdot LNQ_{i,t}^{-\rho_i^{VA}} + \left(1 - \alpha_i^{VA}\right) \cdot KLQ_{i,t}^{-\rho_i^{VA}} \right)^{-1/\rho_i^{VA}}$

5. $\theta_{i,t} = \left[\dfrac{(IM_{i,t} + EX_{i,t}) / VA_{i,t}}{(IM_i^0 + EX_i^0) / VA_i^0} \right]^{\sigma^{PT}}$ or $\theta_{i,t} = 1$ if $EX_i^0 = IM_i^0 = 0$

6. $LNQ_{i,t} = \left[\dfrac{\alpha_i^{VA}}{(1 - \alpha_i^{VA})} \cdot \dfrac{PKLQ_{i,t}}{wnq_{i,t}} \right]^{\sigma_i^{VA}} \cdot KLQ_{i,t}$

7. $LNQ_{i,t} = A_i^{LNQ} \cdot \left(\alpha_i^{LNQ} \cdot LDT_{UNQ,i,t}^{-\rho_i^{LNQ}} + \left(1 - \alpha_i^{LNQ}\right) \cdot LDT_{RNQ,i,t}^{-\rho_i^{LNQ}} \right)^{-1/\rho_i^{LNQ}}$

8. $LDT_{UNQ,i,t} = \left[\dfrac{\alpha_i^{LNQ}}{\left(1 - \alpha_i^{LNQ}\right)} \cdot \dfrac{wt_{RNQ,i,t}}{wt_{UNQ,i,t}} \right]^{\sigma_i^{LNQ}} \cdot LDT_{RNQ,i,t}$

9. $KLQ_{i,t} = A_i^{KL} \cdot \left(\alpha_i^{KL} \cdot LQ_{i,t}^{-\rho_i^{KL}} + \left(1 - \alpha_i^{KL}\right) \cdot KD_{i,t}^{-\rho_i^{KL}} \right)^{-1/\rho_i^{KL}}$

10. $LQ_{i,t} = \left[\dfrac{\alpha_i^{KL}}{\left(1 - \alpha_i^{KL}\right)} \cdot \dfrac{r_{i,t}}{wq_{i,t}} \right]^{\sigma_i^{KL}} \cdot KD_{i,t}$

11. $LQ_{i,t} = A_i^{LQ} \cdot \left(\alpha_i^{LQ} \cdot LDT_{UQ,i,t}^{-\rho_i^{LQ}} + \left(1 - \alpha_i^{LQ}\right) \cdot LDT_{RQ,i,t}^{-\rho_i^{LQ}} \right)^{-1/\rho_i^{LQ}}$

12. $LDT_{UQ,i,t} = \left[\dfrac{\alpha_i^{LQ}}{\left(1 - \alpha_i^{LQ}\right)} \cdot \dfrac{wt_{RQ,i,t}}{wt_{UQ,i,t}} \right]^{\sigma_i^{LQ}} \cdot LDT_{RQ,i,t}$

13. $LDT_{l,i,t} = A_{l,i}^{LG} \cdot \left(\alpha_{l,i}^{LG} \cdot FLDT_{l,i,t}^{-\rho_{l,i}^{LG}} + \left(1 - \alpha_i^{LG}\right) \cdot MLDT_{l,i,t}^{-\rho_{l,i}^{LG}} \right)^{-1/\rho_{l,i}^{LG}}$

14. $FLDT_{l,i,t} = \left[\dfrac{\alpha_{l,i}^{LG}}{\left(1 - \alpha_{l,i}^{LG}\right)} \cdot \dfrac{wm_{l,t}}{wf_{l,t}} \right]^{\sigma_{l,i}^{LG}} \cdot MLDT_{l,i,t}$

15. $GDP_t = \sum\limits_i PV_i^0 \cdot VA_{i,t}$

Income and Savings Equations

16. $YH_{h,t} = \sum\limits_l \left(wf_{l,t} \times FLS_{h,l,t} + wmf_{l,t} \times MLS_{h,l,t} \right) + \left(\dfrac{KH_{h,t}}{KS_t} \right)$
$\times \sum\limits_i r_{i,t} \times KD_{i,t} + PINDEX_t \times TG_{h,t} + DIV_{h,t}$
$+ e_t \times TROW\_H_{h,t}$

17. $YDH_{h,t} = YH_{h,t} - DTH_{h,t}$

18. $SH_{h,t} = \psi_h \cdot \left[\dfrac{rmoy_t / PINDEX_t}{rmoy^0 / PINDEX^0} \right]^{\sigma_h^{HS}} \cdot YDH_{h,t}$

19. $YF_t = \left(\dfrac{KF_t}{KS_t}\right) \cdot \displaystyle\sum_i r_{i,t} \cdot KD_{i,t} + PINDEX_t \cdot TG\_F_t$
$\qquad + e_t \cdot TROW\_F_t$

20. $SF_t = YF_t - DTF_t - \displaystyle\sum_h DIV_{h,t} - DIV\_ROW_t$

21. $DIV_{h,t} = \dfrac{DIV_h^0}{YF^0} \cdot YF_t$

22. $DIV\_ROW_t = \dfrac{DIV\_ROW^0}{YF^0} \cdot YF_t$

23. $YG_{h,t} = \displaystyle\sum_i \left(TI_{i,t} + TIP_{i,t}\right) + \sum_h DTH_{h,t} + \sum_x TIX_{x,t} + \sum_m TIM_{m,t}$
$\qquad + DTF_t \left(\dfrac{KG_t}{KS_t}\right) \cdot \displaystyle\sum_i r_{i,t} \cdot KD_{i,t} + e_t \cdot TROW\_G_t$

24. $SG_t = YG_t - \displaystyle\sum_i PC_{i,t} \cdot G_{i,t} - \sum_h PINDEX_t \cdot TG_{h,t}$
$\qquad - PINDEX_t \cdot TG\_F_t - e_t \cdot TG\_ROW_t$

25. $SG_t = \dfrac{SG^0}{GDP^0} \cdot GDP_t$

26. $TI_{m,t} = \left(tx_m + tx_t^{NEW}\right) \times PL_{m,t} \times D_{m,t} + \left(tx_m + tx_t^{NEW}\right) \times \left(1 + tm_m\right)$
$\qquad \times e_t \times PWM_{m,t} \times IM_{m,t}$

27. $TI_{nm,t} = \left(tx_{nm} + tx_t^{NEW}\right) \cdot PL_{nm,t} \cdot D_{nm,t}$

28. $TIP_{i,t} = tp_i \cdot P_{i,t} \cdot XS_{i,t}$

29. $TIM_{m,t} = tm_m \cdot PWM_{m,t} \cdot e_t \cdot IM_{m,t}$

30. $TIX_{x,t} = tex_x \cdot PE_{x,t} \cdot EX_{x,t}$

31. $DTH_{h,t} = tyf_h \cdot YH_{h,t}$

32. $DTF_t = tyf \cdot YF_t$

Demand Equations

$$33.\ C_{i,h,t} \cdot PC_{i,t} = C_{i,h,t}^{MIN} \times PC_{i,t} + \gamma_{i,h}$$
$$\times \left(YDH_{h,t} - SH_{h,t} - \sum_j C_{j,h,t}^{MIN} \times PC_{j,t} \right)$$

$$34.\ INV_{i,t} \cdot PC_{i,t} = \mu_i \cdot IT_t$$

$$35.\ \frac{IND_{i,t}}{KD_{i,t}} = \phi_i \left[\frac{r_{i,t}}{U_t} \right]^{\sigma_i^K}$$

$$36.\ DIT_{i,t} = \sum_j DI_{i,j,t}$$

Price Equations

$$37.\ (1 - tp_i) \cdot P_{i,t} \cdot XS_{i,t} = PV_{i,t} \cdot VA_{i,t} + \sum_j PC_{j,t} \cdot DI_{j,i,t}$$

$$38.\ PV_{i,t} \cdot VA_{i,t} = r_{i,t} \cdot KD_{i,t} + \sum_l wt_{l,i,t} \cdot LDT_{l,i,t}$$

$$39.\ PKLQ_{i,t} \cdot KLQ_{i,t} = r_{i,t} \cdot KD_{i,t} + wq_{i,t} \cdot LQ_{i,t}$$

$$40.\ wq_{i,t} \cdot LQ_{i,t} = \sum_{qu} wt_{qu,i,t} \cdot LDT_{qu,i,t}$$

$$41.\ wnq_{i,t} \cdot LNQ_{i,t} = \sum_{nq} wt_{nq,i,t} \cdot LDT_{nq,i,t}$$

$$42.\ wt_{l,i,t} \cdot LDT_{l,i,t} = wm_{l,t} \cdot MLDT_{l,i,t} + wf_{l,t} \cdot FLDT_{l,i,t}$$

$$43.\ PC_{m,t} \cdot Q_{m,t} = PD_{m,t} \cdot D_{m,t} + PM_{m,t} \cdot IM_{m,t}$$

$$44.\ PC_{nm,t} = PD_{nm,t}$$

$$45.\ P_{x,t} \cdot XS_{x,t} = PL_{x,t} \cdot D_{x,t} + PE_{x,t} \cdot EX_{x,t}$$

$$46.\ P_{nx,t} = PL_{nx,t}$$

47. $PD_{i,t} = PL_{i,t} \cdot \left(1 + tx_i + tx_t^{NEW}\right)$

48. $PM_{m,t} = e_t \cdot PWM_{m,t} \cdot \left(1 + tm_m\right) \cdot \left(1 + tx_m + tx_t^{NEW}\right)$

49. $PE_{x,t} = \dfrac{e_t \cdot PWE_{x,t}}{\left(1 + tex_x\right)}$

50. $PINDEX_t = \dfrac{\sum\limits_{i,b} PC_{i,t} \cdot C_{i,b}^0}{\sum\limits_{i,b} PC_i^0 \cdot C_{i,b}^0}$

51. $rmoy_t = \dfrac{\sum\limits_i r_{i,t} \cdot KD_i^0}{\sum\limits_i r_i^0 \cdot KD_i^0}$

52. $PK_t = \prod\limits_i \left[\dfrac{PC_{i,t}}{\mu_i}\right]^{\mu_i}$

53. $U_t = PK_t \cdot (ir_t + \delta)$

International Trade Equations

54. $XS_{x,t} = B_x^E \cdot \left(\beta_x^E \cdot EX_{x,t}^{\kappa_x^E} + \left(1 - \beta_x^E\right) \cdot D_{x,t}^{\kappa_x^E}\right)^{1/\kappa_x^E}$

55. $XS_{nx,t} = D_{nx,t}$

56. $EX_{x,t} = \left[\dfrac{\left(1 - \beta_x^E\right)}{\beta_x^E} \cdot \dfrac{PE_{x,t}}{PL_{x,t}}\right]^{\tau_x^E} \cdot D_{x,t}$

57. $Q_{m,t} = A_m^M \cdot \left(\alpha_m^M \cdot IM_{m,t}^{-\rho_m^M} + \left(1 - \alpha_m^M\right) \cdot D_{m,t}^{-\rho_m^M}\right)^{-1/\rho_m^M}$

58. $Q_{nm,t} = D_{nm,t}$

59. $IM_{m,t} = \left[\dfrac{\alpha_m^M}{\left(1 - \alpha_m^M\right)} \cdot \dfrac{PD_{m,t}}{PM_{m,t}}\right]^{\sigma_m^M} \cdot D_{m,t}$

60. $CAB_t = e_t \cdot \sum_m PWM_{m,t} \cdot IM_{m,t} + \left(\dfrac{KROW_t}{KS_t}\right) \cdot \sum_i r_{i,t} \cdot KD_{i,t}$

$\qquad + e_t \cdot TG\_ROW_t + DIV\_ROW_t - e_t \cdot \sum_x PWE_{x,t} \cdot EX_{x,}$

$\qquad - e_t \cdot TROW\_F_t - e_t \cdot TROW\_G_t - e_t \cdot \sum_h TROW\_H_{h,t}$

61. $CAB_t = \dfrac{CAB^0}{GDP^0} \times \left[\dfrac{rmoy_t / PINDEX_t}{rmoy^0 / PINDEX^0}\right]^{\sigma^{FSR}}$

$\qquad \times \left[\dfrac{(IM_t + EX_t)/GDP_t}{(IM^0 + EX^0)/GDP^0}\right]^{\sigma^{FSO}} GDP_t$

Equilibrium Equations

62. $Q_{i,t} = \sum_h C_{i,h,t} + G_{i,t} + DIT_{i,t} + INV_{i,t}$

63. $\sum_h MLS_{h,l,t} = \sum_i MLDT_{l,i,t}$

64. $\sum_h FLS_{h,l,t} = \sum_i FLDT_{l,i,t}$

65. $KS_t = \sum_i KD_{i,t}$

66. $IT_i = \sum_h SH_{h,t} + SG_t + SF_t + CAB_t$

67. $IT_i = PK_t \cdot \sum_i IND_{i,t}$

Dynamic Equations

68. $KD_{i,t+1} = KD_{i,t}(1-\delta) + IND_{i,t}$

69. $KH_{h,t+1} = KH_{h,t}(1-\delta) + \left(\dfrac{SH_{h,t}}{PK_t}\right)$

70. $KF_{t+1} = KF_t \left(1 - \delta\right) + \left[\dfrac{SF_t}{IT_t}\right] \cdot \sum_i IND_{i,t}$

71. $KG_{t+1} = KG_t \left(1 - \delta\right) + \left[\dfrac{SG_t}{IT_t}\right] \cdot \sum_i IND_{i,t}$

72. $KROW_{t+1} = KROW_t \left(1 - \delta\right) + \left[\dfrac{CAB_t}{IT_t}\right] \cdot \sum_i IND_{i,t}$

73. $MLS_{h,l,t+1} = MLS_{h,l,t} \cdot \left(1 + n\right)$

74. $FLS_{h,l,t+1} = FLS_{h,l,t} \cdot \left(1 + n\right)$

75. $C_{i,h,t+1}^{MIN} = C_{i,h,t}^{MIN} \cdot \left(1 + n\right)$

76. $TG_{h,t+1} = TG_{h,t} \cdot \left(1 + n\right)$

77. $TG\_F_{t+1} = TG\_F_t \cdot \left(1 + n\right)$

78. $TG\_ROW_{t+1} = TG\_ROW_t \cdot \left(1 + n\right)$

79. $TROW\_G_{t+1} = TROW\_G_t \cdot \left(1 + n\right)$

80. $TROW\_F_{t+1} = TROW\_F_t \cdot \left(1 + n\right)$

81. $TROW\_H_{h,t+1} = TROW\_H_{h,t} \cdot \left(1 + n\right)$

82. $G_{i,t+1} = G_{i,t} \cdot \left(1 + n\right)$

Parameters

A_i^{KL}: scale coefficient (CES capital–skilled labor)

$A_{l,i}^{LG}$: scale coefficient (CES labor gender function)

A_i^{LNQ}: scale coefficient (CES unskilled labor)

A_i^{LQ}: scale coefficient (CES skilled labor)

A_m^{M}: scale parameter (CES import function)

A_i^{VA}: scale coefficient (CES value added)

$aij_{i,j}$: input-output coefficient

α_i^{KL}: share parameter (CES capital–skilled labor)

$\alpha_{l,i}^{LG}$: share parameter (CES labor by gender)

α_i^{LNQ}: share parameter (CES unskilled labor)

α_i^{LQ}: share parameter (CES skilled labor)

α_m^{M}: share parameter (CES import function)

α_i^{VA}: share parameter (CES value added)

B_x^{E}: scale parameter (CET function)

β_x^{E}: share parameter (CET function)

δ: depreciation rate of capital

$\gamma_{i,b}$: marginal share of good I in household H consumption

io_i: coefficient (Leontief total intermediate consumption)

κ_x^{E}: transformation parameter (CET export function)

μ_i: share of the value of good TR in total investment

n: population growth rate

ϕ_i: coefficient in investment demand function

ψ_b: propensity to save for household H

ρ_i^{KL}: substitution parameter (CES capital–skilled labor)

$\rho_{l,i}^{LG}$: substitution parameter (CES labor gender function)

ρ_i^{LNQ}: substitution parameter (CES unskilled labor)

ρ_i^{LQ}: substitution parameter (CES skilled labor)

ρ_m^{M}: substitution parameter (CES import function)

ρ_i^{VA}: substitution parameter (CES value added)

σ^{FS}: elasticity of foreign savings to rate of return

σ^{HS}: elasticity of household savings to rate of return

σ_i^{K}: investment demand elasticity

σ_i^{KL}: substitution elasticity (CES capital–skilled labor)

$\sigma_{l,i}^{LG}$: substitution elasticity (CES function between gender)

σ_i^{LNQ}: substitution elasticity (CES unskilled labor)

σ_i^{LQ}: substitution elasticity (CES skilled labor)

σ_m^M: substitution elasticity (CES import function)

σ^{PT}: elasticity of scale parameter to openness

σ_i^{VA}: substitution elasticity (CES value added using old capital)

τ_x^E: transformation elasticity (CET export function)

tm_m: import duties on good i

tex_x: tax on exports

tp_i: tax rate on production of sector i

tx_i: tax rate on good i

tyf: direct income tax rate for firms

tyh_h: direct income tax rate for household h

v_i: coefficient (Leontief value added)

Endogenous Variables

$C_{i,b,t}$: household b consumption of good i (volume)

CAB_t: current account balance

$C_{i,t}$: total intermediate consumption of sector I

$D_{i,t}$: demand for domestic good I

$DI_{i,j,t}$: intermediate consumption of good I in sector J

$DIT_{i,t}$: intermediate demand for good I

$DIV_{b,t}$: dividends paid to households

DIV_ROW_t: dividends paid to foreigners

DTF_t : receipts from direct taxation on firms' income

$DTH_{b,t}$: receipts from direct taxation on household H income

$EX_{x,t}$: exports of good X

$FLDT_{l,i,t}$: sector I demand for female labor L

$FLS_{b,l,t}$: household H female labor L supply

GDP_t : gross domestic product at factor cost

$IM_{m,t}$: imports of good M

$IND_{i,t}$: investment by destination

$INV_{i,t}$: investment in good I (origin)

ir_t : interest rate

IT_t : total investment (value)

$KLQ_{i,t}$: sector I demand for capital skilled labor aggregate

KS_t : total capital stock

$LDT_{l,i,t}$: sector I demand for labor L

$LNQ_{i,t}$: sector I demand for unskilled labor

$LQ_{i,t}$: sector I demand for skilled labor

$MLDT_{l,i,t}$: sector I demand for male labor L

$MLS_{h,l,t}$: household H male labor L supply

$P_{i,t}$: producer price of good I

$PC_{i,t}$: price of composite good I

$PD_{i,t}$: domestic price of good I including tax

$PE_{x,t}$: domestic price of exported good X

$PINDEX_t$: consumer price index

PK_t : capital replacement price

$PKLQ_{i,t}$: price of the capital skilled labor aggregate

$PL_{i,t}$: domestic price of good I excluding tax

$PM_{m,t}$: domestic price of imported good I

$PV_{i,t}$: value added price for sector I

$Q_{i,t}$: demand for composite good I

$r_{i,t}$: rate of return to capital in sector I

$rmoy_t$: average rate of return

SF_t : firms' savings

SG_t : government savings

$SH_{h,t}$: household H savings

$\theta_{i,t}$: productivity factor

$TI_{i,t}$: receipts from indirect tax

$TIP_{i,t}$: receipts from tax on production

$TIM_{m,t}$: receipts from import duties

$TIX_{x,t}$: receipts from tax on production

tx_t^{NEW}: new tax on goods and services to keep SG constant

U_t: capital user cost

$VA_{i,t}$: value added in sector I (volume)

$wf_{l,t}$: wage rate for male worker of type L

$wm_{l,t}$: wage rate for male worker of type L

$wnq_{i,t}$: average wage rate for unskilled workers

$wq_{i,t}$: average wage rate for skilled workers

$wt_{l,i,t}$: average wage rate for sector I and labor type L

$XS_{i,t}$: production of sector I

$YDH_{h,t}$: household H disposable income

YF_t : firms' income

YG_t : government income

$YH_{h,t}$: household H income

Exogenous Variables

$C_{i,h,t}^{MIN}$: household H minimum consumption of good I (volume)

e_t : exchange rate (*numeraire*)

$G_{i,t}$: total public consumption (volume)

$KD_{i,t}$: sector I demand for capital

KF_t : firms' capital

KG_t : government capital

$KH_{h,t}$: household H capital

$KROW_t$: ROW capital

$PWE_{x,t}$: world price of export X (foreign currency)

$PWM_{m,t}$: world price of import M (foreign currency)

$TG_{h,t}$: public transfers to households

TG_F_t: public transfers to firms

TG_ROW_t: public transfers to ROW

$TROW\_F_t$: transfers from ROW to firms

$TROW\_G_t$: transfers from ROW to government

$TROW\_H_{h,t}$: transfers from ROW to households

Sets

i, j	sectors, goods and services
m	imported goods
x	exported goods
l	labor category
h	household type
t	time (year)

Notes

Funding for this study was provided by the World Bank–Netherlands Partnership Program (BNPP) and the Poverty and Economic Policy (PEP) research network, which is financed by the government of Canada through the International Development Research Centre (IDRC) and the Canadian International Development Agency (CIDA) and by the Australian Agency for International Development (AusAID). The authors express their thanks to André Martens for his review of the empirical literature on trade, foreign direct investment, and growth, as well as to Erwin Corong for his excellent research assistance. They also thank Maurizio Bussolo, Rafael De Hoyos, André Martens, Will Martin, and participants at the "Gender Aspects of the Trade and Poverty Nexus: A Macro-Micro Approach" workshop, held February 22, 2008, at the World Bank, in Washington DC, for comments and suggestions. They also thank Charles Ackah, Joseph Cabral, Fatou Cissé, Jann Lay, Hans Lofgren, Denis Medvedev, Emmanuel Mensah, Dino Moretto, Oscar Nunez, and James Thurlow for help in obtaining country data and information. John Cockburn is the corresponding author; his e-mail address is jcoc@ecn.ulaval.ca.

1. For compact elaborations of these issues, see Keller (2000), Kim (2000), and Winters (2004).

2. For important contributions in this area, see, among others, Bernard and others (2003); Melitz (2003); Helpman, Melitz, and Yeaple (2004); Baldwin (2005); Baldwin and Robert-Nicoud (2006); and Gustafsson and Segerstrom (2007).

3. This discussion is based on Martens (2008b).

4. See, for example, Elson and Pearson (1981); Standing (1989); Wood (1991); Cagatay and Ozler (1995); Joekes (1995, 1999); and Ozler (2000, 2001). Typical female labor–intensive, export-oriented industries include textiles, garments, electronics, leather, and agricultural-processing industries.

5. See, for example, the work by Lemelin and Decaluwe (2007) on investment demand equations. Abbink, Braber, and Cohen (1995) use a sequential dynamic CGE model for Indonesia in which total investment is distributed as a function of base-year sectoral shares in total capital remuneration and sectoral profit rates.

6. The model is formulated as a system of nonlinear equations solved recursively as a nonlinear programming system with GAMS/Conopt3 solver.

7. The index m (x) represents the subset of importable (exportable) sectors.

8. For empirical studies, see Jonsson and Subramanian (2001) and Arora and Bhundia (2003), both on South Africa.

9. Note that the causality may also be reversed. As trade and foreign investment are determined simultaneously in a CGE model, what is important is that they are complements rather than substitutes.

10. For a more sophisticated presentation of household behavior, see Lemelin and Decaluwe (2007).

11. See, for example, the Senegalese results presented in chapter 7 of this volume.

12. The food-processing and textiles industries have higher protection rates (roughly 12 percent) in Honduras.

13. This is caused primarily by larger mining (10 percent of GDP) and forestry (5 percent) production in Ghana's primary sector, both of these sectors being strongly export oriented.

14. This figure is misleading, because Honduras lists exports from its *maquila* industries (factories that import inputs exempt from tariffs in order to produce exports) as service exports.

15. Recall that the exchange rate is the numeraire of the models. Thus the real exchange devaluation is obtained through a fall in domestic prices.

16. This category corresponds to ILO category 9 ("laborers, elementary service workers, etc.").

17. Because of lack of data, a rural–urban breakdown of workers is not available for Uganda. It is likely that rural workers are primarily elementary workers.

18. Because the Senegal model has only one representative household, this result is arrived at implicitly, by comparing the changes in urban and rural factor returns.

19. Other nonfactor incomes include transfers from abroad (such as remittances) and dividends. Transfers from abroad are constant, as they are indexed to the exchange rate, which is the model numeraire. Dividends are a

fixed share of firm income, which essentially follows the variation in the average returns to capital.

20. The decline in Honduras can be seen by comparing the changes in the rates of returns to capital to changes in consumer prices in the last period in table 5.4.

References

Abbink, G. A., M. C. Braber, and S. I. Cohen. 1995. "A SAM–CGE Demonstration Model for Indonesia: Static and Dynamic Specifications and Experiments." *International Economic Journal* 9 (3): 15–33.

Agarwal, J .P. 1980. "Determinants of Foreign Direct Investment: A Survey." *Weltwirtschaftliches Archiv* 116 (4): 739–73.

Arora, V., and A. Bhundia. 2003. "Potential Output and Total Factor Productivity Growth in Post-Apartheid South Africa." IMF Working Paper WP/03/178, International Monetary Fund, Washington, DC.

Asiedu, E. 2002. "On the Determinants of Foreign Direct Investment to Developing Countries: Is Africa Different?" *World Development* 30 (1): 107–19.

Baldwin, R. E. 2005. "Heterogeneous Firms and Trade: Testable and Untestable Properties of the Melitz Model." NBER Working Paper 11471, National Bureau of Economic Research, Cambridge, MA.

Baldwin, R. E., and F. Robert-Nicoud. 2006. "Trade and Growth with Heterogeneous Firms." CEP Discussion Paper 727, 1–22, Centre for Economic Performance, London.

Becker, G. S. 1959. "Union Restrictions on Entry." In *The Public Stake in Union Power*, ed. P. D. Bradley, 209–24. Charlottesville: University of Virginia Press.

Bernard, A., J. Eaton, J. Jensen, and S. Kortum. 2003. "Plants and Productivity in International Trade." *American Economic Review* 93 (4): 1268–90.

Bhalla, S. 2002. *Imagine There's a Country: Poverty, Inequality and Growth in the Era of Globalization.* Institute of International Economics, Washington, DC.

Blake, A., A. Mckay, and O. Morrissey. 2001. "The Impact on Uganda of Agricultural Trade Liberalisation." Credit Research Paper 01/07, Center for Research in Economic Development and International Trade, Nottingham, United Kingdom.

Bourguignon, F., W. H. Branson, and J. de Melo. 1989 *Macroeconomic Adjustment and Income Distribution: A Macro-Micro Simulation Model.* Technical Paper, Organisation for Economic Co-operation and Development, Paris.

Cagatay, N., and S. Ozler. 1995. "Feminization of the Labor Force: The Effects of Long-Term Economic Development and Structural Adjustment." *World Development* 23 (8): 1883–94.

Cockburn, J., B. Decaluwé, and V. Robichaud. 2007. "Trade Liberalization and Poverty: Lessons from Africa and Asia." In *Future Trade Research Areas That Matter to Developing Country Policymakers*. Studies in Trade and Investment 61, Trade and Investment Division, United Nations Economic Commission for Asia and the Pacific, Bangkok. www.unescap.org/publications/detail.asp?id=1254.

Cuesta, J. 2004. "The 1997 Social Accounting Matrix (SAM) for Honduras." Institute of Social Studies, the Hague, the Netherlands.

De Melo, J., and J.-M. Grether. 1997. *Commerce international: Théories et applications*. Brussels: De Boeck Université.

Dollar, D., and A. Kraay. 2001. "Growth Is Good for the Poor." World Bank Policy Research Department Working Paper 2587, Washington, DC.

EC (European Commission). 2004. *EU Market Access Opportunities for Ghana and Position for EPA Negotiations*. Capacity Building in Support of Preparation of Economic Partnership Agreement, 8 ACP TPS 110/Project043, Final Report, Brussels.

Elson, D., and R. Pearson. 1981. "Nimble Fingers Make Cheap Workers." *Feminist Review* 7: 87–107.

Fofana, I., and F. Cabral. 2007. *La matrice de comptabilité sociale du Sénégal pour l'année 2004*. Poverty and Economic Policy (PEP) Research Network, Université Laval, Quebec.

Fontana, M., S. Joekes, and R. Masika. 1998, *Global Trade Expansion and Liberalization: Gender Issues and Impacts*. Bridge Report 42, Institute of Development Studies, Brighton, United Kingdom.

Gladwin, C., ed. 1991. *Structural Adjustment and the African Women Farmers*. Gainesville: University of Florida Press.

GSS (Ghana Statistical Services) and IFPRI (International Food Policy Research Institute). 2006. "A 2004 Social Accounting Matrix (SAM) for Ghana."

Gustafsson, P., and P. Segerstrom. 2007. "Trade Liberalization and Productivity Growth." CEPR Discussion Paper 5894, Centre for Economic Policy Research, London.

Helpman, E., M. Melitz, and S. R. Yeaple. 2004. "Export versus FDI with Heterogeneous Firms." *American Economic Review* 94 (1): 300–17.

Joekes, S. 1995. *Trade-Related Employment for Women in Industry and Services in Developing Countries*. UNRISD Occasional Paper 5, United Nations Research Institute for Social Development, Geneva.

———. 1999. "A Gender-Analytical Perspective on Trade and Sustainable Development." In *Trade Sustainable Development and Gender*, United Nations Conference on Trade and Development, 33–59. New York and Geneva: UNCTAD.

Jonsson, G., and A. Subramanian. 2001. "Dynamic Gains from Trade: Evidence from South Africa." IMF Staff Paper 48 (1): 197–224, International Monetary Fund, Washington, DC.

Jung, H. S., and E. Thorbecke. 2000. "The Impact of Public Education Expenditure on Human Capital, Growth, and Poverty in Tanzania and Zambia: A General Equilibrium Approach." IMF Working Paper 01/106, International Monetary Fund, Washington, DC.

Kandiero, T., and M. Chitiga. 2006. "Trade Openness and Foreign Direct Investment in Africa." *South African Journal of Economic and Management Sciences* 9 (3): 335–70.

Keller, W. 2000. "Do Trade Patterns and Technology Flows Affect Productivity Growth?" *World Bank Economic Review* 14 (1): 117–47.

Kim, E. 2000. "Trade Liberalization and Productivity Growth in Korean Manufacturing Industries: Price Protection, Market Power, and Scale Efficiency." *Journal of Development Economics* 62 (1): 55–83.

Lemelin, A., and B. Decaluwé. 2007. *Issues in Recursive Dynamic CGE Modeling: Investment by Destination, Savings, and Public Debt. A Survey.* Poverty and Economic Policy (PEP) Research Network, Université Laval Québec.

Lizondo, J. S. 1990. "Foreign Direct Investment." WP/90/63, International Monetary Fund, Washington, DC.

Markusen, J. R., and J. R. Melvin. 1988. *The Theory of International Trade.* New York: Harper and Row.

Markusen, J. R., and L. E. O. Svensson. 1985. "Trade in Goods and Factors with International Differences in Technology." *International Economic Review* 26 (1): 175–92.

Martens, A. 2008a. "Elasticity of Total Factor Productivity with Respect to Trade Openness in the Case of Emerging Countries: A Survey of Estimates." Department of Economics, University of Montreal.

———. 2008b. "Trade Liberalization and Foreign Direct Investment (FDI) in Emerging Countries: An Empirical Survey." Department of Economics, University of Montreal.

Melitz, M. 2003. "The Impact of Trade on Intra-Industry Reallocations and Aggregate Industry Productivity."*Econometrica* 71 (6): 1695–726.

Morrissey, O., N. Rudaheranwa, and L. Moller. 2003. *Trade Policies, Performance and Poverty in Uganda.* Overseas Development Institute, Uganda Trade and Poverty Project, London.

Onyeiwu, S., and H. Shrestha. 2004. "Determinants of Foreign Direct Investment in Africa." *Journal of Development Studies* 20 (1–2): 89–106.

Ozler, S. 2000. "Export Orientation and Female Share of Employment: The Evidence from Turkey." *World Development* 28 (7): 1239–48.

———. 2001. "Export-Led Industrialization and Gender Differences in Job Creation and Destruction: Micro Evidence from the Turkish

Manufacturing Sector." Department of Economics, University of California, Los Angeles.

Sala-i-Martin, X. 2002. "15 Years of New Growth Economics: What Have We Learnt?" Discussion Paper 0102–47, Department of Economics, Columbia University, New York.

Standing, G. 1989. "Global Feminization through Flexible Labor." *World Development* 17 (7): 1077–95.

Wade, R. 2004. "Is Globalization Reducing Poverty and Inequality?" *World Development* 32 (4): 567–89.

Winters, A. 2004. "Trade Liberalization and Economic Performance: An Overview." *Economic Journal* 114 (493): F4–F21.

Winters, A., N. McCulloch, and A. McKay. 2004. "Trade Liberalization and Poverty: The Evidence So Far." *Journal of Economic Literature* 43 (1): 72–115.

Wong, K. 1986. "Are International Trade and Factor Mobility Substitutes?" *Journal of International Economics* 21 (1–2): 25–44.

Wood, Adrian. 1991. "North-South Trade and Female Labour in Manufacturing: An Asymmetry." *Journal of Development Studies* 27 (2): 168– 89.

Zhu, E., and J. Thurlow. 2007. "A 2005 Social Accounting Matrix for Uganda." International Food Policy Research Institute, Washington DC.

PART II

The Micro Approach: Household Models of Trade, Gender, and Poverty

6

Higher Prices of Export Crops, Intrahousehold Inequality, and Human Capital Accumulation in Senegal

Maurizio Bussolo, Rafael E. De Hoyos, and Quentin Wodon

Since the 1994 devaluation of the CFA franc, Senegal has benefited from a high level of economic growth, which has resulted in an average rate of growth of per capita income of about 2 percent a year. As Azam and others (2007) note, the devaluation of the CFA franc has enabled the public sector to decrease its wage bill in real terms and allocate the resulting savings to an increase in public investment. This in turn has helped create conditions for faster growth and poverty reduction. The share of the population living in poverty decreased substantially from an initial level of 67.9 percent in 1994/95 to 57.1 percent in 2001/02 and 50.8 percent in 2005/2006 (Ndoye and others 2008). But not all sectors of the population have benefited equally from poverty reduction and growth. As Loayza and Raddatz (2006) and others show, the sectoral composition of economic growth matters for poverty reduction in most countries. Poverty reduction will typically be larger if growth is biased toward the more labor-intensive agricultural sector. In Senegal growth was higher in sectors such as manufacturing, construction, and transportation than in the labor-intensive agricultural sector. Although farmers also benefited from growth, poverty reduction was stronger in urban areas.

The limited poverty reduction observed in rural areas is caused by a number of factors. One is the fact that agriculture remains highly cyclical, depending on weather and other shocks. Droughts occur at regular intervals; recently locust attacks also led to a decline in agricultural production. Another factor is the fact that monopsonistic structures in key export markets for agricultural products are such that producer prices remain low in comparison with world market prices. The elimination or reduction of such distortions could help bring domestic producer prices closer to international prices, thereby increasing incomes and consumption levels for rural households, a majority of whom remain poor.

The case for connecting rural farmers more closely with international trade opportunities has been made repeatedly. The standard argument maintains that liberalizing agricultural markets would reduce inefficiencies created by the large transfers between tax payers and farmers. In many developing countries, these transfers are the results of policies that privilege urban dwellers by protecting their industries and maintaining low prices for food items, to the disadvantage of (usually poorer) local farmers. The taxation of export crops can also cause inefficiencies. Given that poverty incidence is highest among farmers, the poverty reduction potential of liberalizing agricultural markets looks promising.[1]

Rather than considering the direct impacts on poverty of a trade shock or, more specifically, an increase in the price of groundnuts, Senegal's main export crop, this chapter focuses on another, less obvious welfare impact of such trade-related shocks: the potential change in bargaining power within the household and the concomitant change in consumption choices. It is often argued that incomes from cash crops, including export crops, are controlled mostly by men. It is also well known that preferences in consumption patterns differ between men and women, with women allocating a larger share of their resources to the well-being of their children—through higher spending on education, for example (Hoddinot and Haddad 1995). Changes in producer prices for export crops may then redistribute resources within the household in favor of men (Ghosh and Kanbur 2008). This means that an increase in groundnut income could lead to a decrease in the income share of the household controlled by women, decreasing the share (and perhaps even the level) of spending allocated to investments in human capital for children. This in turn could lead to a reduction in long-term prospects for poverty reduction caused by a less well-educated population especially in rural areas.

Given that men in Senegal control most groundnut income (Gray 2002; Sullivan 2002), the effect of changes in groundnut producer prices on consumption patterns—and thereby human capital investments—could be gender related.[2] The objective of this chapter is to assess whether this is indeed the case in Senegal. The next section provides some additional background information on agricultural markets in Senegal. The following section describes the conceptual framework and empirical methodology used to test the framework. The third section presents the empirical results, using the nationally representative Senegalese Household Survey (Enquête Sénégalaise Auprès des Ménages [ESAM] I). The last section summarizes the chapter's main conclusions.

Agriculture and Poverty in Senegal

Agricultural production in Senegal is specialized in millet as the main food crop and groundnuts as the main export commodity. These two products use about 80 percent of total cultivated land (Boccanfuso and Savard 2005), with production of groundnuts providing income to about a third of the population in rural areas. Most groundnuts are not exported as peanuts but are instead purchased by the Société Nationale de Commercialisation des Oléagineux (SONACOS) (recently renamed Suneor). Suneor is a recently privatized firm that purchases and controls, through various means, a large share of the country's groundnut production. The company refines groundnuts and exports vegetable groundnut oil to European markets. It also runs a separate business by importing palm oil, refining it, and selling the product for consumption in the local Senegalese market. Here the firm benefits from a high degree of monopolistic power as well as from duties imposed on direct imports of refined palm oil, which costs less than its own production. While there are some arguments for maintaining special taxes on imported refined palm oil, these taxes make vegetable oil consumed in the country more expensive. One of the key arguments for maintaining these tariffs is that by helping the consumption side of Suneor's business, the tariffs also support the producer side of its business and thereby groundnut producers. Suneor argues that it could not survive in the short to medium term if it were not able to generate profits from its refining activities for the local market and that its demise would have large negative consequences for groundnut producers. Yet the evidence that Suneor pays high prices to groundnut producers is meager: producer prices have fallen in real terms in recent years. As a consequence, many groundnut producers still cannot emerge from poverty, while consumers continue to suffer from high prices for the vegetable oil they consume (Tsimpo and Wodon 2008).

This discussion makes it clear that in Senegal, as in other countries, the well-being of households is influenced by international commodity markets as well as domestic distortions in export and import prices. These distortions are far from negligible. Masters (2007) suggests that distortions in Senegal's food and agricultural export markets during the 1990s amounted to 17 percent of the domestic price of groundnuts. He estimates that import distortions were responsible for raising the price of rice (another market with monopolistic features in Senegal) about 22 percent higher than it otherwise would have been. One could argue that these estimates may be too high. But there is little doubt that better-functioning and more competitive markets could translate into significant increases in the price of groundnuts for producers as well as significant declines in the price of rice and vegetable oil for consumers. Interestingly, there were no significant distortions in the market for millet (Masters 2007). This is not surprising, because this is a highly decentralized market without large firms controlling its exports (as is the case for groundnut-related products) or imports (as is the case for rice and vegetable oils).

From the point of view of poverty reduction—the government's main objective, according to the principles laid out in Senegal's latest Poverty Reduction Strategy, adopted in 2006—an increase in producer prices for groundnuts could have large positive impacts on producers, many of whom are poor. Estimations of poverty measures among groundnut producers by Tsimpo and Wodon (2008) suggest that these producers are among the poorest groups in the country and that they have benefited less than other groups from the growth that took place after the 1994 devaluation. The authors also suggest that relatively small changes in producer prices could have a large impact on poverty among producers.

The issues related to the groundnut sector in Senegal are complex. A detailed discussion of a reform of the Suneor business model is beyond the scope of this chapter, which instead simply assumes that a well-designed reform would result in an increase in the price received by farmers. Similarly, the positive relation between producer price increases and poverty reduction has been established elsewhere (see, for instance, Tsimpo and Wodon 2008). Instead of focusing on these two issues—deregulation of the groundnuts' market and the poverty effects of changes in the price of this export crop—this chapter considers the effects of producer price changes on income distribution within households and the consequences for household consumption decisions.

Methodology

Using data for Côte d'Ivoire, Hoddinott and Haddad (1995) show that gender-specific control of income translates into changes in expenditures. This result rejects the income-pooling hypothesis (a key implication of the unitary model), suggesting that household consumption patterns are the outcome of complex bargaining processes among household members.[3] A change in relative prices caused by trade shocks or changes in market structure can thus redistribute income between men and women. If the income-pooling hypothesis is rejected, a change in income controlled by men and women can translate into a change in intrahousehold consumption patterns and resource allocation.

To account for the intrahousehold gender effects of trade shocks, we use a simple noncooperative model of the bargaining process based on Hoddinott and Haddad (1995).[4] Total household income Y is separated into income earned by women (Y_F) and income earned by men (Y_M). Define $\mathbf{Q}_F$ and $\mathbf{Q}_M$ as the vectors of consumption being financed with Y_F and Y_M, respectively. Assume that household members F and M differ in their preferences and hence disagree about what the optimal household consumption basket should look like. In this setting household members F and M have to choose their consumption basket based on prices, household income, and intrahousehold bargaining power. Following Hoddinott and Haddad (1995), F and M optimize their own consumption vector taking their counterpart's as given (a Nash noncooperative solution). Hence F will select $\mathbf{Q}_F$ and M will select $\mathbf{Q}_M$ such that:

(6.1a) $$\max_{Q_F} U_F(\bar{\mathbf{Q}}_M, \mathbf{Q}_F) \quad \text{subject to } P\mathbf{Q}_F \leq Y_F$$

(6.1b) $$\max_{Q_M} U_M(\bar{\mathbf{Q}}_F, \mathbf{Q}_M) \quad \text{subject to } P\mathbf{Q}_M \leq Y_M.$$

Notice that the bars on top of $\mathbf{Q}_M$ and $\mathbf{Q}_F$ in expressions (6.1a) and (6.1b) indicate that F and M take those values as given (this is the noncooperative feature of the model). The solution to these expressions yields a set of demand functions that could also be interpreted as reaction functions:

(6.2a) $$\mathbf{Q}_F = R_F(\mathbf{Q}_M, Y_F, P)$$

(6.2b) $$\mathbf{Q}_M = R_M(\mathbf{Q}_F, Y_M, P).$$

It can be shown that, under reasonable assumptions, $\mathbf{Q}_F^*$ and $\mathbf{Q}_M^*$ will yield a Nash equilibrium satisfying equations (6.2a) and (6.2b):

(6.3a) $$\mathbf{Q}_F^* = R_F^*(Y_M, Y_F, P)$$

(6.3b) $$Q_M^* = R_M^*(Y_M, Y_F, P).$$

Using results from Ulph (1988), Hoddinott and Haddad (1995) argue that under this setting, as the income share of one of the members rises, the share of household expenditures on the set of commodities preferred by that individual will rise. Therefore trade price shocks can redistribute household income (bargaining power) between men and women, changing household expenditure patters. Assume for example, that $Q_M^* = R_M^*(Y_M, Y_F, P)$ includes more elements improving children's quality of life (such as education and health) than does Q_M^* (see Haddad 1999). Under this condition a trade shock generating higher incomes for export crops traditionally controlled by men could increase gender inequality within the household and hence reduce women's bargaining power, human capital accumulation, and long-term development progress.

In order to test this hypothesis, we need to estimate an empirical model in order to assess if ceteris paribus an increase in women's income share translates into changes in household expenditure patterns, in particular expenditures favoring human capital formation (through spending on health and education). Following Hoddinot and Haddad (1995), we use an expanded version of the Working-Leser expenditure system as the empirical specification. In this econometric model, the budget share allocated to expenditure category j is a function of the log of household size, the log of per capita expenditure, the share of total income controlled by women (Y_F/Y), demographic variables, regional variables, and other controls:

(6.4)
$$s_j = \alpha_j + \beta_{j,1} \ln(H) + \beta_{j,2} \ln(E) + \beta_{j,3}\left(\frac{Y_F}{Y}\right)$$
$$+ \sum_{l=1}^{L} \gamma_{j,l}\left(\frac{K_l}{H}\right) + \delta_j X + \varepsilon,$$

where H is household size; E is per capita household expenditure; K_l is the number of household members within demographic category l; X is a vector with regional location variables and other controls; α, β, γ, and δ are parameters to be estimated; and ε is a random component assumed to be normally distributed. Because $\sum_j s_j = 1$, ordinary least squares (OLS) estimates of equation (6.4) imply that $\sum_j \theta_j = 0$ and $\sum_j \alpha_j = 1$, where θ_j are the estimated parameter slopes. This feature of the model is known as the adding up restriction.[5]

The novelty introduced to the expenditure functions by Hoddinot and Haddad (1995) is the variable Y_F/Y, which in the framework provided in equations (6.3a) and (6.3b) captures the bargaining power of women within the household. If women have a stronger preference for expenditure categories that directly benefit their children (education or health), an increase in Y_F/Y will cause an increase in the expenditure shares allocated to these categories. Finding that $\beta_{j,3}$ is statistically different from zero would represent enough evidence to reject the income-pooling hypothesis in favor of the more complex intrahousehold bargaining process described in expressions (6.1)–(6.3). Such a process would imply that changes in relative prices will change the intrahousehold distribution of power and hence the allocation of resources (Kanbur 2003).[6]

The impact of an increase in Y_F/Y on the share of spending allocated to different types of consumption is straightforward to estimate from equation (6.4). The impact of a change in income from export crops is a bit more complex to derive because part of the export crop income may be obtained by women, while part may be obtained by men. Even in the extreme situation, in which all income from export crops is captured by men, the increase in household income brought about by higher export prices affects consumption patterns, through a change in total expenditure (E). To see this, consider that total income is derived from K income sources and that women's share of income differs across these sources. Total income and total income for women can be expressed as

$$(6.5) \qquad Y = \sum_{k=1}^{K} Y_k, \qquad Y_F = \sum_{k=1}^{K} Y_{Fk}.$$

The impact of an increase in income from source k on the share of spending allocated to consumption good j is computed as

$$(6.6) \qquad \frac{\partial s_j}{\partial Y_k} = \beta_{j,2} \frac{1}{E} \frac{\partial E}{\partial Y} \frac{\partial Y}{\partial Y_k} + \beta_{j,3} \frac{1}{Y^2} \left(\frac{\partial Y_F}{\partial Y_k} Y - \frac{\partial Y}{\partial Y_k} Y_F \right).$$

Denoting by s_F and s_{kF} the shares of total income obtained by women and the share of income from source k received by women, we can show that the share of total consumption allocated to good j will increase after a positive income shock for source k if the following condition is respected:

$$(6.7) \qquad \frac{\partial s_j}{\partial Y_k} > 0 \quad \textit{iff} \quad \beta_{j,2} \frac{Y}{E} \frac{\partial E}{\partial Y} > \beta_{j,3} \left(s_F - s_{kF} \right).$$

The interpretation is straightforward. The left-hand side of expression (6.7) is typically positive, because it depends on three terms: the impact of total consumption on the share of expenditure devoted to good j (for normal and luxury consumption items one expects a zero or positive relation); the ratio of total income to total consumption; and the impact of an increase in income on total consumption. If $\beta_{j,3}$ is positive, as expected for categories in which women may have stronger preferences than men, the right-hand term is negative when the share of income from source k obtained by women is larger than the share of total household income obtained by women. In this case, an increase in income from source k will increase the share of income allocated to good j. If the share of income source k obtained by women is smaller than the total share of income obtained by women, the condition in expression (6.7) may still be respected if the difference between the share of income from source k and the share in total income obtained by women is not too large. This is so because although an increase in income from source k may reduce the total share of income controlled by women (and thereby the share of consumption allocated to their preferred expenditure category), the counterbalancing effect through higher household income (and thereby consumption) tends to result in a higher share of total consumption allocated to those same categories.

It is interesting to assess the impact of a change in an income source on total spending for various consumption goods. Indeed, what matters for future poverty reduction is the total investment made by households in, say, the education of children rather than the share of consumption allocated to education per se. The impact of an increase in income from source k on the total spending allocated to consumption good j is given by

$$(6.8) \quad \frac{\partial(s_j E)}{\partial Y_k} = s_j \frac{\partial E}{\partial Y} \frac{\partial Y}{\partial Y_k}$$
$$+ E\left[\beta_{j,2} \frac{1}{E} \frac{\partial E}{\partial Y} \frac{\partial Y}{\partial Y_k} + \beta_{j,3} \frac{1}{Y^2} \left(\frac{\partial Y_F}{\partial Y_k} Y - \frac{\partial Y}{\partial Y_k} Y_F \right) \right].$$

Total spending allocated to good j will therefore increase after a positive income shock for income source k if the following condition is respected:

$$(6.9) \quad \frac{\partial(s_j E)}{\partial Y_k} > 0 \quad \textit{iff} \quad \frac{\partial E}{\partial Y}(s_j + \beta_{j,2})Y > \beta_{j,3}(s_F - s_{kF}).$$

Clearly, this condition is much more likely to be respected than condition (6.7), so in the case of Senegal, one might expect that a positive income shock on groundnuts would increase total spending for health and education even if it reduces the share of total income obtained by women. Even in this case, the opposing effects determining conditions (6.7) and (6.9) illustrate the benefits of a positive income shock in the absence of a deterioration on women's bargaining power.

Empirical Results

We use the 1994/95 ESAM I survey from Senegal to estimate our empirical model, using the specification provided in equation (6.4). The (older) ESAM I data are used because subsequent national surveys, such as the 2001/02 ESAM II and the 2005/06 Enquête de Suivi de la Pauvreté au Sénégal (ESPS), do not include income data.

We consider many different types of expenditure categories, four of which are expected to have a positive effect on human capital formation: food, health, education, and children's clothing. The other seven expenditure categories are adults' clothing, alcohol, tobacco, accommodations, transportation, entertainment, and other expenditures. The share of household members in different age and gender categories as a proportion of total household size are used as demographic controls. In particular, we use gender and age to form eight demographic categories: females under 6, females 6–14, females 15–59, females 60 and older, and the same age categories for men. Other controls include a dummy variable for each of the 10 regions in Senegal, a dummy variable for female-headed households, and a rural/urban control. The ratio Y_F/Y is formed by dividing the monetary income of female spouses by the sum of the monetary incomes of the household head and the spouse. Only the personal income of the spouses is included because we assume that the bargaining process described above takes place between the household head and his or her spouse without necessarily involving other household members.

Table 6.1 provides summary statistics for the variables of interest. According to ESAM I, the average Senegalese household spends more than half of its total budget on food and almost a quarter of its budget on accommodations. Health accounts for 6 percent of the total household budget; just 1 percent is allocated to education. This proportion falls short even when compared with the shares allocated to education in countries with similar levels of development, such as Ghana and Uganda. The average household in Senegal has 14 members, each consuming about CFAF 132,000 a year.[7] In 1995, 15 percent of households in Senegal were headed by women, and 61 percent were located in rural areas. The women's bargaining proxy Y_F/Y shows that

Table 6.1 Summary Statistics

Item	Mean	Standard deviation	Minimum	Maximum
Expenditure category (percentage of total expenditures)				
Food	57.8	15.3	0	99.1
Health	5.6	4.4	0	66.0
Education	0.9	1.9	0	28.9
Children's clothing	0.5	0.7	0	6.7
Adults' clothing	8.2	5.3	0	35.7
Alcohol	0.1	0.8	0	20.9
Tobacco	0.6	1.5	0	23.9
Accommodations	21.2	11.2	1	90.9
Transport	3.0	4.6	0	51.9
Entertainment	0.1	0.6	0	34.1
Other	2.1	3.0	0	34.4
Household controls				
Per capita expenditure (thousands of CFA)	132	158	13	6,741
Household size	14	8	1	65
Percentage of female-headed household	15.2	35.9	0	100
Percentage of rural households	61.0	48.8	0	100
Bargaining power proxy Y_F/Y	38.0	42.3	0	100
Demographic controls (percentage of household members)				
Males 0–6	10.6	9.4	0	67
Males 6–15	13.4	10.6	0	67
Males 15–59	20.9	12.9	0	100
Males 60 and over	2.8	5.2	0	100
Females 0–6	10.2	9.1	0	67
Females 6–15	13.0	10.1	0	75
Females 15–59	26.1	10.8	0	100
Females 60 or over	3.0	5.6	0	100

Source: Authors' compilation based on data from ESAM I.

Note: Sample size is 3,278, except for bargaining power proxy, for which sample size is 2,849. The consumption aggregate is slightly different from the aggregate used to compute official poverty measures in Senegal.

female spouses contributed 38 percent of total personal monetary income brought by either the household head or the spouse.

The results of the estimations of equation (6.4) are presented in table 6.2. The first thing to notice is the high degree of variation in

Table 6.2 Estimates of the Determinants of Consumption Shares in Senegal

Item	Food	Health	Education	Children's clothing	Adults' clothing	Alcohol	Tobacco	Accommodations	Transport	Entertainment	Other
Log of household size	-5.344***	1.205***	0.274***	0.047*	3.045***	-0.061***	-0.213***	-0.048	0.530**	0.032*	0.533***
Log of per capita expenditure	-0.893	1.030***	0.365***	-0.008	1.036***	-0.022	-0.132**	-5.125***	2.137***	0.109***	1.502***
Rural household	17.248***	0.072	-0.336***	-0.080**	0.1	0.018	0.003	-17.500***	0.253	0.026	0.196
Female-headed household	-2.243**	-0.435	-0.224	-0.026	0.754*	0.015	-0.167*	2.734***	-0.663**	-0.022	0.277
Women's income share	-0.1	0.232	0.364***	0.014	-0.251	-0.037	-0.062	0.363	-0.326	-0.005	-0.192
Demographic controls											
Males 0–6	15.070***	-5.022***	-1.181***	0.654***	-8.419***	-0.079	0.771**	-4.703*	0.789	0.123	1.998***
Males 6–15	7.643**	-4.773***	0.980**	0.855***	-6.235***	-0.04	0.629**	-2.54	0.954	0.220**	2.307***
Males 15–59	4.780*	-6.968***	0.3	0.104	-3.365***	0.209	1.914***	0.505	0.564	0.454***	1.505**
Males 60 and over	4.244	-6.173***	-2.057***	-0.304	-6.513***	0.199	0.849	16.499***	-5.214***	-0.023	-1.506
Females 0–6	15.217***	-4.084***	-0.883*	1.156***	-6.089***	0.1	0.493	-8.472***	0.369	0.333***	1.861**
Females 6–15	12.047***	-3.959***	1.436***	0.888***	-7.141***	-0.208	0.152	-4.262*	0.268	0.158	0.62
Females 60 or over	-1.632	-4.046**	-0.969*	-0.039	-9.358***	-0.354**	0.264	17.632***	-2.928**	0.018	1.411
Intercept	64.4***	-3.89	-3.04***	0.29	-6.41*	0.477	2.05**	86.6***	-21.6***	-1.287***	-17.7***
R-squared	0.463	0.096	0.18	0.109	0.154	0.019	0.111	0.432	0.134	0.049	0.111

Source: Authors' estimates based on data from ESAM I.

Note: The dependent variable is the household expenditure percentage share in each of the categories in the first row. The demographic controls are the share of household members within the different categories as a proportion of total household size. Regional controls are included throughout. Sample size is 2,848.

*** Significant at the 1 percent level, ** significant at the 5 percent level, * significant at the 10 percent level, all with Huber-White robust standard errors.

the R-squared across expenditure categories. Specification (6.4) captures 47 percent of the total variation in food expenditure shares across households but as little as 2 percent in the case of alcohol. The results show that larger and richer households tend to invest more in health and education. Not surprisingly, rural households allocate a larger budget share to food and a smaller share to education than their urban counterparts. Expenditure shares for clothing (both children's and adults'), transport, and entertainment increase with household per capita expenditure, indicating that these goods can be classified as luxuries in Senegal. Female-headed households tend to spend a smaller proportion of the household's budget on food, tobacco, and transport and a larger share on adults' clothing and accommodations.

The results on Y_F/Y reject the income-pooling hypothesis. Women and men differ in their preference for education of their children; a bargaining process is undertaken to determine how much of their resources should be allocated to this important human capital determinant. Controlling for differences in household size, total expenditure, demographic composition, gender of the household head, and regional variations, an increase in women's income increases the level of resources allocated to education. This result implies that a 1 percent redistribution of monetary income from the male head to his spouse increases the education expenditure share by 0.36 percentage points. Can these results shed light on the potential long-term welfare effects of trade shocks in Senegal through a reduction in human capital accumulation?

The data support the claim that income from groundnut activities is controlled largely by men. Indeed, the gender income gap in the agricultural sector is by far the largest of any sector in Senegal. Moreover, the proportion of monetary income controlled by women Y_F/Y is substantially lower in groundnut-producing households (0.27) than among nongroundnut producers (0.45). Trade shocks favoring the groundnut sector, which increase the income of its producers, would therefore reduce women's intrahousehold bargaining power. An exogenous increase in the price of groundnuts—triggered by a market liberalizing reform or any other trade shock—could thus reduce human capital accumulation in Senegal. As noted earlier, the relation between the expenditure share s_j and the male-controlled income source f will be the outcome of two opposing forces: a positive effect working through the increase in total expenditure and a negative impact caused by the deterioration in women's bargaining power.

Using the regression results together with the analytical solution developed above, we can compute the change in education shares given an exogenous increase in the income of groundnut producers.

Because $\beta_{j,2} = \beta_{j,3}$ for the education expenditure function (see table 6.2),[8] condition (6.7) depends on the comparison between the income elasticity of expenditure $((Y/E)(\partial E/\partial Y))$ and the share differential $(S_F - S_{KF})$. In the extreme case in which women obtain zero income from groundnut production, given that the income elasticity of expenditure is close to 1 and that $s_F = 0.38$, condition (6.7) is still satisfied. Therefore, even if groundnut income is entirely controlled by men, the share of total household budget allocated to education expenditure increases as a result of an increase in the income of groundnut producers, despite deterioration in women's bargaining power. Because the budget share allocated to education increases as a result of an increase in groundnut income (condition 6.7), total expenditure in education also rises as a result of the same shock (condition 6.9).

These results suggest that the loss of women's intrahousehold bargaining power that could result from a trade-mandated increase in commodity export prices is not strong enough to jeopardize long-term human capital accumulation. Nevertheless, although education expenditure would rise as a consequence of an increase in the price of groundnuts, the benefits would have been even larger had the gender effect not been present.

To illustrate this point, the continuous line in figure 6.1 shows the ceteris paribus change in the share of total budget allocated to education that would result from a 10 percent increase in income from groundnut production, ignoring the reduction in women's bargaining power.[9] Figure 6.1 displays different changes in education shares between households located at different points in the distribution of household per capita expenditure (percentiles). It shows that the largest increase in education expenditure brought about by a 10 percent increase in groundnut income occurs in households in the 20th–40th percentile—that is, where groundnut producers are located. Figure 6.1 shows that the education effects of an increase in groundnut income are positive regardless of where the household is located in the distribution. The discontinuous line shows the changes in education expenditure share after taking into account the reduction in women's intrahousehold bargaining power using the results for β_3 in the education expenditure equation presented in table 6.2. The largest losses in women's bargaining power (measured by the difference between the continuous and the dashed lines in figure 6.1) take place in households that benefit most from the increase in groundnut income.[10] In households in the 20th–40th percentile, all of which are below the national poverty line, the loss in education expenditure share is almost half a percentage point of their total budget share. Therefore, even though relatively poor households

Figure 6.1 Estimated Education Expenditure Effect of a 10 Percent Increase in Groundnut Income

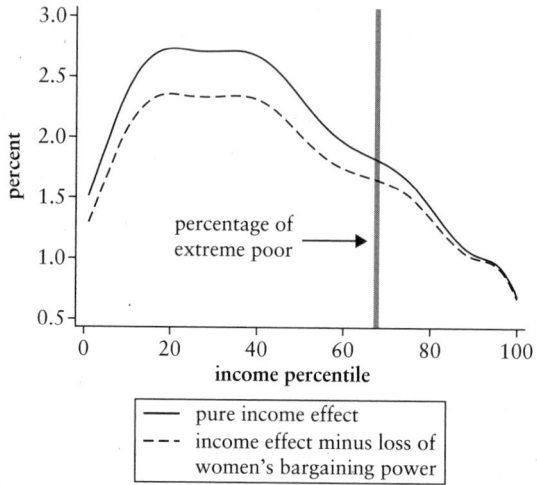

Source: Authors' estimations based on estimates in table 6.2.
Note: Sample is restricted to families with children. The vertical rule indicates the percentage of extreme poor.

benefit from an increase in the price of groundnuts, the loss caused by intrahousehold inequalities are significant and should be taken into account in designing and evaluating trade policy.

These results are robust to several specifications. By including an interaction term between the rural dummy and women's income share, we tested the hypothesis that women's bargaining power had a different impact in rural and urban households. We also included a similar interaction for women working in the agricultural sector. Neither of these interactions was significant. In a different specification, we tested the hypothesis that differences in daughters' income shares lead to different expenditure patterns. The results show that, indeed, daughters behave differently from female spouses. Increases in daughters' income shares do not lead to an increase in education expenditure but instead to larger expenditure shares for adults' clothing.

In a third specification, we interacted Y_F/Y with the levels of per capital consumption to allow for different effects of the bargaining process across different levels of household welfare (measured as household per capita expenditure) (table 6.3). This specification shows that although women have a stronger preference for food than do men, this difference narrows as household welfare increases. Quite the contrary can be said about education: at very low income levels, women and men do not differ significantly over how much to allocate

Table 6.3 Difference in Preferences, Bargaining Power, and Welfare Levels, by Expenditure Category

Item	Food	Health	Education	Children's clothing	Adults' clothing
Women's income share (Y_F/Y)	24.668**	−1.292	−2.685	−0.279	−14.85***
$(Y_F/Y)^*E$	−2.143**	0.132	0.264*	0.025	1.26***
R-squared	0.464	0.096	0.182	0.109	0.158

Source: Authors' estimates based on data from ESAM I.

Note: Includes all the controls presented in table 6.2. Sample size is 2,848.

*** Significant at the 1 percent level, ** significant at the 5 percent level, * significant at the 10 percent level, all with Huber-White robust standard errors.

to this expenditure category, but as welfare increases, women reveal a stronger preference for education. These results find support in the studies discussed in Duflo (2005) and chapter 8 of this volume.

Given the parametric constraint imposed by equation (6.4) $\left(\sum_j \theta_j = 0\right)$, it seems odd that only 1 of 11 parameters estimated on Y_F/Y is significantly different from zero. To explore this anomaly, we estimated specification (6.4) within a system of equations using seemingly unrelated regressions (SUR), as described in Zellner (1962). Because the regressors used in equation (6.4) are the same for all expenditure categories, the SUR results are identical to the OLS ones presented in table 6.2 (Greene 2000). The SUR estimator allows for testing the hypothesis that the parameters on women's income are jointly zero in all equations: $H_0 = \beta_{j,3} = 0, \forall j$. The hypothesis test shows that $\chi_{10} = 24.05$ which rejects the null at the 99 percent confidence level, suggesting that at least one of the coefficients in system (6.4) is significantly different from zero.

A final econometric caveat must be addressed. The simplest microeconomic framework would show that the choice of goods consumed and leisure are the outcome of the same utility-maximizing process. For example, caring mothers concerned about their children's education living in households with a very low budget allocated to this category might be prompted to join the labor market in order to boost Y_F/Y. If this is true, then Y_F/Y is endogenous and the results presented are biased.

To overcome this problem, we undertook a two-stage least squares or instrumental variables (IV) approach in which the ratio of women's to men's education and age were used as instruments for Y_F/Y. Although the overidentification test suggests that these are valid instruments, they are rather weak ones: the point estimators of the parameters change with the IV estimation, but the qualitative effects remain unchanged. Given the weakness of the instruments, we believe that the intrahousehold bargaining effects produced by Y_F/Y are better described by the simple OLS specification (6.9).

Conclusions

As they are in other developing regions in West Africa, export crops in Senegal tend to be controlled by men. The results presented here show that women tend to allocate larger shares of their resources to investments that benefit their children, such as education. These findings suggest that by increasing the share of total income controlled by men, higher groundnut prices could reduce women's bargaining power and potentially reduce household's total spending on education. The resulting lower human capital accumulation could threaten future growth and poverty reduction.

In Senegal the negative impact of higher groundnut prices on the share of total spending for education caused by a worsening of women's bargaining power is likely to be more than compensated by the positive impact of higher total income on household consumption. In addition, even if the share of total consumption allocated to education were to decline (which is not the case in Senegal), the total level of spending for education would still rise.

That said, some qualifications on this strong conclusion should be considered. The magnitude of the links between trade shocks, producer prices, male versus female bargaining power, consumption decisions, future growth, and poverty reduction are not large. This should not be surprising, as groundnut prices are just one factor determining farmers' incomes—and an even less important factor in affecting the share of women's income in total household income. Even given these limitations, however, about 20 percent of the total effect on education expenditures generated by an increase in groundnut incomes is erased by the worsening distribution of power within the household.[11]

The evidence unequivocally shows that the unitary household hypothesis does not hold for Senegal. This chapter brings additional evidence to a growing body of micro literature that has shown that the income-pooling hypothesis—namely, that what matters to household expenditure patterns is not who brings in the income but the total available resources—is not supported by the data. This result signals that gender inequalities encompass not just inequalities of opportunities outside the households—such as inequalities in education, employment, labor remuneration, access to credit, and other dimensions—but also inequalities within the household, manifested mainly by inequality of power. As Kanbur (2003, p. 21) concludes:

[As] long as the unitary model dominates economics teaching and discourse, inequalities of power will naturally get secondary importance.... This is something that needs to be tackled at the core of mainstream economics through yet more evidence on violations of the unitary model assumption, but also through the increased deployment of nonunitary approaches, in modeling and in empirical analysis, to "conventional" topics such as optimal taxation policy, *consequences of trade for income distribution*, composition of public expenditure. [emphasis added]

By using a nonunitary approach and providing evidence of the effects of trade on income distribution through a gender inequality channel, this chapter moves in exactly the direction Kanbur is calling for.

Notes

This chapter was prepared as a contribution to a poverty assessment for Senegal prepared by the Africa Region Vice Presidency of the World Bank, as well as for a research project on trade, gender, and poverty organized by the Development Prospects Group of the World Bank.

1. Krueger, Schiff, and Valdés (1991) is perhaps the best-known study documenting this antiagriculture bias in developing counties. For the 18 countries included in the study, policy interventions induced a 30 percent decline in a price index of agricultural products relative to a nonagricultural price index. For a more recent global study, see Bussolo, De Hoyos and Medvedev (2009).

2. On gender issues in Senegal, see the World Bank's 2006 strategic gender assessment. According to the gender-related development index of the Organisation of Economic Co-coperation and Development (OECD 2006), Senegal has one of the worst gender equality profiles, ranking 118th out of 135 countries included in the sample. For a description of the data, methodologies, and working papers on this topic, see www.oecd.org/dac/gender.

3. The unitary model assumes that the household acts as if it were a single utility-maximizing individual with defined preferences and a budget constraint (see Singh, Squire, and Strauss 1986). In contrast, the bargaining model assumes that household members differ in their preferences and hence

engage in a negotiation process to maximize their personal utility. Haddad and Kanbur (1990, p. 866) show that "neglect of intrahousehold inequality is likely to lead to a considerable understatement of the levels of inequality and poverty."

4. Alternative collective (cooperative) models of intrahousehold allocation have been developed since the paper by Hoddinot and Haddad (1995) (see, for instance, Bourguignon and Chiappori 1992 and Browning and Chiappori 1998). Estimation of the collective model requires reliable price information from the household survey, information that is not available on Senegal.

5. For details on the properties and limitations of this model, see Deaton and Muellbauer (1980).

6. Based on equations (6.3a) and (6.3b) and allowing one of the consumption items to capture leisure, women's income could be endogenous, thereby biasing the OLS parameters of equation (6.4). This simultaneity problem is addressed in the next section.

7. To contextualize this figure, consider that the annual per capita expenditure needed to the poverty line in Senegal was CFAF 143,445 in 1995.

8. Put another way, the positive effect on education expenditure share caused by a 1 percent increase in household per capita expenditure is equivalent to the effect brought about by a 1 percent increase in women's bargaining power.

9. Only households with members of schooling age are included.

10. The continuous and dotted lines converge as income rises, because the importance of income from groundnuts in total income decreases with household per capita income. Therefore, in richer households the loss in women's bargaining power—and in forgone expenditure in education—after an increase in incomes from groundnuts is smaller than in poorer households.

11. The figure of "about 20 percent" is calculated as 0.5 divided by 2.5 (multiplied by 100), where 0.5 is the average distance between the two lines in figure 6.2 for the segment of the population between percentiles 20 and 40. Most groundnut producers are found in this part of the distribution.

References

Azam, J. P., M. Dia, C. Tsimpo, and Q. Wodon. 2007. "Has Growth in Senegal after the 1994 Devaluation Been Pro-Poor?" In *Growth and Poverty Reduction: Case Studies from West Africa*, ed. Q. Wodon, 45–67. World Bank Working Paper 79, Washington, DC.

Boccanfuso, D., and L. Savard. 2005. "Impacts Analysis of the Liberalization of Groundnut Production in Senegal: A Multiple Household Computable General Equilibrium Model." GREDI Working Paper 05–12, Groupe de

Recherche en Économie et Développement International, University of Sherbrooke, Quebec.

Bourguignon, F., and P.-A. Chiappori. 1992. "Collective Models of Household Behavior: An Introduction." *European Economic Review* 36 (2–3): 355–64.

Browning, M., and P.-A. Chiappori,1998. "Efficient Intra-Household Allocations: A General Characterization and Empirical Tests." *Econometrica* 66 (6): 1241–278.

Bussolo, M., R. De Hoyos, and D. Medvedev. 2009. "Global Income Distribution and Poverty in the Absence of Agricultural Distortions." Policy Research Working Paper 4849, World Bank, Washington, DC.

Deaton, A., and J. Muellbauer. 1980. *Economics and Consumer Behavior.* New York: Cambridge University Press.

Duflo, Esther. 2005. "Gender Equality in Development." BREAD Policy Paper 001, Bureau for Research and Economic Analysis of Development, Massachusetts Institute of Technology, Cambridge, MA.

Ghosh, Suman, and Ravi Kanbur. 2008. "Male Wages and Female Welfare: Private Markets, Public Goods, and Intrahousehold Inequality." *Oxford Economic Papers* 60 (1): 42–56.

Gray, J. K. 2002. "The Groundnut Market in Senegal: Examination of Price and Policy Changes." Ph.D. diss., Department of Agricultural and Applied Economics, Virginia Polytechnic Institute and State University, Blacksburg, VA.

Greene, W. H. 2000. *Econometric Analysis,* 4th ed. Upper Saddle River, NJ: Prentice-Hall.

Haddad, L. 1999. "The Income Earned by Women: Impacts on Welfare Outcomes." *Agricultural Economics* 20 (1): 135–41.

Haddad, Lawrence, and Ravi Kanbur. 1990. "How Serious Is the Neglect of Intra-Household Inequality?" *Economic Journal* 100 (402): 866–81.

Hoddinott, John, and Lawrence Haddad. 1995. "Does Female Income Share Influence Household Expenditures? Evidence from Côte d'Ivoire." *Oxford Bulletin of Economics and Statistics* 57 (1): 77–96.

Kanbur, Ravi. 2003. "Education, Empowerment and Gender Inequalities." In *The New Reform Agenda,* ed. B. Pleskovic and N. Stern. Washington, DC: World Bank.

Krueger, A., O. M. Schiff, and A. Valdes, eds. 1991. *The Political Economy of Agricultural Price Policy.* Baltimore, MD: Johns Hopkins University Press for the World Bank.

Loayza, Norman, and Claudio Raddatz. 2006. "The Composition of Growth Matters for Poverty Alleviation." Policy Research Working Paper Series 4077, World Bank, Washington, DC.

Masters, W. 2007. "Distortions to Agricultural Incentives in Senegal." Agricultural Distortions Working Paper 41, World Bank, Washington, DC.

Ndoye, D., F. Adoho, P. Backiny-Yetna, M. Fall, P. Thiecouta Ndiane, and Q. Wodon. 2008. *Tendances et déterminants de la pauvreté au Sénégal de 1994 à 2006.* World Bank, Washington, DC.

OECD (Organisation for Economic Co-Operation and Development). 2006. *The Gender, Institutions and Development Data Base.* OECD Development Centre, Paris.

République du Sénégal. 2006. *DSRP II : Document de strategie pour la croissance et la reduction de la pauvreté 2006–2010.* Dakar.

Singh, I., L. Squire, and J. Strauss. 1986 *Agricultural Household Models: Extensions, Applications and Policy.* Baltimore, MD: Johns Hopkins University Press for the World Bank.

Sullivan, Amy. 2002. "Gender, Household Composition, and Adoption of Soil Fertility Technologies: A Study of Women Rice Farmers in Southern Senegal." *African Studies Quarterly: The Online Journal for African Studies* 6 (1–2). http://web.africa.ufl.edu/asq/v6/v6i1a6.htm.

Tsimpo, C., and Q. Wodon. 2008. *Indirect Taxation and Poverty in Senegal's Groundnut Sector.* World Bank, Poverty Reduction and Economic Management, Africa Region, Washington, DC.

Ulph, D. 1988. "A General Non-Cooperative Nash Equilibrium Model of Household Consumption Behaviour." Department of Economics, University of Bristol, United Kingdom.

World Bank. 2006. *Genre et développement au Sénégal: Garçon ou fille, ils se valent.* Poverty Reduction and Economic Management, Africa Region, Washington, DC.

Zellner, A. 1962. "An Efficient Method of Estimating Seemingly Unrelated Regressions and Tests for Aggregation Bias." *Journal of the American Statistical Association* 57 (298): 348–68.

7

More Coffee, More Cigarettes? Coffee Market Liberalization, Gender, and Bargaining in Uganda

Jennifer Golan and Jann Lay

This chapter extends the trade and gender debate to the agricultural economies of sub-Saharan Africa by looking at the gender consequences of cash crop market liberalization. It investigates the effects of coffee market liberalization in Uganda, with a focus on intra-household allocation.

By affecting households' production and consumption structure, trade reforms can have an important effect on households' resource allocation patterns and gender relations. The evidence on the gender-specific effects of cash crop market liberalization is scarce, however, although some anecdotal evidence in various policy documents suggests negative effects and the exclusion of women. Most gender analyses tend to focus on barriers to women from a static perspective and have very little to say about whether these barriers may have changed.[1]

This chapter aims to fill these empirical gaps by investigating the case of coffee in Uganda, a country where thorough sector reforms have triggered a substantial supply response. It draws on data from three household surveys conducted between 1992 and 2006 to quantitatively examine the impact of the expansion of coffee production from a gender perspective. In order to assess changes in intrahousehold resource allocation related to changes in coffee income, we examine whether the share of coffee income positively (negatively) affects the expenditure shares on male (female) goods by estimating Engel curves for a number of more or less gender-related goods. We find that the share of household income derived from coffee had some impact on household expenditure patterns in the early 1990s but that this effect appeared to have vanished by 2005. As a result, coffee income seems to have been more equally distributed between men and women in the early 2000s than it was earlier. As increased income pooling may indicate more cooperative household consumption behavior, we expect men and women to cooperate better in coffee production. However, coffee yield—and in particular labor input—estimates indicate that intrahousehold struggles over resources for coffee production as well as agricultural gender roles persist.

This chapter is organized as follows. The first section provides a short review of the literature on gender roles in agriculture, intrahousehold resource allocation, and bargaining processes that is relevant to understanding the transmission channels of trade reform in the rural context. The following section presents the methodological frameworks and the empirical results. The last section summarizes the chapter's main conclusions.

Review of the Literature

Analyzing the welfare impact of trade reforms and increased trade flows disaggregated by gender in a poor agricultural economy requires in-depth understanding of household decision processes. The unitary model of household behavior provides a useful starting point for this discussion. The model assumes that household members behave as if they maximize a well-defined and uniform household welfare function and that within the household all resources (land, labor, and capital)—and consequently all production and incomes from factor markets—are pooled. If the unitary model of household behavior were to apply, the gender effects of trade reforms would be negligible, because all household members would benefit equally from possible efficiency improvements.

Not surprisingly, plenty of evidence rejects the unitary model and the resource pooling assumption in particular. Using data for Côte d'Ivoire from the late 1980s, Hoddinott and Haddad (1995) show that the income share earned by female household members raises expenditure on food and reduces expenditure on alcohol and tobacco. This evidence is inconsistent with income pooling. Quisumbing and Maluccio (2003) use more recent datasets for Bangladesh,

Ethiopia, Indonesia, and South Africa to test the income-pooling hypothesis, which they, too, reject.

These findings lend support to household models in which the household's interests are not pursued by maximizing a uniform welfare function. Rather, individuals have diverse preferences, and household as well as individual welfare result from bargaining struggles over household resources. If individuals have diverse preferences, there is no a priori reason to give up control over individually earned income. In bargaining models there is hence no supposition of income pooling within the household.

Different bargaining models have been proposed in the context of household resource allocation. In contrast to the unitary model, cooperative household models allow household decision makers to have different preferences. Outcomes of the bargaining process are assumed to be Pareto efficient, which under preference diversity implies that households dispose of efficient sharing rules (that is, they are able to negotiate adequate compensations to achieve efficient resource allocations). Several researchers (Bourguignon and others 1993, 1994; Thomas and Chen 1994; Browning and Chiappori 1998) have found evidence of Pareto-efficient household allocations in developed countries; no such evidence has been found for sub-Saharan Africa.

In his examination of farm households in Burkina Faso, for example, Udry (1996) finds that female plots have substantially lower yields, because they are less intensively farmed. Because of diminishing returns, households could increase production by reallocating inputs, primarily labor, from male to female plots. The yield differential that remains after "household-year-crop fixed effects" are controlled for implies that prevailing bargaining processes (that is, sharing rules and negotiated compensations) do not lead to efficient outcomes.

Jones (1983) documents inefficient allocations in northern Cameroon. Her findings suggest that married women do not allocate enough labor to rice production because of inadequate compensation. Both men and women would gain if married women were compensated for allocating less time to "their" sorghum and more time to "men's" paddy rice production.

Duflo and Udry (2004) analyze cooperative behavior in Ivorian households using panel data from 1985–88. Assuming that efficiency requires household members to insure against short-term income fluctuation caused by rainfall, they reject Pareto efficiency. Using rural Ethiopian data from the late 1990s and applying a variety of stochastic efficiency estimations, Seebens and Sauer (2007) find that relative bargaining asymmetries within the household (as captured by the distribution of land and livestock brought to marriage) adversely affect household efficiency in production.

Taken together, this evidence suggests the lack of both Pareto-efficiency and income pooling, particularly in agrarian settings. Thus at least partly noncooperative behavior within rural households seems to prevail.

These results may be explained by three factors, which often complicate negotiations in the sub-Saharan African context. First, household members typically jointly contribute to agricultural production. While wages of individual household members are easily observed, this does not hold for individual marginal agricultural product. Second, the number of tasks is much larger in poorer countries. In addition to agricultural and nonagricultural activities, these tasks include the labor-intensive production of a number of household public goods, such as water fetching, cooking, and herding. These activities need to be taken into account when compensation agreements are achieved. Third, households have to negotiate under strong cultural gender roles, which, for example, exclude women from certain agricultural activities.

Intrahousehold processes and changes therein are of utmost importance for evaluating the impact of trade reform on women (Alderman and others 1995; Alderman, Haddad, and. Hoddinott 1997). Yet very few empirical assessments have been conducted on changes in bargaining processes and gender. roles, particularly in response to policy shocks. One exception is Newman's (2002) study on the impact of increased female employment in the cut flower industry in Ecuador. She reports important behavioral change and finds a reallocation of housework to husbands caused by increased bargaining power of wives in cut-flower regions.

There is very little evidence on the impact of trade reform on gender discrimination in general and coffee market liberalization in particular in Uganda. Some rather anecdotal evidence can be found in policy documents (Baden 1993; Elson and Evers 1996; World Bank 2005). Elson and Evers (1996, p. 21), for example, suggest that "the economic reform programme has not only failed to reduce . . . gender distortions and barriers—it has intensified many of them."

It seems to be fairly well established that coffee production in Uganda relies heavily on female labor input in the production process, while marketing and control over coffee income lie in male hands (Elson and Evers 1996; Kasente 1997; Evers and Walters 2000; Evers and Walters 2001; Bantebya and Keniston 2006; EPRC 2007). The gender division of tasks is not limited to cash crop production. The production of food crops and specific tasks (such as weeding) required to produce other crops are typically performed by women (Kasente and others 2000; Dolan 2001). In addition, men exert control over their spouses' labor to some extent, a tradition also reflected by the practice of paying a bride price (Evers and Walters 2001). Finally, women bear the burden of housework, which comprises a number of time-consuming duties other than domestic tasks, including fetching water and collecting firewood.

In light of the nature of gender relations and the discussion of intrahousehold decision making, it may be instructive to think about two scenarios when considering policy change that leads to higher prices for cash crops (in this case coffee). In the first scenario, there is no change in intrahousehold decision making. In this case higher incomes from coffee may result in increased struggles over household resources. By controlling a larger share of household income, males may increase their bargaining power, reinforcing existing bargaining asymmetries. More income under male control may bias expenditure patterns toward higher consumption of "male" goods, some of which may be harmful to other household members' welfare. Moreover, increased male bargaining power could be used to exert pressure on female labor to contribute more labor to cash crop production, thereby squeezing women's labor time (Elson and Evers 1996). In extreme cases more intense bargaining struggles may even cause a higher incidence of domestic violence (Dolan 2001).

In the second scenario, instead of favoring the male position within the household, increased coffee income may increase the importance of female participation in the production process, which may raise women's relative bargaining strength and lead household negotiations toward more equitable compensation agreements. Alternatively, other socioeconomic changes, especially the increased market participation of farmers and the growing importance of non-agricultural income sources in rural areas in Uganda (Kappel, Lay, and Steiner 2005), may lead to female empowerment and cause a modification of the household allocation rules (Haddad and Reardon 1993). Together these facets of possible change in household decision-making processes would tend to move households toward more cooperative behavior, increasing the likelihood of efficient bargaining outcomes.

It is difficult to identify the precise causes of changes in household allocation rules. But why rules change may be less important than whether they change; what matters is whether women are excluded from the benefits coffee income. In the following, we therefore attempt to trace empirically possible changes in Ugandan households' resource allocation rules during a period of remarkable economic transformation and structural change.

Household Survey Evidence from Uganda

Coffee sector deregulation was one of the core pieces of Uganda's economic reform program of the 1990s.[2] These reforms triggered a considerable supply response, which improved the living standards of coffee farming households (Baffes 2006; Bussolo and others 2007). This section examines the effect of these reforms from a gender perspective by drawing on three survey datasets: the Integrated Household Survey of 1992/93 and the Uganda National Household Surveys of 1999/2000 and 2005/06, made available by the Uganda Bureau of Statistics. In contrast to most studies on gender relations, this study draws on relatively comparable datasets, which allow behavioral change to be examined.

Effect of Increase in Coffee Income on Household Income Pooling

Based on these surveys, we examine the effect of the coffee income share on household expenditure over time. If coffee income is indeed controlled by men and men are assumed to tend to favor private over public consumption, the rise in income from coffee should be expected to bias expenditure toward male consumption goods. In a manner similar to Hoddinott and Haddad (1995), we estimate Engel curves for a number of goods following the specifications used by Deaton (1989) and Deaton, Ruiz-Castillo, and Thomas (1989), originally introduced by Working (1943):

$$(7.1) \qquad w_i = \frac{p_i q_i}{x} = \alpha + \beta_i \ln\left(\frac{x}{n}\right) + \eta_i \ln(n) + \sum_{j=1}^{J-1} \gamma_{ij}\left(\frac{n_j}{n}\right)$$
$$+ \delta_i z + \lambda_i cof + u_i,$$

where total household expenditure is expressed as x and the number of people in the same household as n. The variable w_i is the expenditure share on good i, which is linearly related to the logarithm of the household per capita expenditure (see Deaton and Muellbauer 1980), household size (see Working 1943), and the demographic household composition $\sum_{j=1}^{J-1} \gamma_{ij}(n_j/n)$ (the proportion of household members in demographic group j). The variable z captures additional information presumably influencing the overall expenditure pattern, such as the educational level of the head of the household or the "type of community" (Working 1943). Expenditure functions are estimated for each survey, following Deaton's specification, with only minor modifications. Following Appleton, Chessa, and Hoddinott (1999), we alter the demographic categories and included some additional variables, such as urban, regional, and month dummies, to capture income fluctuations, expenditure seasonality, and regional price variations.

The primary variable of interest is the household's income share from coffee production, *cof*. We test the finding that women are heavily involved in the coffee production process (harvesting, seeding, and so forth) but that men dominate selling activities and thus typically control coffee proceeds (EPRC 2007).

To capture the importance of bargaining processes beyond coffee income, we include a dummy capturing male or female "excess education"; we also control for the educational level of the household head and spouse.[3] We test a range of other possible bargaining proxies that could be constructed for all survey years, including the age difference between heads and their spouses and variables related to women's age at birth of their first child. Given the problems arising in the construction and qualitative adequacy of these variables, it is not surprising that these alternative proxies do not yield any further insights.[4] They are therefore disregarded in what follows.

Being less concerned with comparability across years, we draw on particular questions asked in the surveys of 1999/2000 and 2005/06 to construct better bargaining proxies. For 1999/2000 we use information on the inheritance rules applied in each community (that is, which household or family member typically inherits the fathers' or mothers' land and other assets).[5] We aggregate this information by creating dummy variables for communities in which the rules exclusively favor women or men. Based on the question in the 2005/06 survey "Who mainly manages/controls the output from this parcel among the household members?" we construct dummy variables indicating whether output (from all parcels of the household) is controlled only by the household head or only by the spouse.[6]

We estimate the shares of four "male" expenditure items (tobacco, alcohol, beef [proxied by the aggregate expenditure share on beef and goat meat], and meat [also including poultry]) and two "female" expenditure categories (women's clothing and children's clothing). For the sake of homogeneity, we drop urban areas and the northern part of the country.[7] For these reduced samples, we estimate Engel curves using different subsamples.

The bargaining problems described above will not apply to female-headed households or households with no female spouse at all, and they may be altered in a fundamental manner in polygamous households. To cope with these different structures, we first drop households with no spouses and include a female-head dummy in the estimation. The second subsample excludes female-headed households altogether, while the third leaves only male-headed coffee farmers with a female spouse. Polygamy is taken into account by including a dummy variable for households headed by husbands with multiple spouses. Given the relative robustness of the results across subsamples, we report only the results of the preferred specification, based on the sample excluding female-headed households and male-headed households without a female spouse.[8] Given the large number of zero observations caused by the nonconsumption of alcohol and tobacco as well as semidurables and meat during the survey, we estimate Tobit models. The results are corrected for heteroskedasticity using robust estimates.

The results indicate that an increase in the share of coffee income increased the expenditure share of alcohol and reduced the share of children's and women's clothing in the early 1990s (table 7.1). These results lose their statistical significance in subsequent years (the full results are provided in annex tables 7A.1–7A.3). This implies that higher proceeds from coffee have not been associated with a disproportionate increase in household expenditure on "male" consumption goods. Thus during the 1990s, income from coffee appears to have been increasingly pooled.

The "educational excess" variables have the expected sign in most cases, and 10 of the 36 coefficients are statistically significant at the 10 percent level. The results can be taken as an indication that education does play some role in household expenditure decisions.[9] No particular time trend is observed, and there is no indication that the nature of the bargaining process follows a certain path. Yet while the polygamy dummy has a negative and statistically significant impact on alcohol and positive impacts on women's clothing in 1992 and 1999, it does not exhibit any statistically significant impact on any expenditure share in 2005 (see annex tables 7A.1–7A.3). This may be interpreted as a sign of cultural change.

We use the information on control over output in the most recent available survey to examine whether there is a detectable pattern of male control over coffee income, a result that would be somewhat at odds with increased income pooling. The results indicate that joint management/control of agricultural output is much more common on coffee farms than on noncoffee farms (table 7.2). This pattern does not vary with the degree of intercropping: even output from almost pure coffee parcels typically appears to be controlled jointly.

Table 7.1 Estimated Impact of Increased Share of Coffee Income on Expenditure Patterns in Uganda, 1992–2006

Year/item	Alcohol	Tobacco	Children's clothing	Women's clothing	Meat	Beef
1992/93						
Coffee share	0.0329*	−0.0103	−0.00424	−0.0122**	0.0141	0.00495
	(0.018)	(0.019)	(0.0028)	(0.0053)	(0.015)	(0.015)
Male excess education	0.0102	0.00483	−0.00198**	−0.00493***	−0.000292	0.00294
	(0.0078)	(0.0076)	(0.00097)	(0.0019)	(0.0056)	(0.0055)
Female excess education	−0.0182	−0.0149	0.00350**	0.0112***	−0.0136*	−0.0110
	(0.012)	(0.011)	(0.0015)	(0.0036)	(0.0075)	(0.0071)
1999/2000						
Coffee share	0.0135	−0.0397	−0.00678	−0.0150***	0.000430	0.0513*
	(0.031)	(0.027)	(0.0047)	(0.0051)	0.00941	(0.030)
Male excess education	−0.00149	−0.00264	−0.00314*	0.00156	0.0031	−0.00624
	(0.013)	(0.012)	(0.0017)	(0.0019)	(0.013)	(0.013)
Female excess education	−0.0374*	−0.00560	0.00168	0.00375	−0.00551	−0.0197
	(0.021)	(0.015)	(0.0019)	(0.0027)	(0.021)	(0.021)
2005/06						
Coffee share	−0.0565*	−0.00552	−0.00522*	−0.00615	−0.0438	−0.0218
	(0.034)	(0.019)	(0.0030)	(0.0038)	(0.030)	(0.028)
Male excess education	0.0181*	0.0153**	0.0000555	0.00231*	−0.00192	0.000553
	(0.010)	(0.0067)	(0.0010)	(0.0013)	(0.0074)	(0.0069)
Female excess education	−0.0135	−0.00511	0.00252	0.00307**	0.0194*	0.0183
	(0.017)	(0.0092)	(0.0025)	(0.0015)	(0.012)	(0.011)

Source: Authors' calculations based on survey data.

Note: Excess education refers to a dummy variable that assumes a value of one when the schooling gap (in years) between spouses exceeds five years. Figures in parentheses are robust standards errors. Full regression results are reported in annex tables 7A.1–7A.3.

*** Significant at the 1 percent level; ** significant at the 5 percent level; * significant at the 10 percent level.

Table 7.2 Control over Agricultural Output on Coffee and
Noncoffee Farms in Uganda, 2005/06

Type of farm	Only male head	Only female spouse	Joint
Coffee not grown	0.38	0.24	0.38
Coffee grown	0.33	0.15	0.52
Total	0.36	0.20	0.43

Source: Authors' calculations based on survey data.
Note: Table includes only households headed by males. Values represent relative
frequencies of farms by output control and farm type.

Unfortunately, comparable data are not available for earlier
years. However, the high share of jointly managed/controlled coffee
parcels in 2005, taken together with the income-pooling results and
the widespread perception that coffee income is (or has been) controlled by men, may be interpreted as a sign that production modes
have changed.

Effect of Increase in Coffee Income on Cooperation in Coffee Production

As a result of increased coffee income pooling since the early 1990s,
one would expect household members to cooperate more in production, raising production efficiency. To test whether this was actually
the case in Uganda, we estimate coffee yield equations for 1999 and
2005.[10] The specification combines Udry's (1996) approach for
detecting output inefficiencies caused by the distribution of plot ownership within the household and the analysis by Lim, Winter-Nelson,
and Arends-Kuenning (2007) of the importance of female bargaining
power on coffee production. Our bargaining proxies are the male and
female "excess education" variables,[11] the proxy for gender-biased
inheritance rules (for 1999/2000), and the dummies for male head– or
female spouse–controlled parcels (for 2005/06).

We expect bargaining asymmetries captured by those proxies to
lead to less cooperative production behavior and inefficiencies. In
general, production decisions should be made in accordance with
price signals and endowments to achieve efficient allocations. If
influenced by bargaining processes, such influence will lead to sub-
optimal outcomes.

More specifically, the female power proxy may negatively affect
coffee yields, because a woman may use her bargaining power to
reduce labor input into male-controlled coffee production. As suggested above, however, men seem to have lost control over coffee
income to a certain extent, which could in principle be interpreted as

a change in the compensation for increased female labor input into coffee production. An improvement in the compensation rule ought to render relative bargaining power less important in determining productive resource allocation, thereby increasing production efficiency. The effect of male bargaining power is thus theoretically ambiguous. Coffee production may benefit from men using their relative strength to force or convince their spouses to contribute to it, leading to an inefficient outcome.

As in the previous estimations, we use the geographically reduced sample, which is further restricted to married male household heads who are coffee farmers. The results (reported in annex table 7A.4) reveal that coffee output to the area devoted to its production is inversely related to plot size. The first and second production area quantiles positively affect output in both years examined; the last three are associated with output declines, although not in a statistically significant manner (the third is the reference category within the total of six quantiles). These results may be explained by decreasing returns to scale or by phenomena such as rigid cost structures (Udry 1996). Additional controls include land quality, approximated by the value of the land parcel (per acre); agricultural assets; the number of male and female prime-age adults; coffee area as a share of total cropped area; a dummy for the application of manure; dummies for intercropping; and the educational achievement of household heads and their spouses.

The static effects of the bargaining proxies correspond to expectations (table 7.3). In all estimations, female bargaining power has a negative effect on coffee yield. The effect of male bargaining

Table 7.3 Impact of Bargaining Proxies on Coffee Yields in Uganda, 1999/2000 and 2005/06

	1999/2000		2005/06	
Balance of power within household	*Excess education as bargaining proxy*	*Gender-biased inheritance rules*	*Excess education as bargaining proxy*	*Control over output as bargaining proxy*
Male more powerful	−57.03	32.08	20.44	−29.64
	(68.5)	(68.8)	(41.0)	(29.1)
Female more powerful	−253.7**	−111.0*	−140.2**	−35.56
	(104)	(59.4)	(59.3)	(36.1)

Source: Authors' calculations based on survey data.

Note: Figures in parentheses are robust standard errors. Full regression results are reported in annex.

*** Significant at the 1 percent level; ** significant at the 5 percent level; * significant at the 10 percent level.

power proxies is ambiguous across specifications and years and not significantly different from zero. Between 1999 and 2005, these relations appear to have weakened slightly. For 2005 whether output from the coffee plot is controlled only by the male head or only by the female spouse does not make a significant difference in yield. Coffee production decisions may hence still be influenced by bargaining proxies, which can be taken as a sign of the presence of inefficiencies.[12]

These results rest on relatively weak empirical evidence, as the number of comparable control variables available in both surveys is limited. In particular, the 1999/2000 survey does not report labor input by plot, a key determinant of agricultural output. The 2005/06 survey allows for a more detailed analysis, because it provides information on male, female, child, and hired labor input as well as nonlabor input by plot. It also asked farmers about the share of intercropped crops (the 1999/2000 survey only ranks the crops according to relative importance). For 2005 we can hence estimate an "augmented" coffee yield equation, the results of which are reported in annex table 7A.5. Once different types of labor input, the quantity of applied manure, the intercropped share, and the intercrop are controlled for, the effect of neither female nor male bargaining power proxied by plot control is significant.

If control over the proceeds from coffee does not affect coffee yields, intrahousehold compensation mechanisms seem to allow coffee-farming households to achieve Pareto-efficient allocations. Such a mechanism would, for example, link plot control to the respective labor contribution.

To examine this bargaining process more closely, we estimate labor input equations for male, female, and child labor. We regress labor input into coffee production on the same set of variables as in the yield equation, including the plot control dummy. The results (reported in annex table 7A.6) highlight the sexual division of tasks within rural agricultural production. While intercropping with "female" crops (such as root and potato tubers) increases female labor input, intercropping with other cash crops (such as cocoa and tea) is associated with higher male labor input. As expected, male control over output is associated with higher male and lower female labor input. If output from the plot is controlled by a woman, males contribute significantly less labor to this plot. Yet women do not expend significantly more labor effort on plots they control. These findings show that output control and labor input are indeed linked. While the "augmented" coffee yield equation suggests no influence of bargaining processes on coffee yields—and hence Pareto-efficiency— the asymmetries between male- and female-controlled plots point toward inefficiencies in the compensation mechanism. A final judgment on whether these results reflect an efficient compensation mechanism has to be left to future research.

Taken together, the results on coffee production suggest that bargaining processes, in particular over labor allocation, may still undermine production efficiency. Yet no significant impact of bargaining proxies in the "augmented" yield equation is found in the most recent survey, and control over coffee output is on average more equally distributed between husbands and wives than control of other crops. The empirical analysis hence also gives some hints at more cooperative household behavior in coffee production.

Conclusion

This chapter analyses the impact of coffee market liberalization in Uganda between 1992 and 2006 from a gender perspective. Estimation of Engel curves, including the coffee income share (as a proxy for male bargaining power), reveals that income has been increasingly pooled. Proceeds from coffee did not increase male welfare disproportionately but appear to have been shared more equally among household members.

Increased pooling of coffee income should be reflected in more cooperative behavior in production. Unfortunately, the data may be too imperfect to allow a firm conclusion to be reached in this regard. The detailed analysis of coffee production for the most recent survey suggests that rigid gender roles and struggles over resources persist in Ugandan agriculture. These phenomena can obstruct increasing agricultural efficiency, especially in the cash crop sector. Given the strong public as well as academic perception of coffee as a "male" crop, however, the results may also be interpreted as an indication that households may have moved toward more efficient compensation rules.

There is no evidence that liberalization of cash crops strengthens existing bargaining asymmetries: overall, the opportunities created by liberalized markets and a growing economy appear to have altered households' consumption allocation rules and provided incentives for households to move toward more cooperative consumption behavior. Coffee market liberalization alone plays only a minor role in explaining behavioral change, however, which is deeply embedded in Uganda's cultural and social structure. This becomes particularly apparent in the analysis of household production processes. One should therefore be prudent about drawing general conclusions from the Ugandan case.

Annex Tables

Table 7A.1 Engel-Curve Estimates for 1992/93

Item	Alcohol	Tobacco	Children's clothing	Women's clothing	Meat	Beef
Log per capita epxenditure	0.00871*	0.00250	-0.0000174	-0.00219*	0.0257**	0.0221***
	(0.0045)	(0.0038)	(0.00058)	(0.0013)	(0.0034)	(0.0033)
Log household size	0.00120	-0.00740	0.00468***	-0.00716***	0.00874	0.00824
	(0.0075)	(0.0059)	(0.00100)	(0.0018)	(0.0055)	(0.0057)
Coffee share	0.0329*	-0.0103	-0.00424	-0.0122**	0.0141	0.00495
	(0.018)	(0.019)	(0.0028)	(0.0053)	(0.015)	(0.015)
Male excess education	0.0102	0.00483	-0.00198**	-0.00493***	-0.000292	0.00294
	(0.0078)	(0.0076)	(0.00097)	(0.0019)	(0.0056)	(0.0055)
Female excess education	-0.0182	-0.0149	0.00350**	0.0112***	-0.0136*	-0.0110
	(0.012)	(0.011)	(0.0015)	(0.0036)	(0.0075)	(0.0071)
Share of fem. children 0–5	0.00726	-0.00252	0.0294***	-0.000690	-0.00812	-0.00634
	(0.029)	(0.020)	(0.0038)	(0.0064)	(0.020)	(0.020)
Share of fem. children 6–14	0.0254	-0.00807	0.0278***	0.00140	0.00312	-0.00794
	(0.027)	(0.023)	(0.0041)	(0.0075)	(0.021)	(0.022)
Share of male children 0–5	0.0144	-0.0189	0.0304***	0.00152	-0.0172	-0.0152
	(0.028)	(0.020)	(0.0040)	(0.0068)	(0.021)	(0.020)
Share of male children 6–14	0.0572**	-0.0135	0.0194***	-0.00811	-0.0102	-0.0127
	(0.029)	(0.022)	(0.0041)	(0.0069)	(0.022)	(0.023)
Share of male adults 15 plus	0.0624	-0.00857	0.00996*	-0.0120	-0.0340	-0.0237
	(0.040)	(0.026)	(0.0054)	(0.0083)	(0.025)	(0.025)

Polygamous household	−0.0308***	−0.00165	−0.000226	0.0154***	−0.0136**	−0.00510
	(0.010)	(0.010)	(0.0013)	(0.0031)	(0.0067)	(0.0064)
Household head completed primary school	−0.00724	−0.0269***	0.00277***	0.00541***	0.00554	0.00454
	(0.0061)	(0.0060)	(0.00070)	(0.0016)	(0.0043)	(0.0042)
Household head completed at least secondary school	−0.000114	−0.0416***	0.00471***	0.0135***	0.00100	−0.00893
	(0.0090)	(0.0100)	(0.0011)	(0.0024)	(0.0063)	(0.0061)
Spouse completed primary school	−0.0148**	0.00226	0.0000193	0.000909	0.00506	0.00522
	(0.0066)	(0.0059)	(0.00073)	(0.0016)	(0.0045)	(0.0042)
Spouse completed at least secondary school	−0.0387***	−0.00856	80.00131	0.00148	0.00116	0.00298
	(0.015)	(0.014)	(0.0015)	(0.0039)	(0.0089)	(0.0083)
Coffee stratum	−0.0327***	0.00211	−0.000679	0.00165	0.00851	0.0286***
	(0.0080)	(0.0062)	(0.00089)	(0.0018)	(0.0069)	(0.0069)
Share of cash income	−0.0139	−0.0291**	0.00270*	0.00852**	0.0257***	0.0274***
	(0.013)	(0.012)	(0.0015)	(0.0035)	(0.0095)	(0.0091)
Nonagricultural share	0.00681	0.0319**	−0.000127	−0.00512	−0.00716	−0.00599
	(0.014)	(0.013)	(0.0017)	(0.0036)	(0.011)	(0.010)
Other cash crops share	0.0459	0.0298	−0.00113	0.00832	−0.00761	0.0125
	(0.029)	(0.034)	(0.0068)	(0.0087)	(0.025)	(0.022)
Regional dummies	Yes	Yes	Yes	Yes	Yes	Yes
Months dummies	Yes	Yes	Yes	Yes	Yes	Yes
Constant and selection term	Yes	Yes	Yes	Yes	Yes	Yes

Source: Authors' calculations based on survey data.

Note: Figures in parentheses are robust standard errors. Number of observations is 2,783.

*** Significant at the 1 percent level; ** significant at the 5 percent level; * significant at the 10 percent level.

Table 7A.2 Engel-Curve Estimates for 1999/2000

Item	Alcohol	Tobacco	Children's clothing	Women's clothing	Meat	Beef
Log per capita epxenditure	0.0321***	0.00737**	0.00158***	0.00204**	0.0793***	0.0716***
	(0.0048)	(0.0034)	(0.00055)	(0.00079)	(0.0045)	(0.0043)
Log household size	-0.00816	-0.00637	0.00801***	-0.00360***	0.0187***	0.0196***
	(0.0066)	(0.0048)	(0.00077)	(0.0011)	(0.0067)	(0.0067)
Coffee share	-0.00622	-0.0224	-0.00477*	-0.0116***	-0.0150	0.00246
	(0.025)	(0.019)	(0.0026)	(0.0032)	(0.022)	(0.023)
Male excess education	0.0104	0.0146**	-0.000495	0.000752	-0.00831	-0.0110
	(0.0085)	(0.0062)	(0.00086)	(0.0011)	(0.0079)	(0.0082)
Female excess education	-0.0173	-0.00534	-0.0000183	0.000853	0.00380	-0.0101
	(0.015)	(0.0097)	(0.0011)	(0.0018)	(0.012)	(0.012)
Share of fem. children 0–5	-0.0223	-0.0135	0.0169***	-0.00459	0.0902***	0.0539*
	(0.029)	(0.020)	(0.0032)	(0.0042)	(0.029)	(0.030)
Share of fem. children 6–14	0.00599	-0.0265	0.00972***	-0.0127***	0.0431	0.0336
	(0.028)	(0.019)	(0.0032)	(0.0045)	(0.031)	(0.030)
Share of male children 0–5	-0.0346	-0.0382*	0.0138***	-0.00967***	0.0736**	0.0579*
	(0.029)	(0.020)	(0.0033)	(0.0044)	(0.030)	(0.030)
Share of male children 6–14	-0.000717	-0.0195	0.00477	-0.0214***	0.0454	0.0339
	(0.030)	(0.020)	(0.0033)	(0.0046)	(0.029)	(0.029)
Share of male adults 15 plus	-0.0382	-0.00743	0.00391	-0.0238***	-0.0509	-0.0396
	(0.035)	(0.023)	(0.0045)	(0.0052)	(0.037)	(0.038)
Polygamous household	-0.0272*	-0.0117	-0.00419***	0.00512**	0.00497	0.0122
	(0.014)	(0.0097)	(0.0014)	(0.0020)	(0.012)	(0.012)

Household head completed primary school	-0.00804 (0.0064)	-0.0157*** (0.0050)	0.00265*** (0.00061)	0.0000548 (0.00083)	0.00998* (0.0056)	0.00657 (0.0059)
Household head completed at least secondary school	-0.00845 (0.011)	-0.0277*** (0.0080)	0.00348*** (0.00100)	0.00194 (0.0014)	0.00265 (0.0089)	0.00221 (0.0089)
Spouse completed primary school	-0.0147** (0.0071)	-0.00194 (0.0051)	0.000629 (0.00063)	0.00132* (0.00080)	-0.00217 (0.0059)	0.00583 (0.0060)
Spouse completed at least secondary school	-0.0211 (0.015)	-0.00450 (0.011)	0.00291** (0.0014)	0.00366* (0.0021)	-0.00122 (0.010)	0.000186 (0.011)
Coffee stratum	-0.0415*** (0.0082)	0.00673 (0.0049)	0.000406 (0.00067)	0.00130 (0.00092)	-0.0276*** (0.0069)	-0.0154** (0.0069)
Share of cash income	-0.0217 (0.018)	-0.0185 (0.013)	0.00842*** (0.0017)	0.0141*** (0.0023)	0.0497*** (0.016)	0.0465*** (0.0017)
Nonagricultural share	-0.00241 (0.018)	0.000491 (0.013)	-0.00290 (0.0018)	-0.00255 (0.0024)	-0.00246 (0.015)	0.00522 (0.016)
Other cash crops share	-0.148** (0.062)	0.0290 (0.035)	-0.00749 (0.0054)	-0.000647 (0.0075)	0.0852 (0.058)	0.0650 (0.056)
Regional dummies	Yes	Yes	Yes	Yes	Yes	Yes
Months dummies	Yes	Yes	Yes	Yes	Yes	Yes
Constant and selection term	Yes	Yes	Yes	Yes	Yes	Yes

Source: Authors' calculations based on survey data.

Note: Figures in parentheses are robust standard errors. Number of observations is 4,061.

*** Significant at the 1 percent level; ** significant at the 5 percent level; * significant at the 10 percent level.

Table 7A.3 Engel-Curve Estimates for 2005/06

Item	Alcohol	Tobacco	Children's clothing	Women's clothing	Meat	Beef
Log per capita epxenditure	0.0128**	−0.00417	0.00135**	0.000279	0.0579***	0.0494***
	(0.0063)	(0.0034)	(0.00063)	(0.00065)	(0.0049)	(0.0044)
Log household size	−0.00855	−0.00281	0.00511***	−0.00306***	0.0220***	0.0197***
	(0.0095)	(0.0050)	(0.00091)	(0.0011)	(0.0066)	(0.0062)
Coffee share	−0.0565*	−0.00552	−0.00522*	−0.00615	−0.0438	−0.0218
	(0.034)	(0.019)	(0.0030)	(0.0038)	(0.030)	(0.028)
Male excess education	0.0181*	0.0153**	0.0000555	0.00231*	−0.00192	0.000553
	(0.010)	(0.0067)	(0.0010)	(0.0013)	(0.0074)	(0.0069)
Female excess education	−0.0135	−0.00511	0.00252	0.00307**	0.0194*	0.0183
	(0.017)	(0.0092)	(0.0025)	(0.0015)	(0.012)	(0.011)
Share of fem. children 0–5	−0.0612	−0.0156	0.0184***	−0.00527	0.0850***	0.0598**
	(0.040)	(0.022)	(0.0040)	(0.0039)	(0.027)	(0.025)
Share of fem. children 6–14	−0.0437	−0.00894	0.0123***	−0.00858**	0.0589**	0.0594**
	(0.039)	(0.024)	(0.0035)	(0.0040)	(0.027)	(0.026)
Share of male children 0–5	−0.110***	−0.0328	0.0139***	−0.00118	0.0592**	0.0287
	(0.037)	(0.023)	(0.0036)	(0.0040)	(0.027)	(0.025)
Share of male children 6–14	−0.0711*	−0.0198	0.0107***	−0.0124***	0.0234	0.00795
	(0.039)	(0.021)	(0.0036)	(0.0038)	(0.027)	(0.025)
Share of male adults 15 plus	−0.115**	0.0158	−0.000357	−0.0122**	0.0326	0.0328
	(0.048)	(0.026)	(0.0042)	(0.0048)	(0.033)	(0.031)
Polygamous household	0.0000669	−0.00547	−0.00205	0.00295	0.000393	0.00260
	(0.016)	(0.0095)	(0.0014)	(0.0018)	(0.012)	(0.011)

Household head completed primary school	-0.00491	-0.0235***	0.00214***	0.00159*	0.0125**	0.00777
	(0.0073)	(0.0050)	(0.00065)	(0.00088)	(0.0055)	(0.0051)
Household head completed at least secondary school	-0.0244*	-0.0296***	0.00439***	0.00168	0.00284	-0.00356
	(0.013)	(0.0078)	(0.0010)	(0.0013)	(0.0080)	(0.0079)
Spouse completed primary school	-0.0107	-0.00552	0.00121*	0.00310***	-0.0161***	-0.00678
	(0.0076)	(0.0051)	(0.00070)	(0.00096)	(0.0056)	(0.0053)
Spouse completed at least secondary school	-0.0423***	0.000363	0.00343*	0.00685***	-0.0135	-0.00677
	(0.016)	(0.0089)	(0.0019)	(0.0018)	(0.0091)	(0.0086)
Coffee stratum	-0.0000122	-0.00910**	0.000074	0.000173	0.00370	0.0103*
	(0.0082)	(0.0046)	(0.00074)	(0.00087)	(0.0058)	(0.0055)
Share of cash income	-0.00146	-0.0210*	0.000693	0.00513**	0.0458***	0.0377***
	(0.020)	(0.011)	(0.0015)	(0.0022)	(0.014)	(0.013)
Nonagricultural share	-0.0175	0.00262	-0.000270	-0.00156	-0.0278**	-0.0115
	(0.018)	(0.011)	(0.0014)	(0.0019)	(0.013)	(0.012)
Othercash crops share	-0.0701	-0.0224	-0.00861*	-0.0123	-0.0199	0.00130
	(0.052)	(0.035)	(0.0049)	(0.0078)	(0.041)	(0.035)
Regional dummies	Yes	Yes	Yes	Yes	Yes	Yes
Months dummies	Yes	Yes	Yes	Yes	Yes	Yes
Constant and selection term	Yes	Yes	Yes	Yes	Yes	Yes

Source: Authors' calculations based on survey data.

Note: Figures in parentheses are robust standard errors. Number of observations is 2,684.

*** Significant at the 1 percent level; ** significant at the 5 percent level; * significant at the 10 percent level.

Table 7A.4 Comparable Coffee Yield Estimates for 1999/2000 and 2005/06

Bargaining power proxy	1999/2000		2005/06	
	Excess education as bargaining proxy	Gender-biased inheritance rules	Excess education as bargaining proxy	Control over output as bargaining proxy
Household head completed primary school	14.89	38.36	−19.69	3.119
	(55.1)	(49.5)	(33.8)	(28.7)
Household head completed at least secondary school	47.06	49.39	−42.22	−18.09
	(83.3)	(69.0)	(50.2)	(39.4)
Spouse completed primary school	95.87	63.26	43.93	28.62
	(61.9)	(55.3)	(37.8)	(34.3)
Spouse completed at least secondary school	−68.34	−93.05	75.36	44.59
	(93.6)	(83.9)	(62.9)	(54.4)
Experience	0.749	0.317	−1.068	−0.863
	(1.21)	(1.23)	(0.80)	(0.91)
Male adults	−0.863	4.210	30.44*	32.30*
	(25.5)	(28.4)	(16.1)	(16.6)
Female adults	38.85	29.27	−3.220	−3.489
	(28.7)	(29.6)	(13.8)	(14.1)
Area under coffee sixtile 1	279.2**	299.2***	198.3***	213.8***
	(108)	(107)	(53.4)	(56.7)
Area under coffee sixtile 2	50.79	66.16	106.4**	110.2**
	(102)	(102)	(44.1)	(44.9)
Area under coffee sixtile 4	−129.2	−129.8	8.785	14.78
	(93.7)	(92.8)	(41.5)	(42.9)
Area under coffee sixtile 5	−144.7	−132.5	−53.13	−33.40
	(102)	(101)	(37.1)	(40.1)

	(1)	(2)	(3)	(4)
Area under coffee sixtile 6	-192.3*	-181.1*	13.00	17.41
	(101)	(101)	(48.0)	(49.6)
Land quality	5.921	7.788	16.62***	18.28***
	(6.70)	(6.97)	(4.33)	(4.45)
Agricultural asset quartile 2	117.6	107.6	27.86	39.58
	(98.1)	(97.9)	(39.8)	(39.0)
Agricultural asset quartile 3	159.0*	146.5	94.76***	97.30***
	(95.7)	(94.9)	(36.0)	(37.1)
Agricultural asset quartile 4	157.2	162.9*	78.49*	70.45
	(97.8)	(97.5)	(41.4)	(43.0)
Coffee area as share of total cropped area	-404.5***	-419.1***	-110.2**	-124.0**
	(111)	(113)	(49.1)	(50.9)
Plot intercropped	-13.73	-17.47	-139.2***	-136.4***
	(41.4)	(41.7)	(47.0)	(47.1)
Manure applied	99.72	94.23	10.75	23.07
	(71.8)	(72.8)	(32.2)	(37.5)
Male more powerful	-57.03	32.08	20.44	-29.64
	(68.5)	(68.8)	(41.0)	(29.1)
Female more powerful	-253.7**	-111.0*	-140.2**	-35.56
	(104)	(59.4)	(59.3)	(36.1)
Constant	451.6***	463.4***	258.8***	243.3***
	(157)	(155)	(77.1)	(75.3)
Observations	931	933	926	928
R-squared	0.14	0.14	0.13	0.13

Source: Authors' calculations based on survey data.

Note: Figures in parentheses are robust standard errors. Agricultural assets in 2005/06 include a broader class of assets.

*** Significant at the 1 percent level; ** significant at the 5 percent level; * significant at the 10 percent level.

Table 7A.5 Results of Augmented Yield Equation for 2005/06

Variable	Coefficient	Variable	Coefficient
Household head completed primary school	−0.383	Agricultural asset quartile 4	119.0***
	(28.7)		(43.7)
Household head completed at least secondary school	4.643	Manure in kilograms	0.00676
	(42.9)		(0.017)
Household head completed at least higher school	−48.07	Coffee area as share of total cropped area	−159.0***
	(72.0)		(50.0)
Spouse completed primary school	49.78	Plot intercropped	−41.20
	(32.5)		(49.5)
Spouse completed at least secondary school	55.18	Share intercropped with grains	−385.0***
	(54.9)		(95.0)
Male labor	0.438	Share intercropped with beans or peas	−274.6***
	(0.27)		(95.5)
Female labor	0.383*	Share intercropped with other legumes	−293.5*
	(0.23)		(174)
Child labor	−0.446***	Share intercropped with vegetables	−489.7**
	(0.17)		(203)
Hired labor	−0.00581	Share intercropped with cotton/tobacco	−340.7
	(0.15)		(304)
Area under coffee sixtile 1	210.0***	Share intercropped with potato tubers	−281.5*
	(69.9)		(170)
Area under coffee sixtile 2	98.62*		
	(58.4)		

Area under coffee sixtile 4	−17.94 (57.3)	Share intercropped with root tubers	−382.5*** (109)
Area under coffee sixtile 5	−77.46 (53.1)	Share intercropped with tree fruits	−21.37 (286)
Area under coffee sixtile 6	−39.49 (62.0)	Share intercropped with matoke	−291.5 (291)
Land quality	17.54*** (4.50)	Share intercropped with sweet banana	−714.4** (310)
Agricultural asset quartile 2	48.66 (41.6)	Share intercropped with tea/cocoa	−585.4 (357)
Agricultural asset quartile 3	112.8*** (37.7)	Share intercropped with other plants	−411.4 (252)
Male more powerful	−45.14 (30.1)		
Female more powerful	−16.36 (37.1)		
Constant	381.8*** (89.0)		

Source: Authors' calculations based on survey data.

Note: Figures in parentheses are robust standard errors. Number of observations is 927. *R*-squared is 0.17.

*** Significant at the 1 percent level; ** significant at the 5 percent level; * significant at the 10 percent level.

Table 7A.6 Results of Labor Input per Acre Equations

Variable	Male labor per acre	Child labor per acre	Female labor per acre
Male adults	1.504		
	(1.95)		
Children between 6–14		4.526***	
		(0.76)	
Female adults			4.706
			(3.65)
Head completed primary school	−0.807	5.740	5.062
	(4.23)	(3.49)	(8.04)
Head completed at least	8.541	7.669	12.34
secondary school	(7.41)	(5.04)	(12.1)
Head completed at least	1.323	41.37***	24.83
higher school	(12.8)	(14.7)	(19.5)
Spouse completed primary	−15.73***	−10.42***	−19.49**
school	(4.15)	(3.55)	(8.13)
Spouse completed at least	−17.90***	−12.13*	−41.24***
secondary school	(6.43)	(6.19)	(14.5)
Area under coffee sixtile 1	36.71***	12.71	151.8***
	(9.52)	(8.63)	(18.2)
Area under coffee sixtile 2	7.369	3.422	33.57***
	(7.57)	(7.58)	(12.1)
Area under coffee sixtile 4	−15.10**	−5.876	−20.06
	(7.19)	(7.31)	(13.0)

Area under coffee sixtile 5	−23.35***	−2.916	−33.29***
	(7.20)	(7.68)	(11.7)
Area under coffee sixtile 6	−38.20***	−12.20	−57.26***
	(6.93)	(7.75)	(13.1)
Coffee area as share of total cropped area	−25.87***	−19.34***	−52.46***
	(7.75)	(5.47)	(13.4)
Plot intercropped	−9.501	0.180	2.086
	(7.84)	(5.13)	(15.3)
Share intercropped with grains	73.92***	37.43***	136.4***
	(16.0)	(12.4)	(31.3)
Share intercropped with beans or peas	31.05**	28.06**	107.7***
	(14.0)	(10.9)	(25.6)
Share intercropped with other legumes	69.59***	20.08	324.3***
	(26.7)	(24.0)	(77.2)
Share intercropped with vegetables	43.81	42.58***	58.85
	(37.3)	(15.4)	(40.1)
Share intercropped with cotton/ tobacco	193.9***	82.92**	169.5**
	(74.5)	(40.6)	(80.6)
Share intercropped with potato tubers	56.11**	38.02	252.6***
	(27.5)	(26.4)	(61.6)
Share intercropped with root tubers	25.73	28.32**	128.1***
	(18.9)	(14.1)	(34.4)
Share intercropped with tree fruits	154.3***	3.364	39.66
	(55.9)	(31.5)	(73.8)

(Continued on the following page)

Table 7A.6 (*Continued*)

Variable	Male labor per acre	Child labor per acre	Female labor per acre
Share intercropped with matoke	-124.7**	0.143	-18.22
	(54.6)	(30.8)	(74.3)
Share intercropped with sweet banana	-195.1***	25.01	-88.11
	(62.9)	(44.9)	(83.0)
Share intercropped with tea/cocoa	108.9*	13.78	92.07
	(57.7)	(27.1)	(57.1)
Share intercropped with other plants	22.57	31.98	96.83**
	(31.6)	(24.3)	(48.4)
Output controlled by male head	12.99***	-1.021	-18.93**
	(4.57)	(3.35)	(7.92)
Output controlled by female spouse	-34.20***	0.924	13.28
	(5.33)	(4.59)	(10.4)
Constant	57.04***	6.159	61.73***
	(10.2)	(9.37)	(21.1)
Observations	912	921	916
R-squared	0.27	0.15	0.42

Source: Authors' calculations based on survey data.

Note: Figures in parentheses are robust standard errors.

*** Significant at the 1 percent level; ** significant at the 5 percent level; * significant at the 10 percent level.

Notes

The authors gratefully acknowledge funding from the World Bank Netherlands Partnership Program (BNPP)–funded project "Trade, Growth and Poverty in the Developing World" and the research exchange facility of the Poverty Reduction, Equity and Growth Network (PEGNet). The authors thank Rafael De Hoyos, Erik Thorbeke, and Alan Winters for helpful comments on this chapter. They are highly indebted to Sarah Ssewanyana, of the Economic Policy Research Centre, and James Muwonge, of the Uganda Bureau of Statistics, for their help with the Uganda National Household Survey 2005/06 and for making the data available to them. Jann Lay is the corresponding author; his e-mail address is jann.lay@ifw-kiel.de.

1. Some anthropological evidence points to changes in gender roles in East Africa. See, for example, and Dolan (2001) Silberschmidt (2001).

2. See the chapters in Reinikka and Collier (2001) for different aspects of the reforms. Other discussions include Dijkstra and van Donge (2001) and Okidi and others (2006). For details on coffee sector reforms, see Akiyama (2001).

3. The male/female "excess education" variables are dummy variables that equal one for households having an educational disparity between the household head and his or her spouse that exceeds a threshold of five years for males and four years for females. In polygamous households the educational level of the wife with the highest educational achievement is used for the calculation. Female-headed household heads are excluded. The subsample formation is discussed in more detail below.

4. For instance, the Ugandan surveys do not allow assigning children to their biological mother.

5. In some communities, the community leader decides on inheritance matters.

6. Information is given only for parcels, not for plots or crops. Among farm households 27 percent have one parcel, 34 percent have two parcels, and 21 percent have three parcels. There is some variation in control over parcel output. In only about a third of male-headed farms are all parcels controlled exclusively by the head; on a fifth of all male-headed farms, all parcels are controlled mainly by the spouse; in more than 40 percent of farm households is output controlled/managed jointly.

7. The northern region has been shown to suffer from adverse agricultural conditions and to be largely delinked from the rest of the economy.

8. Further restricting the subsample to include only monogamous households with children does not affect the results. Estimates based on the entire sample—including a female-head dummy variable—reveal a negative effect of the coffee income share on both women's and children's clothing in the most recent survey as well. The fact that the effects are weaker than

in earlier years may indicate that men in coffee-farming households are somewhat more powerful in general. The additional regression results are available upon request from the authors.

9. The variables constructed from the survey year–specific information—the gender-biased inheritance rule dummy for 1999/2000 and the output control dummy for 2005/06—yield similar results.

10. Unfortunately, the 1992/93 survey does not comprise information about coffee plot size and does not allow for an estimation of yield equations.

11. The "educational excess"' dummies are somewhat more problematic in the production than in the consumption context, because they also reflect comparative advantages of individual household members (such as comparative advantages in nonfarm activities or work on the field).

12. Too much emphasis should not be put on the strength of the effect between the two years in light of the large variations in the other coefficients, which could, for example, be caused by differences in questionnaire design.

References

Akiyama, T. 2001. "Coffee Market Liberalization since 1990." In *Commodity Market Reforms: Lessons of Two Decades*, ed. T. Akiyama, J. Baffes, D. F. Larson, and P. Varangis, 83–120. Washington, DC: World Bank.

Alderman, H., P-A. Chiappori, L. Haddad, J. Hoddinott, and R. Kanbur. 1995. "Unitary versus Collective Models of the Household: Is It Time to Shift the Burden of Proof?" *World Bank Research Observer* 10 (1): 1–19.

Alderman, H., L. Haddad, and J. Hoddinott. 1997. *Intrahousehold Resource Allocation in Developing Countries: Models, Methods, and Policies*. Baltimore, MD: Johns Hopkins University Press.

Appleton, S., I. Chessa, and J. Hoddinott. 1999. "Are Women the Fairer Sex? Looking for Gender Differences in Gender Bias in Uganda." Centre for the Study of African Economies, University of Oxford, United Kingdom.

Baden, S. 1993. "Gender and Adjustment in Sub-Saharan Africa." Bridge Report 8, Institute of Development Studies, Brighton, United Kingdom.

Baffes, J. 2006. "Restructuring Uganda's Coffee Industry: Why Going Back to Basics Matters." *Development Policy Review* 24 (4): 413–36.

Bantebya, G., and M. Keniston. 2006. *Women, Work and Domestic Virtue in Uganda 1900–2003*. Oxford: James Currey Ltd.

Bourguignon, F., M. Browning, P.–A. Chiappori, and V. Lechene. 1993. "Intra-Household Allocation of Consumption: A Model and Some

Evidence from French Data." *Annales d'economie et de statistique* 29: 137–56.

———. 1994. "Income and Outcomes: A Structural Model of Intrahousehold Allocation." *Journal of Political Economy* 102 (6): 1067–96

Browning, M., and P.-A. Chiappori. 1998. "Efficient Intra-Household Allocations: A General Characterization and Empirical Tests." *Econometrica* 66 (6): 1241–78.

Bussolo, M., O. Godart, J. Lay, and R. Thiele. 2007. "The Impact of Commodity Price Changes on Rural Households: The Case of Coffee in Uganda." *Agricultural Economics* 37 (2–3): 293–303.

Deaton, A. 1989. "Looking for Boy-Girl Discrimination in Household Expenditure Data." *World Bank Economic Review* 3 (1): 1–15.

Deaton, A., and J. Muellbauer. 1980. *Economics and Consumer Behaviour.* Cambridge: Cambridge University Press.

Deaton, A., J. Ruiz-Castillo, and D. Thomas. 1989. "The Influence of Household Composition on Household Expenditure Patterns: Theory and Spanish Evidence." *Journal of Political Economy* 97 (1): 179–200.

Dijkstra, A., and J. van Donge. 2001 "What Does the 'Show Case' Show? Evidence of and Lessons from Adjustment in Uganda." *World Development* 29 (5): 841–63.

Dolan, C. 2001. "The 'Good Wife': Struggles over Resources in the Kenyan Horticultural Sector." *Journal of Development Studies* 37 (3): 39–70.

Duflo, E., and C. Udry. 2004. "Intrahousehold Resource Allocation in Côte d'Ivoire: Social Norms, Separate Accounts and Consumption Choices." NBER Working Paper 10498, National Bureau of Economic Research, Cambridge, MA.

Elson, D., and B. Evers. 1996. *Uganda: Gender Aware Country Strategy Report.* School of Social Sciences, University of Manchester, United Kingdom.

EPRC (Economic Policy Research Centre). 2007. *International Trade and Gender in East Africa: The Ugandan Case Study.* Kampala.

Evers, B., and B. Walters. 2000. "Extra-Household Factors and Women Farmers' Supply Response in Sub-Saharan Africa." *World Development* 28 (7): 1341–45.

———. 2001. "The Model of a Gender-Segregated Low-Income Economy Reconsidered: Evidence from Uganda." *Review of Development Economics* 5 (1): 76–88.

Haddad, L., and T. Reardon. 1993. "Gender Bias in the Allocation of Resources within Households in Burkina Faso: A Disaggregated Outlay Equivalent Analysis." *Journal of Development Studies* 29 (2): 260–76.

Hoddinott, J., and L. Haddad. 1995. "Does Female Income Share Influence Household Expenditures? Evidence from Côte d'Ivoire. *Oxford Bulletin of Economics and Statistics* 57 (1): 77–96.

Jones, C. 1983. "The Mobilization of Women's Labor for Cash Crop Production: A Game Theoretic Approach." *American Journal of Agricultural Economics* 65 (5): 1049–54.

Kappel, R., J. Lay, and S. Steiner. 2005. "Uganda: More Pro-Poor Growth?" *Development Policy Review* 23 (1): 27–53.

Kasente, D. 1997. "Agricultural Intensification Strategies, Women's Workloads and Well-Being in Uganda." Paper prepared for workshop on "Gender, Poverty and Well-Being" hosted by the United Nations Research Institute for Social Development, the United Nations Development Programme, and the Centre for Development Studies, Kerala, India, November 24–27.

Kasente, D., M. Lockwood, J. Vivian, and A. Whitehead. 2000. "Gender and the Expansion of Non-Traditional Agricultural Exports in Uganda." UNRISD Occasional Paper 12, United Nations Research Institute for Social Development, Geneva.

Lim, S., A. Winter-Nelson, and M. Arends-Kuenning. 2007. "Household Bargaining Power and Agricultural Supply Response: Evidence from Ethiopian Coffee Growers." *World Development* 35 (7): 1204–20.

Newman, C. 2002. "Gender, Time Use, and Change: The Impact of the Cut Flower Industry in Ecuador." *World Bank Economic Review* 16 (3): 375–96.

Okidi, J., S. Ssewanyana, L. Bategeka, and F. Muhumuza. 2006. "Uganda's Experience with Operationalizing Pro-Poor Growth, 1992 to 2003." In *Delivering on the Promise of Pro-Poor Growth*, ed. T. Besley and L. Cord, 169–98. Washington, DC: World Bank/Palgrave.

Quisumbing, A. R., and J. A. Maluccio. 2003. "Resources at Marriage and Intrahousehold Allocation: Evidence from Bangladesh, Ethiopia, Indonesia, and South Africa." *Oxford Bulletin of Economics and Statistics* 65 (3): 283–328.

Reinikka, R., and P. Collier, eds. 2001. *Uganda's Recovery: The Role of Firms, Farms, and Government*. Washington, DC: World Bank.

Seebens, H., and J. Sauer. 2007. "Bargaining Power and Efficiency: Rural Households in Ethiopia." *Journal of International Development* 19 (7): 895–918.

Silberschmidt, M. 2001. "Disempowerment of Men in Rural and Urban East Africa: Implications for Male Identity and Sexual Behavior." *World Development* 29 (4): 657–71.

Thomas, D., and C.-L. Chen. 1994. "Income Shares and Shares of Income: Empirical Tests of Models of Household Resource Allocations." RAND Labor and Population Program Working Paper 94–08. Santa Monica, CA.

Udry, C. 1996. "Gender, Agricultural Production, and the Theory of the Household." *Journal of Political Economy* 104 (5): 1010–46.

Ulph, D. 1988. *A General Non-Cooperative Nash Model of Household Consumption Behaviour*. University of Bristol Discussion Paper 88/205, Department of Economics, University of Bristol, United Kingdom.

Working, H. 1943. "Statistical Laws of Family Expenditure." *Journal of the American Statistical Association* 38 (221): 43–56.

World Bank. 2005. *Uganda: From Periphery to Center. A Strategic Country Gender Assessment*. Report 30136–UG, Washington, DC.

8

Gender Impacts of Agricultural Liberalization: Evidence from Ghana

Charles Ackah and Jann Lay

This chapter examines how female farmers in Ghana responded to trade reform and improved incentives for cocoa production and whether increased income from cocoa reinforced gender imbalances within households. Various studies examine the impact of structural adjustment from a gender perspective in Ghana (Sarris and Shams 1991; Baden and others 1994; Brown and Kerr 1997; World Bank 1999), but evidence on the gender effects of cash crop market liberalization remains scarce. Most gender analyses tend to focus on barriers to women (such as limited access to land, education, and credit) from a static perspective; they have little to say about whether these barriers have changed. Furthermore, only a few studies look at intrahousehold issues in the context of agricultural trade reforms.

This chapter attempts to fill this empirical gap by looking at the evidence on Ghana. Cocoa sector reform, a principal component of the reforms in agriculture, was not as far reaching as reform of the cash crop sectors of other countries (such as the coffee sector in Uganda, described in chapter 7). Reforms nevertheless triggered some supply response.

This chapter tests two hypotheses about that response. The first posits that because female farmers or female-headed households are often disadvantaged in terms of access to productive resources, they may not be able to respond to improved production incentives as well as their male counterparts, which would bias the gains from reform toward males. The second posits that male bias could arise from gender inequalities within the household: as cash crop production is traditionally a male domain in many sub-Saharan African countries, increased income from cocoa farming may have strengthened males' position within households, thereby increasing existing gender inequalities.

We use data from household surveys conducted in 1991/92 and 1998/99 to test these hypotheses. We analyse differences in cocoa supply responses between female- and male-headed rural households and the role of differential access to productive resources in explaining those differences. The analysis suggests that female farmers indeed participate less in the cocoa sector than male farmers. Between 1991 and 1998, it became easier for women to engage in cocoa production (partly because of improved access to productive resources, particularly land), however, so that they, too, benefited from cocoa sector growth.

We examine whether higher cocoa incomes result in stronger male bargaining power by estimating Engel curves for a number of gender-specific goods, including the share of cocoa income, as explanatory variables. Contrary to common perceptions, we find that cocoa income does not bias expenditure patterns in favor of "male" goods. Hence the increase in this income source is not likely to have increased intrahousehold gender inequality.

The chapter is organized as follows. The first section discusses Ghana's agricultural liberalization efforts and reviews the evidence on the corresponding supply response, particularly in the cocoa sector. The second section reviews the literature on gender roles in Ghanaian agriculture. The third section briefly summarizes earlier assessments of the effects of agricultural liberalization from a gender perspective. The fourth section presents our empirical results. The last section summarizes the chapter's main conclusions.

Agricultural Reforms and the Supply Response in Ghana

Like the vast majority of sub-Saharan African countries, Ghana had extremely restrictive and distortionary agricultural policies between independence and the 1980s. These policies were motivated by the desire to protect domestic producers in order to increase food production, provide raw materials and inputs to other sectors, and ensure food security and adequate nutrition by improving the availability of food (Brooks, Croppenstedt, and Aggrey-Fynn 2007).

These policies included price controls, input and credit subsidies, obligatory credit allocations, and heavy state involvement in production, distribution, and marketing.

Trade and agricultural liberalization were the main focus of Ghana's economic reform program (Aryeetey, Harrigan, and Nisanke 2000). Reforms since 1983 have removed price distortions on crops; eliminated subsidies for agricultural inputs, including fertilizer; and reduced the role of parastatals (Sarris and Shams 1991; Nyanteng and Seini 2000). The reforms were introduced gradually, gaining momentum only with the Agricultural Services Rehabilitation Project, initiated in 1987. This joint government/World Bank project aimed at improving the institutional capacity of the country's agricultural policy bodies, mainly through privatization. A number of successes were recorded in agricultural research, extension, and irrigation (Brooks, Croppenstedt, and Aggrey-Fynn 2007).

The elimination of guaranteed minimum prices paid to farmers for food crops (mainly maize and rice) in 1990 initiated the next set of reforms in the agricultural sector. In collaboration with the World Bank, between 1991 and 2000 the government embarked on a Medium-Term Agricultural Development Program, with the key objective of increasing productivity and competitiveness in the agricultural sector. The program further reduced government interventions in input and output markets, increased government support for selected key institutions, and improved rural infrastructure. A key measure was the abolishment of subsidies on inputs (mainly fertilizer) in 1992.

Although growth in agriculture is considered the key determinant of the substantial reduction in poverty achieved in the 1990s (World Bank 2007), overall performance of the sector has been only modest. Yields improved only slightly, with agricultural growth stemming mainly from area expansion (World Bank 2007). Slow agricultural growth has been attributed to a lack of improvement in the productivity of Ghana's main food crops, particularly as a result of poor transport and distribution channels and lack of support for innovation in small-scale agriculture (Aryeetey 2005).

Nyanteng and Seini (2000) stress the very limited use of fertilizer following the withdrawal of government subsidies on agricultural inputs. They point to the vacuum in the procurement, supply, and distribution of inputs following the withdrawal of government support and the failure of the private sector to assume such responsibilities. One of the consequences of this vacuum is the decreased availability and large increases in the real prices of such critical inputs as fertilizers, insecticides, and fungicides. Following the withdrawal of government subsidies, the average price of fertilizer increased 74–277 percent, with particularly large price rises in the three Northern regions (the poorest) and the Brong Ahafo region (Ackah and Appleton 2007). After removal of the subsidies, the real prices of inputs thus rose much more rapidly than the consumer price index (Teal and Vigneri 2004).

The parastatal monopoly in cocoa marketing has not been eliminated and still handles overseas shipment and export (World Bank 1995; IMF 2000) The liberalization of internal cocoa marketing, however, has ensured that cocoa farmers receive a higher share of world market prices (Kanbur 1994). The upward trend in cocoa output since 2002 has been attributed in part to improved agronomic practices as well as price incentives.

Evidence on the supply responsiveness of the cocoa sector is limited. Using time-series data on cocoa production and prices from 1960 to 1989, Abdulai and Rieder (1995) find a fairly low price elasticity of cocoa supply in both the short and the long run. In a cross-sectional study, Hattink, Heerink, and Thijssen (1998) find a low short-run elasticity using farm-level data for 1987/88. Teal and Vigneri (2004) assess cocoa production changes in the 1990s based on the Ghana Living Standards Survey (GLSS) 3 (conducted in 1991) and the GLSS 4 (conducted in 1998). Their study is the first to evaluate farmers' responses to the reforms over a longer time span.

The GLSS 3 provides a reasonable baseline for such an assessment, as the most important pieces of agricultural reforms were not yet or had just been implemented at the time the survey was conducted. In line with macro statistics on cocoa production, Teal and Vigneri find a considerable increase in cocoa output between 1991 and 1998. The data suggest that this increase can be almost entirely attributed to an expansion of land under cocoa, driven mainly by the increasing number of households engaged in cocoa farming.

Teal and Vigneri report strong regional variation. This may be interpreted as a sign that under less distortive pricing regimes cocoa production shifts into regions that exhibit better conditions for growing cocoa. The data on average production by farm suggest that smaller—and possibly less competitive—cocoa farmers exit the cocoa sector. Total factor productivity remained more or less constant, while important changes in single-factor productivities were registered. Perhaps somewhat surprisingly, labor seems to be the limiting production factor: labor productivity rose considerably in the period under investigation, as the ratio of both land and other nonlabor inputs to labor increased. Land productivity remained unchanged. No innovation in cocoa production was detected.

Gender and Agriculture

It has long been recognized that the organization of agricultural production has important implications for gender relations and vice versa in sub-Saharan Africa. Yet the role of women in agriculture differs markedly across regions as well as across ethnic, cultural, and religious groups. These differences also apply to the claim that cash crops in sub-Saharan Africa are typically controlled by males while food crops are controlled by females. Review of the empirical evidence on gender roles in Ghanaian agriculture, with a focus on female farmers, indicates that, while there is some justification for considering cash crops as "male" crops, doing so oversimplifies rural reality and the changing political economy in Ghana, particularly in the cocoa-producing regions of the country.

In precolonial, traditional, subsistence agriculture–based Ghana, men and women farmed together on the same plots of land, producing exclusively for home consumption. Specific agricultural tasks were confined to certain age and gender groups. Men were responsible for producing food crops, while women were responsible for weeding and assisting during harvest. Women were also responsible for most domestic tasks, including cooking, fetching water, collecting firewood, and taking care of their children. While these domestic tasks remain in the female domain today, the advent of cash crops, principally cocoa, and the increasing importance of market exchange in agriculture has significantly changed gender roles in agriculture.

Cocoa production in Ghana dates back to the mid-19th century. For most of the 20th century until the 1970s, the country was the world's leading cocoa producer. Initially, it was primarily men who became cash crop producers, while women's responsibility shifted toward the production of food crops for home consumption. The main traditional food crop (yam) was replaced by less labor-intensive maize and cassava. As the proceeds from cocoa production accrued to men, women soon started to sell part of the production of food crops to ensure cash income for themselves. The rise of the market economy hence contributed to the establishment of separate male and female agricultural income accounts.

Control over income seems to be very closely linked to the organization of agricultural production. As Carr (2008, p. 905) notes:

> once … land is allocated to individuals within the household … the person who is farming that land has control over what is planted, what is harvested, and the crops and income

generated by that plot of land ... As a result of this land tenure
arrangement, the household is not an economic unit as much
as it is a social unit that houses autonomous economic
producers.... This division seems to be mirrored by patterns of
control over NFE [nonfarm employment] income, where the
person earning that income has control over its use.

Takane (2002) suggests that even if a woman establishes her
"own farm" on her husband's land, the husband maintains some
control over farm management, products, and, eventually, income;
income control is closely related to decision-making power over the
allocation of household expenditure. This observation is consistent
with the claim by Sarris and Shams (1991) that males dominate
expenditure decisions despite women's considerable contribution to
household income. The review of the anthropological literature on
gender roles in Ghana by Lloyd and Gage-Brandon (1991) suggests
that men have considerable authority over household resources.

There are three important limitations to male dominance over
agricultural activities and intrahousehold decision-making processes
in Ghana. First, Ghana is ethnically and culturally diverse; the position of women among the Akan, Ghana's largest ethnic group, differs from that of women from other ethnic groups. Second, cash
crop production is not an exclusively male activity, as Ghanaian
women traditionally operated an important share of cocoa farms.
Third, it is not usually possible to fully separate income, production,
and consumption accounts within a household.

So far we have assumed that Ghanaian rural households can be
treated as a homogeneous group. This assumption does not hold in
light of the ethnic and cultural diversity of the country. In some
regions, particularly in the north, women are not even allowed to till
land or hire labor; in other regions they run farms on their own. In
general, women are more restricted in the northern regions, where
their contribution to agricultural production is confined to certain
tasks. The roots of these cultural norms may well be climatic, as the
arid climate in those regions implies that many household tasks
(such as fetching water) require much more time than they do in
milder climates.

What make the cocoa-growing regions of Ghana special are the
gender relations among the Akan, the predominant ethnic group
in those regions. In contrast to many other ethnic groups, their
clans (abusua) are based on the maternal line (Grier 1992; Mikell
1989; Takane 2002). Although households are headed by males,
male heads in a matrilineal society may have less control over
their wives, children, and grandchildren than those in patrilineal

societies. Wives and offspring belong to their clan and seek advice and assistance from their clan's head (Rattray 1929, cited in Grier 1992).[1]

Migration into cocoa-growing areas may also have played a role in increasing female autonomy. According to Mikell (1989), the introduction of cocoa triggered significant migration flows into cocoa-growing regions, which allowed Akan women to maintain their cocoa farms by establishing conjugal ties with migrants. Such mechanisms and the high regard for and strong position of women in Akan societies make cocoa farming in Ghana a special case.[2]

Data from household surveys confirm the autonomy of Akan women in agriculture. Some 45 percent of Akan-speaking farmers are women (women represent just 12 percent of Ewe-speaking farmers and 6 percent of Ga-speaking farmers) (Doss 2002, based on GLSS 3).[3] About 15 percent of female Akan-speaking farmers are engaged in cocoa farming (the figure for men is 24 percent) (authors' calculations based on data from the GLSS 3). This pattern is consistent with national figures, which indicate that 12 percent of female farmers and 18 percent of male farmers grow cocoa. Thus while it may not be possible to classify crops clearly as either "male" or "female" crops, there is a tendency for male farmers to be engaged more heavily in cocoa production than female farmers.[4]

The literature reviewed above suggests that men and women tend to have separate income and expenditure streams, with "conventional divisions of responsibility for household expenditure" (Baden and others 1994, p. ii). How separate are income and expenditure streams within households?

The GLSS data suggest that most male-headed rural households do not run more than one farm; if they do, the farms are usually controlled by the (male) household head. If reported control over a farm were to imply exclusive access to agricultural income, women in those households would not have any access to agricultural income. This seems unrealistic. It seems more likely that household members bargain over access to income and the related allocation of expenditures between "male" and "female" private goods as well as expenditure on household public goods.[5] Moreover, even if a man and woman in the same household maintain separate farms, they often rely on each other's labor input and tend to share a number of joint expenses.

The evidence from Ghana suggests the need to modify some prior assumptions about the gender analysis of cash-crop production. Women do play an important role as autonomous farmers, mainly because of the role of women in Akan society. In addition, although there is evidence for the absence of income pooling, it is unlikely that households keep completely separate male and female income and expenditure accounts.

Household Responses to Trade Reform from a Gender Perspective

A number of policy documents and reports examine the gender impact of agricultural and trade reforms in Ghana (Baden 1993; Baden and others 1994; Brown and Kerr 1997; World Bank 1999). Most of these assessments focus on gender-linked constraints to responding to changing price incentives and highlight women's limited access to productive resources in the process of reallocating resources, especially land, from nontradable to tradable sectors.[6] The prevailing view on the effects of the reforms from a female farmer's perspective is summarized by Baden and others (1994, p. iii):

> In agriculture, the benefits of adjustment have largely accrued to medium and larger farmers in the cocoa sector, of whom few are women. There is limited evidence as yet of women own account producers switching to cocoa production under the influence of adjustment; the benefits of female producers under adjustment may be largely confined to those women already in the cocoa sector.

The ability to respond to improved incentives requires access to resources, including land, labor, capital, and complementary agricultural inputs. Quisumbing and others (2001) and Goldstein and Udry (1999, 2005) have studied female access to land in Ghana. These studies reveal that inheritance rules are very complex, particularly among the matrilineal Akan. Eventually, the transfer of land rights depends on, among other factors, an individual's land use history (for example, planting of cocoa trees), contribution to land improvements, and status within the family (Goldstein and Udry 2005). Structural adjustment seems to have caused a shift toward more individualized land rights (Baden and others 1994; Quisumbing and others 2001). There are conflicting views on whether these developments favor men (Mikell 1986) or increasingly allow women to gain access to land (Quisumbing and others 2001). Regarding access to other agricultural inputs, Doss and Morris (2001) find important gender differences for the adoption of modern maize varieties and the use of chemical fertilizer, which they attribute to differential access to complementary inputs, particularly land, labor, and extension services. Once one controls for resource access, gender per se does not play a role in explaining adoption patterns.

New Evidence from Household Surveys

The empirical analysis presented in this chapter complements the literature by analyzing female and male farmers' responses to reforms in the cocoa sector. It adds a new perspective by examining the intra-household allocation of cocoa income. We first present some general trends in cocoa farming from a gender perspective, based on the results of the GLSS 3 and GLSS 4.[7] We then examine male and female farmers' decision to participate in cocoa production. Finally, we test the hypothesis that cocoa is a "male" crop, in the sense that income from this source is used primarily for male consumption.

Both surveys cover a series of topics on household expenditures and incomes, agricultural production, prices, and community characteristics. The GLSS 3 covers 4,552 households, with an average household size of 4.5 members, implying a total of 20,403 individuals.[8] The GLSS 4 covers 5,998 households, with an average household size of 4.3 members, implying a total of 25,855 individuals

Male and Female Cocoa Farmers

Female farmers play an increasingly important role in Ghana. Among households owning land being used for agriculture, the percentage of households headed by women rose from 28 percent in 1991 to 32 percent in 1998 (table 8.1).[9] Fourteen percent of female farmers and 17 percent of male farmers grew cocoa in 1991.[10] The share of cocoa-growing households increased slightly, to 15 percent for female-headed households and 18 percent for male-headed households in 1998. These figures hide important variations across regions (see Teal and Vigneri 2004 for details).

The average share of household income earned from cocoa farming stood at 36 percent in 1991, rising to 38 percent in 1998. This share is higher for male- than for female-headed households in both years, although the difference is somewhat smaller in 1998. Much larger are the differences in cocoa output: male-headed households on average produce more than twice as much cocoa as female-headed households in both years. Average cocoa output increased 41 percent among male-headed households and 9 percent among households headed by women. Median cocoa production declines among men and remains constant for women. Output gains thus seem to more equally distributed among female farmers.

Table 8.1 Cocoa Farming among Female- and Male-Headed Farm Households, 1991 and 1998

	1991			1998		
Item	Male-headed farms	Female-headed farms	Both	Male-headed farms	Female-headed farms	Both
Share of all farms	0.72	0.28	1.0	0.68	0.32	1.0
Share of cocoa farmers	0.17	0.14	0.16	0.18	0.15	0.17
Share of cocoa income, cocoa farmers only	0.38	0.29	0.36	0.42	0.34	0.38
Cocoa output in kilograms, cocoa farmers only	758	347	661	1,069	381	881
farmers only (median)	500	200	400	350	200	300
Average farm size in acres	6.0	3.3	5.3	7.2	6.3	6.9
acres (median)	3.0	2.0	3.0	4.0	2.5	3.5
Average farm size in acres, cocoa farmers only	12.9	6.8	11.4	12.8	8.9	11.8
cocoa farmers only (median)	7.0	4.0	7.0	8.5	5.0	7.0
Share of all farmers with secondary or higher education	0.06	0.01	0.04	0.10	0.03	0.08
Share of cocoa farmers with secondary or higher education	0.05	0.00	0.04	0.07	0.02	0.06
Poverty headcount, all Ghana	0.52	0.47	0.51	0.43	0.37	0.41
Poverty headcount, cocoa farmers only in Ghana	0.49	0.49	0.49	0.31	0.26	0.30

Source: Authors' calculations.
Note: Farm households are those households that report some land used for agricultural purposes.

The main reason for the huge difference in cocoa output is that female-headed households farm much smaller farms. In 1991 the average farm run by a woman was about half the size of the average farm run by a man. This gap in farm size narrowed considerably by 1998.

The fact that area expansion was the driving force of the production increase (Teal and Vigneri 2004) is difficult to discern from the average figures provided in table 8.1. Average farm size increased only slightly in Ghana between 1991 and 1998, despite a growing number of farms. The increase was due almost entirely to increased farm size of female-headed farms, confirming the results of Quisumbing and others (2001). Average farm size of female-headed households increased a whopping 90 percent, while farms owned by male-headed households grew just 20 percent. For cocoa-farming households, this tendency is less: the average farm size of female-headed cocoa-farming households increased by about 30 percent, while it declined slightly for male-headed households.[11] This possibly reflects the fact that women are in a position to continue with cocoa farming if the husband ceases to grow cocoa or moves.

The stark differences in farm size do not imply lower welfare in female-headed households: in both years the headcount ratio is lower among these households than among male-headed households. Female-headed households are much smaller, many of them benefit from remittance flows, and many are engaged in nonfarm activities as secondary occupations. Poverty reduction between 1991 and 1998 is much more pronounced among cocoa-farming households than for other households. The group that experiences the strongest reduction in the headcount index are female-headed cocoa-farming households.

This analysis confirms the important role of Ghanaian women as independent farmers. It also suggests that women farmers have not been excluded from the benefits of reforms. These benefits seem to have accrued only to female farmers already in the cocoa sector, however (Baden and others 1994). Agricultural reforms seem to have had a positive impact on the living standards of cocoa farmers. Improved access to land may have played a vital role in this process.

The Role of Access to Land

This section uses a multivariate framework to explain why participation in cocoa farming is lower for females than for males. We estimate a very simple cocoa participation equation that models the decision to produce cocoa as a function of farms' asset endowments (specifically, land and the household head's educational achievement) using a logit-model.[12] The model includes the household head's age, a dummy variable for Akan-speaking households (proxied by the language used by the respondent), and dummies for divorced and widowed household heads. It also controls for the demographic structure of the household and for regional dummies.

The key variable of interest is a dummy for female-headed households, which we interact with all the other explanatory variables. In light of the evidence on gender roles and the very different characteristics of female- and male-headed households (in terms of land endowments and household composition, for example), it seems plausible that the decision to participate in cocoa production differs for the two groups.

We estimate the model separately for each survey year, because the parameters governing the participation choice are likely to have changed in response to the reforms implemented between 1991 and 1998. We then use the estimated parameters to illustrate direct (gender–dummy effect) and indirect (through access to productive resources) sources of female discrimination and quantify their importance. The estimations are based on subsamples of the GLSS 3 and GLSS 4 that include only households that own land for farming (this includes almost all rural households). It excludes three northern regions (Northern Region, Upper East, and Upper West) as well as the Greater Accra Region, because these regions do not have suitable climatic conditions for growing cocoa. (The detailed estimation results are reported in annex table 8A.1.)

Of the main variables, only land endowments and the female-head dummy turn out to be significant. Land size has the expected positive effect on cocoa participation probabilities, with the negative coefficient of the squared term implying that the strength of the effect declines with increasing land size. The coefficient of the female-head dummy is negative. As expected, Akan households are more likely to participate in cocoa production that non-Akan households (although the coefficient is significant only for 1991).

Most of the results on the effects of additional participation determinants correspond to expectations, although very few turn out to be significant. In 1991 households headed by older and better-educated individuals were more likely to be engaged in cocoa farming. The education coefficients change sign in 1998, possibly reflecting better opportunities for educated individuals outside agriculture.[13]

The effect of land size, the only significant determinant, differs significantly between male- and female-headed households. The coefficients for land size (and land size squared) as well as for regional dummies (not reported) are different for both years. Although we cannot test this formally on a pooled dataset (because the model does not converge), the 95 percent confidence intervals do not overlap for the interaction terms of land and female head.

As the coefficients cannot be readily interpreted in nonlinear models with interaction terms, table 8.2 shows the changes in predicted probabilities of being a cocoa farmer that correspond to discrete changes in the key explanatory variables (land and the female-head dummy). This way of presenting the results allows the strengths of the effects of changes in explanatory variables to be quantified.

The first "male to female experiment" sets the female-head dummy variable from 0 to 1, thereby taking into account the interaction effects. For 1991 this reduces the probability of being a cocoa farmer by 15.1 percentage points, a considerable reduction. The processes that determine farmers' cocoa participation decision hence seem to discriminate heavily against female farmers. Discrimination against female-headed households decreases over time, with the effect 10.1 percentage points lower in 1998 than in 1991. This is

Table 8.2 Changes in Predicted Cocoa Participation Probabilities

Experiment	1998	1991
Predicted probability for average male farmer (reference farmer)	0.273	0.312
Male to female head (dummy only)	−0.151	−0.100
Changes in land endowments for cocoa farmers		
1991 average female to male land endowments	0.094	0.080
1998 average female to male land endowments	0.037	0.030

Source: Authors' calculations based on data from the GLSS 3 and GLSS 4.

Note: The table reports point changes in predicted probabilities. The reference probability is predicted for a farmer with average age, median land endowments (except for land effects), and basic education. This "reference farmer" is Akan, resides in the Central Region, and is neither divorced nor widowed. Changes in predicted probabilities are evaluated holding all other variables constant at the values of the relevant reference farmer.

particularly remarkable because the reference probability of the average male farmer rises 4 percentage points.

The second set of experiments endows a female farmer with male land endowments, answering the question "what would the cocoa participation of female-headed households be if they were endowed with the same land as their male-headed counterparts?" The difference in land endowments between male- and female-headed household has a large impact on cocoa participation probabilities (table 8.2). In 1991 female farmers' cocoa participation would have been almost 10 percentage points higher. Between 1991 and 1998, the closing of the gap between male- and female-headed households in terms of land holdings reduces this figure to less than 4 percentage points, regardless of whether the 1991 or 1998 parameters are used.

Computing probabilities based on the average male and female land endowments using both the 1991 and the 1998 parameters allows us to distinguish an "endowment" and a "process" effect. The endowment effect reflects changes in gender inequalities in land holdings; the process effect captures how land endowments translate into production choices. The endowment effect is clearly more important, but the process effect in 1998 is also more female friendly, as the same land endowment results in a higher participation probability for females.

Some words of caution on the method are in order. The analysis relies on a fairly simple model, estimated on two cross-sections. It does not allow more than rough conclusions to be drawn regarding the relation between asset endowments and participation behavior. The experiments are no more than simple illustrations. Furthermore, the estimates may well be biased by unobserved heterogeneity and the likely endogeneity of land endowments.

Despite these caveats, we believe that the multivariate regression complements the descriptive statistics of the previous section and provides some insight into the order of magnitude of and changes in discrimination following agricultural reforms in Ghana. The analysis suggests a fair amount of discrimination against female farmers with regard to access to the cocoa sector. This discrimination is reinforced by gender inequalities in access to land. These findings are in line with earlier claims that female farmers have been excluded from the benefits of trade reform in the cash-crop sector. Our analysis also suggests that obstacles for female farmers to engage in cocoa production have been reduced: between 1991 and 1998 both the degree of direct discrimination and discrimination in access to land seem to have declined somewhat.

Control over Cocoa Income and the Impact on Expenditure Patterns

Although female-headed households with female farmers account for an important share of the rural population in Ghana, the majority of women live in households headed by a male. In these households the supply response may be constrained by intrahousehold struggles over resources for production, as explored in chapter 9. The Ghanaian data do not allow us to dig deeper into these issues. We therefore restrict our analysis of intrahousehold resource allocation to the influence of cocoa income, often considered to be controlled by men, on expenditure patterns.

The income-pooling assumption of the neoclassical household model can be empirically tested by detecting the influence of individually earned income on expenditure patterns. If such an influence is found, income is not being pooled. Because it is difficult to identify individually earned income in poor agricultural economies, the income-pooling test typically relies on anthropological evidence that assigns income from certain crops to male or female individuals (Haddad and Hoddinott 1995; Duflo and Udry 2004). Here the same empirical approach has a slightly different interpretation. Given that households bargain over expenditure allocation, the effect of income from a presumably "male" or "female" crop on the allocation can be considered to reflect the extent of (individual) control over this income source.

Like Haddad and Hoddinott (1995), we adopt the Engel-curve specification of Deaton (1989) and Deaton, Ruiz-Castillo, and Thomas (1989) to examine the influence of the cocoa income on expenditure patterns:

$$(8.1) \qquad w_i = \frac{p_i q_i}{x} = \alpha + \beta_i \ln\left(\frac{x}{n}\right) + \eta_i \ln(n) + \sum_{j=1}^{J-1} \gamma_{ij} \left(\frac{n_j}{n}\right) + z$$

$$+ \lambda_i cocoash + \rho_i fnfincsh_i + u_i,$$

where total household expenditure is expressed as x and the number of people in the same household as n. The variable w_i is the expenditure share on good i, which is linearly related to the logarithm of household per capita expenditure (see Deaton and Muellbauer 1980), household size (see Working 1943), and the demographic household composition, $\sum_{j=1}^{J-1} \gamma_{ij}(n_j / n)$. This composition is captured by the proportion of household members in demographic group j by age and gender (eight groups). The vector z comprises additional information presumably influencing the overall expenditure pattern, particularly the gender of the household head, the ethnic group the household belongs to, and the educational levels of the household head and spouse. We also include regional dummies, an urban dummy, and dummies for different ecological zones.

The primary variables of interest on the right-hand side of the equation are the household's income shares from two distinct sources: cocoa production (*cocoash*) and the share of female non-farm income from either self- or wage employment (*fnfincsh*). Following the literature, we hypothesize that household members have different preferences with regard to consumption of some categories of goods. Given egoistic preferences, relative bargaining power determines the allocation of expenditure. If cocoa income is controlled by men, it proxies for male bargaining power. We then expect the share of cocoa income in total income to have an impact on household consumption choices in favor of "male" consumption goods, suggesting that incomes are not pooled. The female income from nonfarm activities can be seen as a reference point for the impact of the cocoa income share (that is, it shows whether privately earned/controlled income influences expenditure patterns).

For each survey we estimate Engel curves for a number of goods that can be thought of as representing either private male or female goods or household public goods that females may have preferences for. Alcohol and tobacco are primarily consumed by males, while female clothing can be considered a private female good. According to conventional wisdom, females are more likely than males to prefer household public goods, including children's clothing and health; female health (which is, of course, also a private female good); education; and food. Analysis of the literature, however, suggests that this is not always the case. As most of the expenditure categories are left-censored, we estimate the Engel curves using a Tobit model (with robust standard errors).

The first set of results is for the entire nationally representative sample for 1991 and 1998. The second set of results is based on a subsample of rural male-headed households with one spouse. This subsample is motivated by the notion that the bargaining processes require at least two parties, a head and a spouse. It is unlikely that differences in consumption behavior between rural and urban areas can be fully captured by a dummy variable for urban residence, as in the first specification. Accordingly, the second sample requires a slightly different specification, as the urban dummy as well as the dummy for female heads define the sample. (The detailed results of the Engel-curve estimates are reported in annex tables 8A.2 and 8A.3.)

For the full sample, the cocoa share does not seem to systematically affect expenditure patterns (table 8.3). In 1991 the cocoa income share significantly increased expenditure for female clothing and women's health and decreased expenditure on food. The effect on food is the largest observed effect in both years. The only additional significant—albeit small—impact of the cocoa income share is a positive effect on kitchen utensils.

In contrast, the effect of nonfarm income earned by females and the effect of the female-head dummy are much more in line with expectations, particularly for 1998. Both variables tend to influence expenditure patterns toward female consumption goods or household public goods possibly preferred by females. While income from cocoa does not appear to systematically influence expenditure patterns, the share of female nonfarm income does affect expenditure patterns, an indication that the data are inconsistent with the income-pooling hypothesis underlying the unitary model.

The estimates on the reduced sample yield similar results, although the results on the female nonfarm income share are less clear cut (table 8.4). Overall, although the share of female nonfarm income biases household expenditure patterns toward female private or specific household public goods, cocoa income does not seem to be used primarily for male consumption purposes. The results with regard to nonfarm income do not support the unitary household model. Although the results do not support any particular nonunitary model, they do indicate that rural households in Ghana may not always act as single economic units. This finding reinforces the finding that cocoa income, in contrast to nonfarm income, is indeed pooled.

Conclusion

The empirical analysis presented in this chapter suggests that trade reforms in Ghana are not biased against females. This result is at odds with claims frequently made with regard to the consequences of structural adjustment for gender inequalities.

Cocoa sector reforms have clearly benefited cocoa farmers, many of whom are female in Ghana. The benefits appear to be confined to women already in the sector before the reforms, however. The analysis also points to discrimination against females in cocoa sector participation and access to productive resources, particularly land.

Table 8.3 Impact of Cocoa Share and Other Bargaining Power Proxies on Expenditure Patterns: Engel-Curve Estimations for the Full Sample, 1991 and 1998

Year	Alcohol	Tobacco	Male clothing	Female clothing	Kitchen utensils	Women's health	Children's health	Education	Food
1991									
Cocoa income share	0.023	0.016	0.013	0.006*	0.001	0.009*	0.001	0.001	−0.042**
	(0.015)	(0.017)	(0.011)	(0.003)	(0.002)	(0.006)	(0.001)	(0.009)	(0.017)
Female non-farm income	−0.027***	−0.009	−0.013**	0.001	0.001	−0.004	0.001*	0.003	0.013
	(0.009)	(0.010)	(0.006)	(0.001)	(0.001)	(0.003)	(0.000)	(0.006)	(0.009)
Female head	−0.085***	−0.106***	−0.035**	−0.004**	−0.002*	−0.006	−0.000	0.037***	0.054***
	(0.011)	(0.013)	(0.008)	(0.002)	(0.001)	(0.004)	(0.001)	(0.005)	(0.010)
1998									
Cocoa income share	−0.000	−0.004	−0.009	0.001	0.004**	−0.004	−0.002	0.001	−0.050***
	(0.009)	(0.014)	(0.007)	(0.003)	(0.002)	(0.003)	(0.002)	(0.010)	(0.018)
Female non-farm income	−0.001	−0.038***	−0.012**	0.003**	0.001	−0.004**	−0.001	0.011**	−0.010
	(0.004)	(0.012)	(0.005)	(0.001)	(0.001)	(0.002)	(0.001)	(0.005)	(0.006)
Female head	−0.060***	−0.075***	−0.033***	0.000	−0.002	−0.010***	−0.001*	0.034***	0.038***
	(0.007)	(0.013)	(0.006)	(0.001)	(0.001)	(0.003)	(0.001)	(0.006)	(0.007)

Source: Authors' calculations based on data from the GLSS 3 and GLSS 4.

Note: Figures in parentheses are robust standards. Full regression results are reported in the annex.

*** Significant at the 1 percent level; ** significant at the 5 percent level; * significant at the 10 percent level.

Table 8.4 Impact of Cocoa Share and Other Bargaining Power Proxies on Expenditure Patterns: Engel-Curve Estimations for a Reduced Sample of Male-Headed Rural Households with One Spouse, 1991 and 1998

Year	Alcohol	Tobacco	Male clothing	Female clothing	Kitchen utensils	Women's health	Children's health	Education	Food
1991									
Cocoa income share	0.000	0.012	0.016	0.004	0.001	0.013***	0.001	-0.004	-0.008
	(0.022)	(0.028)	(0.012)	(0.004)	(0.003)	(0.004)	(0.001)	(0.008)	(0.023)
Female non-farm income	-0.066***	-0.006	0.000	-0.003	-0.001	0.001	0.001	0.037***	0.046**
	(0.017)	(0.018)	(0.010)	(0.003)	(0.002)	(0.004)	(0.001)	(0.009)	(0.019)
1998									
Cocoa income share	-0.002	-0.000	-0.028***	0.002	0.002	-0.003	-0.002	0.002	-0.031
	(0.010)	(0.018)	(0.010)	(0.002)	(0.003)	(0.004)	(0.002)	(0.011)	(0.024)
Female non-farm income	-0.025*	-0.044**	-0.042***	0.003	-0.000	-0.001	-0.001	0.030**	-0.007
	(0.014)	(0.020)	(0.012)	(0.003)	(0.002)	(0.004)	(0.002)	(0.014)	(0.018)

Source: Authors' calculations based on data from the GLSS 3 and GLSS 4.
Note: Figures in parentheses are robust standards. Full regression results are available from the authors upon request.
*** Significant at the 1 percent level; ** significant at the 5 percent level; * significant at the 10 percent level.

235

This implies that liberalization could have had much higher payoffs for women if they had been allowed to and provided with the means to respond to these incentives. The situation of women in Ghana seems to have improved in this regard, as demonstrated by the decrease in discrimination in the 1990s, partly as a result of their better access to land.

From a policy perspective, our results underline the scope for and the importance of policy interventions aimed at empowering women. Despite some progress between 1991 and 1998 (the timeframe of our analysis), female discrimination remains an important phenomenon in Ghanaian society. The analysis highlights the importance of ensuring enforceable land rights for women in rural areas.

The data on Ghana do not confirm the conjecture that cocoa income is controlled by males. Put somewhat more cautiously, cocoa income is not being spent primarily on male consumption goods. As in chapter 7, the analysis of intrahousehold allocations suggests that one has to be careful about generalizing about control over (increased) proceeds from cash crops. At least for cocoa production in Ghana, it does not seem to be true that cash crop production is a male domain and that reforms that lead to its expansion therefore disproportionately favored males.

Annex Tables

Table 8A.1 Cocoa Participation Estimations, 1991 and 1998

Explanatory variable	1991	1998
Female head dummy	−3.395**	−2.683*
	(1.284)	(1.333)
Basic education	0.137	0.141
	(0.146)	(0.142)
Secondary completed	0.170	−0.527
or higher	(0.397)	(0.304)
Age	0.0182	0.0107
	(0.0281)	(0.0268)
Age squared	−0.0000593	0.000162
	(0.000287)	(0.000272)
Land size	0.0542***	0.0801**
	(0.0137)	(0.0114)
Land size squared	−0.000117***	−0.000337**
	(0.0000306)	(0.0000671)
Widowed	0.104	0.0774
	(0.474)	(0.400)
Divorced	−0.116	−0.152
	(0.267)	(0.230

Table 8A.1 (Continued)

Explanatory variable	1991	1998
Akan dummy (language used	0.482*	0.297
by respondent)	(0.231)	(0.255)
Primary education	0.167	0.141
completed	(0.378)	(0.275)
Interacted with female head dummy		
Secondary completed		−1.019
or higher		(0.677)
Age	0.0468	0.0354
	(0.0474)	(0.0506)
Age squared	−0.000293	−0.000524
	(0.000477)	(0.000529)
Land size	0.244***	0.105**
	(0.0580)	(0.0266)
Land size squared	−0.00576**	−0.00161**
	(0.00177)	(0.000437)
Widowed	−0.175	0.221
	(0.578)	(0.514)
Divorced	0.140	0.114
	(0.402)	(0.351)
Akan dummy (language used	−0.265	0.994
by respondent)	(0.476)	(0.528)
Household composition	Yes (also	Yes (also
controls	interacted)	interacted)
Regional dummies	Yes (also	Yes (also
	interacted)	interacted)
Number of observations	2,409	3,233

Source: Authors' calculations based on data from the GLSS 3 and GLSS 4.

Note: Figures in parentheses are standards errors. No = 0, Yes = 1. "With interaction" means that all explanatory variables are interacted with the female-head dummy.

*** Significant at the 1 percent level; ** significant at the 5 percent level; * significant at the 10 percent level.

(*Chapter continues on the following page.*)

Table 8A.2 Results for Engel-Curve Estimations, 1991 (Full Sample)

Explanatory variable	Alcohol	Tobacco	Male clothing	Female clothing	Kitchen utensils	Women's health	Children's health	Education	Food
Cocoa income share	0.023	0.016	0.013	0.006*	0.001	0.009*	0.001	0.001	-0.042**
	(0.015)	(0.017)	(0.011)	(0.003)	(0.002)	(0.006)	(0.001)	(0.009)	(0.017)
Female nonfarm income	-0.027***	-0.009	-0.013**	0.001	0.001	-0.004	0.001*	0.003	0.013
	(0.009)	(0.010)	(0.006)	(0.001)	(0.001)	(0.003)	(0.000)	(0.006)	(0.009)
Female head	-0.085***	-0.106***	-0.035***	-0.004**	-0.002*	-0.006	-0.000	0.037***	0.054***
	(0.011)	(0.013)	(0.008)	(0.002)	(0.001)	(0.004)	(0.001)	(0.005)	(0.010)
Ln per capita expenditure	0.021***	-0.007*	0.019***	0.001	0.001***	0.000	-0.001***	-0.009**	-0.007
	(0.005)	(0.004)	(0.003)	(0.001)	(0.001)	(0.001)	(0.000)	(0.004)	(0.006)
Ln household size	-0.003	-0.012*	0.026***	0.007***	0.001**	0.013***	0.003***	0.083***	-0.026***
	(0.006)	(0.006)	(0.003)	(0.001)	(0.001)	(0.003)	(0.000)	(0.004)	(0.006)
Akan dummy	-0.001	0.018**	-0.006	0.001	0.002**	0.002	-0.000	-0.006	0.012
	(0.010)	(0.009)	(0.004)	(0.001)	(0.001)	(0.003)	(0.000)	(0.005)	(0.010)
Ewe dummy	0.005	-0.012	-0.008	0.002	0.002	-0.000	0.002**	0.011	0.020
	(0.017)	(0.016)	(0.011)	(0.004)	(0.001)	(0.005)	(0.001)	(0.009)	(0.019)
Gaadagbe dummy	0.030**	0.035***	0.001	0.001	0.001	-0.007	-0.000	-0.020***	0.002
	(0.012)	(0.012)	(0.008)	(0.002)	(0.002)	(0.006)	(0.000)	(0.007)	(0.015)
Hausa dummy	-0.170**	-0.022	0.016*	-0.006	-0.009**	0.007	0.000	0.014	0.089***
	(0.067)	(0.034)	(0.010)	(0.005)	(0.004)	(0.008)	(0.001)	(0.016)	(0.028)
Nzema dummy	-0.038	0.065	-0.207***	0.013	-0.003	0.010	-0.006**	-0.047***	0.016
	(0.072)	(0.053)	(0.021)	(0.008)	(0.004)	(0.021)	(0.003)	(0.012)	(0.053)
Share of males 15–59	-0.016	0.016	0.022**	-0.023***	-0.007***	-0.037***	-0.003***	0.031***	-0.011
	(0.016)	(0.018)	(0.010)	(0.003)	(0.002)	(0.008)	(0.001)	(0.011)	(0.014)
Share of males <5	-0.013	0.018	-0.003	-0.005	0.003	0.039***	0.015***	-0.089***	0.032*
	(0.020)	(0.024)	(0.015)	(0.003)	(0.002)	(0.010)	(0.001)	(0.011)	(0.019)

Share of males 6–14	-0.000	0.024	0.003	-0.011***	-0.004**	-0.031***	0.004***	0.093***	0.012
	(0.017)	(0.021)	(0.013)	(0.003)	(0.002)	(0.009)	(0.001)	(0.012)	(0.020)
Share of males >60	0.032	0.039*	0.004	-0.029***	-0.014***	-0.087***	-0.009***	0.021	0.047**
	(0.020)	(0.022)	(0.016)	(0.005)	(0.003)	(0.024)	(0.002)	(0.014)	(0.018)
Share of females <5	-0.028	0.021	0.011	0.013***	0.004	0.053***	0.017***	-0.091***	0.022
	(0.019)	(0.023)	(0.014)	(0.003)	(0.002)	(0.012)	(0.002)	(0.012)	(0.021)
Share of females 6–14	0.014	0.007	-0.014	0.011***	-0.003	-0.035***	0.003***	0.079***	0.014
	(0.017)	(0.022)	(0.014)	(0.003)	(0.002)	(0.010)	(0.001)	(0.011)	(0.018)
Share of females >60	-0.047**	0.043**	-0.041**	-0.016***	-0.009***	-0.043***	-0.005***	-0.041***	0.096***
	(0.019)	(0.019)	(0.018)	(0.004)	(0.002)	(0.012)	(0.001)	(0.013)	(0.016)
Male head education dummies	Yes	Yes	Yes	Yes	Yes	Yes	Yes	Yes	Yes
Female head education dummies	Yes	Yes	Yes	Yes	Yes	Yes	Yes	Yes	Yes
Spouse education dummies	Yes	Yes	Yes	Yes	Yes	Yes	Yes	Yes	Yes
Urban dummy	Yes	Yes	Yes	Yes	Yes	Yes	Yes	Yes	Yes
Regional dummies	Yes	Yes	Yes	Yes	Yes	Yes	Yes	Yes	Yes
Ecozone dummies	Yes	Yes	Yes	Yes	Yes	Yes	Yes	Yes	Yes
Constant	-0.160***	0.077	-0.275***	-0.028***	-0.010	-0.063***	0.003	-0.106**	0.746***
	(0.060)	(0.051)	(0.034)	(0.010)	(0.006)	(0.023)	(0.004)	(0.048)	(0.078)
Ln sigma	-2.182***	-2.281***	-2.934***	-3.895***	-4.193***	-3.382***	-5.144***	-2.641***	-1.944***
	(0.041)	(0.042)	(0.081)	(0.045)	(0.061)	(0.192)	(0.087)	(0.080)	(0.014)

Source: Authors' calculations based on data from the GLSS 3 and GLSS 4.

Note: Figures in parentheses are robust standard errors. Number of observations is 4,497. Full regression results are available from the authors upon request.

*** Significant at the 1 percent level; ** significant at the 5 percent level; * significant at the 10 percent level.

Table 8A.3 Results for Engel-Curve Estimations, 1998 (Full Sample)

Explanatory variable	Alcohol	Tobacco	Male clothing	Female clothing	Kitchen utensils	Women's health	Children's health	Education	Food
Cocoa income share	-0.000	0.004	-0.009	0.001	0.004**	-0.004	-0.002	0.001	-0.050***
	(0.009)	(0. 014)	(0.007)	(0.003)	(0.002)	(0.003)	(0.002)	(0.010)	(0.018)
Female nonfarm income	-0.001	-0.038***	-0.012**	0.003**	0.001	-0.004**	-0.001	0.011**	-0.010
	(0.004)	(0. 012)	(0.005)	(0.001)	(0.001)	(0.002)	(0.001)	(0.005)	(0.006)
Female head	-0.060***	-0.075***	-0.033***	0.000	-0.002	-0.010***	-0.001*	0.034***	0.038***
	(0.007)	(0.013)	(0.006)	(0.001)	(0.001)	(0.003)	(0.001)	(0.006)	(0.007)
Ln per capita expenditure	0.023***	0.005	0.018***	0.006***	0.003***	-0.000	-0.001*	-0.005*	-0.016***
	(0.004)	(0.004)	(0.002)	(0.001)	(0.001)	(0.001)	(0.000)	(0.003)	(0.005)
Ln household size	-0.000	0.002	0.017***	0.009***	0.003***	0.010***	0.006***	0.099***	-0.048***
	(0.003)	(0.006)	(0.003)	(0.001)	(0.001)	(0.001)	(0.002)	(0.005)	(0.005)
Akan dummy	0.011	-0.007	-0.003	0.002	-0.000	0.000	0.001	-0.005	-0.006
	(0.007)	(0.009)	(0.004)	(0.001)	(0.001)	(0.002)	(0.001)	(0.005)	(0.008)
Gaadagbe dummy	0.012	-0.026**	-0.027***	-0.004*	-0.002	0.002	-0.001	-0.004	0.014
	(0.009)	(0.013)	(0.006)	(0.002)	(0.002)	(0.003)	(0.002)	(0.008)	(0.015)
Hausa dummy	0.027***	0.014	-0.003	0.004*	0.002	-0.000	0.002*	-0.021**	-0.001
	(0.007)	(0.014)	(0.006)	(0.002)	(0.001)	(0.003)	(0.001)	(0.009)	(0.013)
Nzema dummy	-0.079**	-0.012	-0.001	0.004	-0.003	0.007*	-0.001	0.007	0.041
	(0.036)	(0.026)	(0.026)	(0.002)	(0.003)	(0.003)	(0.002)	(0.010)	(0.032)
Share of males 15–59	0.009	0.074***	0.009	-0.023***	-0.008***	-0.034***	-0.002	0.037***	0.022**
	(0.006)	(0.017)	(0.007)	(0.002)	(0.001)	(0.004)	(0.002)	(0.010)	(0.010)
Share of males <5	0.010	0.044*	0.011	-0.004	0.003	0.032***	0.034***	-0.141***	0.049***
	(0.010)	(0.025)	(0.011)	(0.003)	(0.002)	(0.004)	(0.010)	(0.013)	(0.016)

Share of males 6–14	0.004 (0.009)	0.041* (0.022)	-0.002 (0.010)	-0.021*** (0.003)	-0.006*** (0.002)	-0.034*** (0.005)	-0.002 (0.002)	0.120*** (0.012)	0.030** (0.013)
Share of males >60	0.008 (0.011)	0.087*** (0.021)	-0.018* (0.011)	-0.027*** (0.004)	-0.012*** (0.002)	-0.072*** (0.011)	-0.012** (0.005)	-0.010 (0.014)	0.088*** (0.014)
Share of females <5	0.006 (0.010)	0.028 (0.027)	-0.002 (0.010)	0.012** (0.003)	0.002 (0.002)	0.031*** (0.005)	0.034*** (0.010)	-0.113*** (0.013)	0.076*** (0.017)
Share of females 6–14	0.008 (0.009)	0.034 (0.022)	-0.009 (0.008)	0.009*** (0.003)	-0.003 (0.002)	-0.029*** (0.004)	-0.000 (0.002)	0.104*** (0.010)	0.017 (0.013)
Share of females >60	-0.027*** (0.007)	-0.022 (0.024)	-0.030** (0.014)	-0.024*** (0.003)	-0.008*** (0.002)	-0.031*** (0.006)	-0.003 (0.002)	-0.054*** (0.010)	0.079*** (0.011)
Male head education dummies	Yes	Yes	Yes	Yes	Yes	Yes	Yes	Yes	Yes
Female head education dummies	Yes	Yes	Yes	Yes	Yes	Yes	Yes	Yes	Yes
Spouse education dummies	Yes	Yes	Yes	Yes	Yes	Yes	Yes	Yes	Yes
Urban dummy	Yes	Yes	Yes	Yes	Yes	Yes	Yes	Yes	Yes
Regional dummies	Yes	Yes	Yes	Yes	Yes	Yes	Yes	Yes	Yes
Ecozone dummies	Yes	Yes	Yes	Yes	Yes	Yes	Yes	Yes	Yes
Constant	-0.184*** (0.053)	-0.159** (0.063)	-0.268*** (0.030)	-0.108*** (0.014)	-0.043*** (0.009)	-0.026* (0.013)	-0.012 (0.011)	-0.107** (0.043)	0.701*** (0.072)
Ln sigma	-2.611*** (0.050)	-2.312*** (0.053)	-3.027*** (0.081)	-3.930*** (0.056)	-4.148*** (0.049)	-3.739*** (0.065)	-4.661*** (0.293)	-2.516*** (0.033)	-2.108*** (0.015)

Source: Authors' calculations based on data from the GLSS 3 and GLSS 4.

Note: Figures in parentheses are robust standard errors. For 1998 the Ewe cannot be identified. Full regression results are available from the authors upon request.

*** Significant at the 1 percent level; ** significant at the 5 percent level; * significant at the 10 percent level.

Notes

The authors gratefully acknowledge funding from the project "Trade, Growth and Poverty in the Developing World," funded by the World Bank Netherlands Partnership Program (BNPP). Jann Lay is the corresponding author; his e-mail address is jann.lay@ifw-kiel.de.

1. Traditionally, Akan women lived with their brothers rather than their husbands (today this practice is rare).

2. Akan women can be considered emancipated only compared with other ethnics groups in Ghana. Men dominate many Akan households (World Bank 1999).

3. Ewe is spoken in Ghana's eastern region. Ga-speaking people live in the central region around Accra.

4. Doss (2002) shows that crops cannot be clearly divided into those grown by women and those grown by men. Yet while women are not excluded from cash crops, such crops tend to be disproportionately grown by men.

5. We could not find much evidence on how the necessary compensation schemes are negotiated between household members. Okali (1983, cited in Grier 1992, p. 322) reports that in the 1970s "some women were refusing to work on their husbands' farms because of the uncertainty of ever benefitting."

6. Very few assessments have looked into intrahousehold issues. Brown and Kerr (1997) stress the increased workload of women following structural adjustment without adequate compensation within the household.

7. A new household survey (GLSS 5) was completed in 2005/06. Its results were not publicly available at the time this chapter was written.

8. For more information on the GLSS, including more details on the sample design, strata weights, and fieldwork, see GSS (2000).

9. Female- versus male-headed households are examined because the number of households that report farms or parcels being farmed by different members of the same household (typically members other than the household head) is small. This finding is somewhat at odds with some of the above accounts.

10. The small difference between these figures and those provided by Doss (2002) lies in the fact that her unit of analysis is farms instead of households.

11. The farm size figures ignore the share of land under cocoa. They therefore provide only a very rough estimate of land under cocoa.

12. We opted for this approach in light of the numerous empirical problems associated with a full-fledged supply response analysis on the basis of the two cross-sections. After experimenting with different models of supply response, we concluded that the database is too weak to estimate such models.

13. The coefficients of the regional dummies (not reported) suggest that females are more likely to be cocoa farmers in the traditional cash crop–growing regions, in particular the Eastern region. This finding is in line with the finding of Mikell (1989) and Grier (1992) that women in those regions were already exposed to export-oriented production, either as own-account producers or workers.

References

Abdulai, A., and P. Rieder. 1995. "The Impacts of Agricultural Price Policy on Cocoa Supply inn Ghana: An Error Correction Estimation." *Journal of African Economies* 4 (3): 315–35.

Ackah, C., and S. Appleton. 2007. *Food Price Changes and Consumer Welfare in Ghana in the 1990s.* CREDIT Research Paper 07/03, University of Nottingham.

Aryeetey, E. 2005. "Globalization, Employment and Poverty in Ghana." Working Paper, Institute of Statistical, Social and Economic Research, University of Ghana.

Aryeetey, E., J. Harrigan, and M. Nisanke, eds. 2000. *Economic Reforms in Ghana: The Miracle and the Mirage.* Oxford: James Currey and Woeli Publishers.

Baden, S. 1993. *Gender and Adjustment in Sub-Saharan Africa.* BRIDGE Report 8, Institute of Development Studies, Brighton, United Kingdom.

Baden, S., C. Green, N. Otoo-Oyortey, and T. Peasgood. 1994. "Background Paper on Gender Issues in Ghana." Report prepared for the Department for Overseas Development, West and North Africa Department, London.

Brooks, J., A. Croppenstedt, and E. Aggrey-Fynn. 2007. "Distortions to Agricultural Incentives in Ghana." Agricultural Distortions Working Paper 47, World Bank, Washington DC.

Brown, L. R., and J. Kerr. 1997. *The Gender Dimensions of Economic Reforms in Ghana, Mali, and Zambia.* North-South Institute, Ottawa.

Carr, E. R. 2008. "Men's Crops and Women's Crops: The Importance of Gender to the Understanding of Agricultural and Development Outcomes in Ghana's Central Region." *World Development* 36 (5): 900–15.

Deaton, A. 1989. "Looking for Boy-Girl Discrimination in Household Expenditure Data." *World Bank Economic Review* 3 (1): 1–15.

Deaton, A., and J. Muellbauer. 1980. *Economics and Consumer Behaviour.* Cambridge: Cambridge University Press.

Deaton, A., J. Ruiz-Castillo, and D. Thomas. 1989. "The Influence of Household Composition on Household Expenditure Patterns: Theory and Spanish Evidence." *Journal of Political Economy* 97 (1): 179–200.

Doss, C. R. 2002. "Men's Crops? Women's Crops? The Gender Patterns of Cropping in Ghana." *World Development,* 30 (11): 1987–2000.

Doss, C. R., and M. L. Morris. 2001. "How Does Gender Affect the Adoption of Agricultural Innovations? The Case of Improved Maize Technology in Ghana." *Agricultural Economics* 25 (1): 27–39.

Duflo, E., and C. Udry. 2004. "Intrahousehold Resource Allocation in Côte d'Ivoire: Social Norms, Separate Accounts and Consumption Choices." NBER Working Paper 10498, National Bureau of Economic Research, Cambridge, MA.

Goldstein, M., and C. Udry. 1999. *Agricultural Innovation and Resource Management in Ghana*. Final report to the International Food Policy Research Institute under MP17, Washington, DC.

————. 2005. *The Profits of Power: Land Rights and Agricultural Investment in Ghana*. Yale University Economic Growth Center Discussion Paper 29, New Haven, CT.

Grier, B. 1992. "Pawns, Porters, and Petty Traders: Women in the Transition to Cash Crop Agriculture in Colonial Ghana." *Signs* 17 (2): 304–28.

GSS (Ghana Statistical Service). 2000. *Poverty Trends in Ghana in the 1990s*. Accra.

Haddad, L., and J. Hoddinott. 1995. "Does Female Income Share Influence Household Expenditures? Evidence from Côte d'Ivoire." *Oxford Bulletin of Economics and Statistics* 57 (1): 77–96.

Hattink, W., N. Heerink, and G. Thijssen. 1998. "Supply Response of Cocoa in Ghana: A Farm-Level Profit Function Analysis." *Journal of African Economies* 7 (3): 424–44.

IMF (International Monetary Fund). 2000. *Ghana: Selected Issues*. IMF Staff Country Report 2, Washington, DC.

Kanbur, R. 1994. "Welfare Economics, Political Economy, and Policy Reform in Ghana." Policy Research Working Paper 1381, World Bank, Washington, DC.

Lloyd, C. B., and A. J. Gage-Brandon. 1993. "Women's Role in Maintaining Households: Family Welfare and Sexual Inequality in Ghana." *Population Studies* 47 (1): 115–31.

Mikell, G. 1989. *Cocoa and Chaos in Ghana*. New York: Paragon House.

Nyanteng, V., and A. W. Seini. 2000. "Agricultural Policy and the Impact on Growth and Productivity 1970–95." In *Economic Reforms in Ghana: The Miracle and the Mirage*, ed. E. Aryeetey, J. Harrigan, and M. Nisanke, 267–83. Oxford: James Currey and Woeli Publishers.

Okali, C. 1983. *Cocoa and Kinship in Ghana: The Matrilineal Akan of Ghana*. London: Kegan Paul.

Quisumbing, A. R., E. Payongayong, J. B. Aidoo, and K. Otsuka. 2001. "Women's Land Rights in the Transition to Individualized Ownership: Implications for Tree-Resource Management in Western Ghana." *Economic Development and Cultural Change* 50 (1): 157–81.

Rattray, R. S. 1929 (reprinted 1969). *Ashanti Law and Constitution*. Oxford: Oxford University Press.

Sarris, A., and H. Shams. 1991. *Ghana under Structural Adjustment: The Impact on Agriculture and the Rural Poor.* International Fund for Agricultural Development. New York: New York University Press.

Takane, T. 2002. *The Cocoa Farmer of Southern Ghana: Incentives, Institutions, and Change in Rural West Africa.* Institute for Developing Economies Occasional Paper 36, Chiba, Japan.

Teal, F., and M. Vigneri. 2004. "Production Changes in Ghana Cocoa Framing Households under Market Reforms." CSAE Working Paper 216, Center for the Study for African Economies, Oxford.

Working, H. 1943. "Statistical Laws of Family Expenditure." *Journal of the American Statistical Association* 38: 43–56.

World Bank. 1995. *Is Growth Sustainable? Ghana Country Assistance Review: A Study in Development Effectiveness.* Washington, DC: World Bank.

———. 1999. *Ghana: Gender Analysis and Policymaking for Development.* World Bank Discussion Paper 403, Washington, DC.

———. 2007. *World Development Report 2008: Agriculture for Development.* Washington, DC: World Bank.

9

Can *Maquila* Booms Reduce Poverty? Evidence from Honduras

Rafael E. De Hoyos, Maurizio Bussolo, and Oscar Núñez

Honduras made progress toward reducing poverty between 1991 and 2006, with the proportion of the population living in extreme poverty falling from 61.5 percent to 47.5 percent. This large decrease in extreme poverty was almost entirely explained by progress in urban areas, where the headcount ratio fell from 52.2 percent in 1991 to 27.9 percent in 2006.[1] Between 1991 and 2006, 6 percent of the population in Honduras left rural areas in search of a better life in the cities; by 2006, 54 percent of the population lived in rural areas, down from 60 percent in 1991. Despite this decline, the fortunes of those left behind did not change much, with the incidence of extreme poverty in rural areas remaining at a high level of 65 percent throughout the period.

Poverty reduction had been taking place in a period of unstable and relatively low economic growth, with per capita income growing at an average annual rate of just 0.9 percent between 1990 and 2005. During this period Honduras' external sector experienced major shocks, the most important of them being the preferential trade agreement with the United States. Preferential access to the U.S. market translated into annual rates of export growth of 2.7 percent. Export growth was led mainly by the manufacturing *maquila*

247

sector, whose value added (in U.S. dollars) grew at an average rate of 33 percent a year between 1990 and 2006.[2]

A special feature of the *maquila* sector in Honduras is the gender-biased nature of its employment mix: during the 1991–2006 period, close to 7 out of 10 *maquila* employees were women. Given the close relation between the performance of the sector and women's income, this study explores how gender shapes the relation between trade expansion and poverty. It tests the hypothesis that the reductions in poverty attributed to the *maquila* expansion are, to a certain extent, explained by gender effects.

The chapter is organized as follows. The next section presents an overview of the Honduran economy between 1991 and 2006. It describes the country's macroeconomic performance, poverty and inequality indicators, and trends in international trade in general and the *maquila* sector in particular. The third section describes the methodology used to identify the poverty impact of an expansion in the *maquila* sector as well as the gender effects embedded in this relation. The fourth section presents the results. The last section summarizes the chapter's main findings.

Trade Expansion and Poverty Alleviation in Honduras, 1990–2006

This section briefly describes international trade and its composition, the importance of the *maquila* industry, and poverty trends in Honduras since 1990. The data suggest that increasing integration with international markets—and its potential poverty-alleviating effect—is associated with Honduras' trade-liberalizing policies.

Trade Policy and the Booming Maquila Sector

Honduras began implementing pro-trade reforms by unilaterally reducing tariffs in 1990; in 1994 it joined the General Agreement on Tariffs and Trade (GATT). The multilateral agreement became the base for Honduras' trade policy granting, at least, Most Favored Nation (MFN) treatment to all its trading partners. Honduras is an active member of the Central American Common Market. It has signed about a dozen bilateral investment treaties and free trade agreements with countries including Canada, Colombia, Chile, the Dominican Republic, Mexico, Panama, Switzerland, Taiwan (China), and the United States. Trade-oriented policies continue to be at the center of the development agenda in Honduras, which is participating in the negotiation of a trade agreement between the European Union and Central America.

As a result of trade policy, the Honduran economy is developing into a more open and liberalized economy. Its tariff structure is low and more uniform than it used to be, and the application of nontariff measures is very limited (figure 9.1). The simple average of implicit tariff rates decreased from more than 16 percent in 1991–92 to about 3.3 percent in 2005–06.[3] In 2002, after the damaging effects of Hurricane Mitch, international trade supported a rapid recovery lead by the exports of *maquila* manufacturing and agroprocessing industries.

Between 1999 and 2006, exports and domestic markets became more diversified and employment and investment (domestic and foreign) grew, particularly in some nontraditional export activities. The United States remains the country's principal trading partner, with Central American, particularly El Salvador and Guatemala, representing the second-most important market. The European Union is third, with exports to Germany particularly high. In recent years, exports to Mexico and Canada have also increased significantly.

Maquila has become the single most important export activity in Honduras. In 2006 it represented 27 percent of total exports of goods and services, up from virtually zero in 1990. Between 1990 and 2006, the value added of exports by the sector rose from $16.2

Figure 9.1 Trade Openness in Honduras, 1990–2006

Source: Authors, based on data from the Banco Central de Honduras and Secretaría de Finanzas.

million to $1,062.2 million, growing at an impressive average annual rate of 33 percent (table 9.1). The percentage of total exports accounted for by the *maquila* sector rose from 1.5 percent in 1990 to 26 percent in 2006 (figure 9.2). During the same period, the share of traditional export crops, such as coffee and bananas, declined from 51 percent to 16 percent. In contrast to the sluggish evolution of coffee and bananas, exports of other nontraditional products—particularly farmed shrimp, minerals, palm oil, and other agroindustries—expanded.[4]

The unilateral trade preference conceded by the United States under the Caribbean Basin Initiative, established in 1983, and a variety of other factors (such as logistics, abundant and low cost of labor, and the granting of export incentives) consolidated Honduras as a major exporter of textiles and apparel to the United States.[5] In 1995 the value added of the *maquila* industry represented 2.2 percent of GDP and 14.5 percent of total manufacturing production; by 2006 the sector accounted for 6.5 percent of GDP and 36.3 percent of manufacturing production (Banco Central de Honduras 2007). During this period the number of *maquila* firms more than doubled, the number of employees working in the sector increased 140 percent, and average annual wages in the sector rose from $1,456 to $3,829 (see table 9.1). In 2001 the expansion of the *maquila* sector came to a halt, mainly as a result of the slowdown in the U.S. economy. The sector resumed growth in subsequent years.

Table 9.1 Dynamic Performance of the *Maquila* Sector in Honduras, 1990–2006

Year	Number of firms	Number of employees (thousands)	Average annual wage (US$)	Value added (US$ millions)
1990	24	9.0	656	16.2
1995	135	55.0	1,456	162.7
2000	218	106.5	3,142	575.4
2001	230	94.4	3,210	560.0
2002	252	105.5	3,041	612.8
2003	273	114.2	3,358	710.0
2004	294	119.9	3,447	815.3
2005	306	125.2	3,669	969.2
2006	313	130.1	3,829	1,062.2

Source: Authors, based on data from the Banco Central de Honduras.

Figure 9.2 Composition of Exports in Honduras, 1990–2006

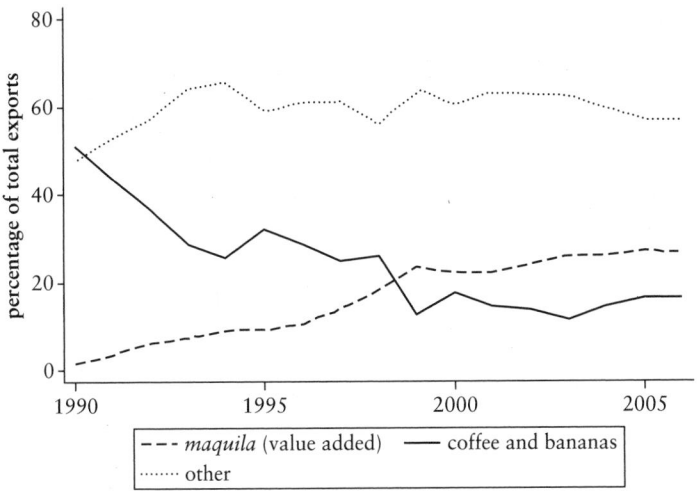

Source: Authors, based on data from the Banco Central de Honduras.

Honduras' *maquila* sector is highly concentrated in the production of textiles and apparel. In 2006, 313 firms belonged to the sector, 51 percent of which produced textiles and apparel. These firms employed 77.2 percent of the total workers in the *maquila* sector. The rest of the *maquila* sector is made up by firms engaged in manufacturing electronic components for automobiles, furniture, and wood products (23.3 percent of all firms); trade-related activities, such as the import and sale of spare parts for machinery (18.8 percent); and services, such as data processing (6.7 percent) (Banco Central de Honduras 2007).

Poverty and Workers in the Maquila *Sector*

In 1990 more than 60 percent of Honduras' population lived in rural areas; by 2006 this figure had fallen to 54 percent. Over the same period, GDP grew at the moderate annual rate of 3.2 percent, and the average annual increase in per capita household expenditure was 0.4 percent. Although Honduras' growth achievements are far from remarkable and disparities in the distribution of income are growing, the proportion of the population classified as poor fell almost 13 percentage points between 1991 and 2006 (table 9.2).

Table 9.2 Poverty Headcount Ratio and Gini Coefficient in
Honduras, 1991–2006

(percent)

Welfare measure	1991	1995	2001	2006
Extreme poverty				
Rural	68.0	65.1	69.2	65.1
Urban	52.2	41.9	32.7	27.9
National	61.5	55.1	51.2	47.5
Moderate poverty				
Rural	80.3	75.6	78.1	73.6
Urban	79.4	74.4	63.5	59.6
National	79.9	75.1	70.9	67.0
Gini coefficient				
National	52.4	55.5	56.6	58.6

Source: Authors, based on data from EPHPM.

Notwithstanding a nationwide reduction in the poverty rates, there has been little poverty alleviation in rural areas, particularly in the number of households below the extreme poverty line.[6] In contrast, urban areas in Honduras have made substantial progress against poverty, with the extreme poverty headcount ratio plummeting from 52.2 percent in 1991 to 27.9 percent in 2006.

How much of the significant reduction in poverty can be explained by the *maquila* boom? The answer depends on the proportion of households in the neighborhood of the poverty line whose incomes depend on the *maquila* sector, the change in real wages of *maquila* workers living in households near the poverty line, and the possibility for people near the poverty line to get jobs in the *maquila* sector. The share of Honduras' workforce working in the *maquila* sector increased from 1.3 percent in 1991 to 4.4 percent in 2006; during this time the prevalence of poverty among *maquila* workers fell 22 percentage points (from 54.6 percent to 32.9 percent, a 40.0 percent decline), an achievement well above the national level (table 9.3). This is an indicator that the overall poverty reduction documented in table 9.2 was at least partly caused by fast-growing labor participation and earnings in the *maquila* sector. The potential contribution of the *maquila* sector to poverty alleviation in Honduras is significant: in 1991 just 3.3 percent of households above the poverty line had a member working in *maquila*; by 2006 this proportion had increased to 10.8 percent. The increase is hardly surprising given the high level of employment created in the *maquila* industry, which had a direct positive income effect for workers who found jobs in this

Table 9.3 Maquila Performance and National Poverty
Rates, 1991–2006

Item	1991	1995	2001	2006
Total number of workers in *maquila*	19,400	45,327	90,016	106,501
Percentage of active population working in *maquila*	1.3	2.6	4.3	4.4
Percentage of *maquila* workers living under the national poverty line[a]	54.6	58.0	37.6	32.9
Percentage of nonpoor households with family member working in *maquila*	3.3	4.4	10.7	10.8

Source: Authors, based on data from the EPHPM.
a. Poverty is the moderate poverty line set by the Instituto Nacional de Estadísticas.

sector and an indirect effect on all workers through the general equilibrium effect on wages in the economy (table 9.3).

An important component of the welfare effect brought about by an increase in activity in the *maquila* sector is given by its capacity to create new jobs. The proportion of total employment in the *maquila* sector increased steadily beginning in 1991 (table 9.4). Although the change in the gender mix in the sector favored men, in 2006 more than half of all *maquila* workers were women. Two other important aspects highlighted by table 9.4 are the increase in the working-age population and the increase in underemployment. These trends suggest that the Honduran economy was unable to create the new jobs needed to satisfy the demographically driven increase in labor supply, contributing to the proliferation of part-time jobs, most of which are in the informal sector. In addition, unable to find jobs in their home country, many young Hondurans have migrated, mainly to the United States.

Methodology

The trade reforms introduced in Honduras during the 1990s could be seen as an external shock redistributing resources to the *maquila* sector. Redistribution of productive factors is given through price mechanisms (that is, increases in labor demand in the *maquila* sector

Table 9.4 Labor Participation and the *Maquila* Contribution,
1991–2006

(percent)

Item	1991	1995	2001	2006
Working-age population (15–65)	51.7	52.1	53.4	56.1
Of which: active population	59.4	61.0	60.8	58.3
Of which: employed	81.1	76.3	78.5	75.1
Men in *maquila*	0.5	0.9	1.9	2.7
Women in *maquila*	1.1	2.4	3.5	3.1
Underemployed	14.4	19.4	17.1	22.6
Unemployed	4.5	4.3	4.3	2.3

Source: Authors, based on data from EPHPM.

causes a rise in the relative wages of labor, an increase in labor participation, or both in that sector). The poverty impact of the changes
brought about by trade reform can be analyzed using the empirical
framework developed in this section.[7]

Household h is defined as poor if its per capita household income
(or expenditure), y_h, is below a predetermined poverty line, z. At the
national level, poverty indices can take into account the proportion,
depth, and severity of poverty. These three aspects of poverty (the
poverty headcount, the poverty gap, and the distance from the poverty line) are estimated using the poverty measures developed by
Foster, Greer, and Thorbecke (1984):

$$(9.1) \qquad P_\alpha = \frac{1}{N} \sum_{h=1}^{N} \left(\frac{z - y_h}{z} \right)^\alpha \qquad \forall (y_h \leq z),$$

where N is the total population and α is a parameter that penalizes
the differences between the income of the poor and the poverty line.
Let us define the income of household h as the sum of incomes of all
household members derived from various sources:

$$(9.2) \qquad y_h = \frac{Y_h}{G_h} = \sum_{g=1}^{G} w_{g,h} + Y_h^o,$$

where $w_{g,h}$ is the wage of member g in household h and Y_h^o represents income from other sources of household h. Hence y_h measures per capita household disposable income, the welfare measure
used here. The *maquila* sector is linked to household welfare—and
hence poverty—by changes in wages and employment attributable
to the sector's performance. Following human capital theory, the
log of wages is defined as a function of personal characteristics and

a random component. In order to identify the conditional gender wage gaps and the wage effects accounted by the *maquila* sector, we introduce a dummy variable for women and for workers in *maquila*:

$$(9.3) \qquad \ln(w_i) = \sum_j \beta_j x_{i,j} + \delta_1 D_w + \gamma D_m + \varepsilon_i.$$

According to equation (9.3), the wage of worker i is a function of j personal characteristics, $x_{i,j}$; a dummy variable, D_w, which takes the value 1 when the worker is a women; a dummy variable for workers in the *maquila* sector, D_m; a set of parameters; and a random component, ε_i.[8] To test the hypothesis that part of the relation between the *maquila* expansion and poverty operates through gender, let us decompose the impact from *maquila* to wages and express this as a linear function of gender:

$$(9.4) \qquad \frac{\partial \ln(w_i)}{\partial D_m} = \gamma = \delta_2 + \delta_3 D_w.$$

Substituting equation (9.4) into equation (9.3) yields the following:

$$(9.5) \qquad \ln(w_i) = \sum_j \beta_j x_{i,j} + \delta_1 D_w + \delta_2 D_m + \delta_3 D_w D_m + u_i.$$

Parameters δ_1 and δ_2 in equation (9.5) measure the gender and *maquila* premium, respectively; δ_3 captures the wage effects of the *maquila* sector (over and above the gender impacts) that operate through gender. An alternative interpretation for the interactive effect, δ_3, can be found in the economics of discrimination literature, which posits that the gender wage gap tends to be smaller in export-oriented sectors (Becker 1971). The gender wage gap is linked to the export-oriented *maquila* sector by the increased competition brought about by trade integration (Artecona and Cunningham 2002; Arbache and Santos 2005). The interactive effect, δ_3, is equal to the difference in the gender wage gap in and out of the *maquila* sector (table 9.5). If the *maquila* sector is more competitive (and hence employers care more about workers' productivity rather than the gender) and there is some degree of discrimination in the labor market, the wage gap between male and female workers in the *maquila* sector should be smaller than in other sectors; δ_3 should thus be greater than zero.

The excluded category in equation (9.5) is men outside the *maquila* sector; the three parameters capturing the gender, *maquila*, and interaction effects are interpreted as shifts in wages with respect to this

Table 9.5. Wage Premia by Subgroup

	Sector of employment	
Item	Maquila	*Non*-maquila
Men	δ_2	Control
Women	$\delta_1 + \delta_2 + \delta_3$	δ_1
Wage gap (men/women)	$-(\delta_1 + \delta_3)$	$-\delta_2$

Source: Authors, based on equation (9.5).

control group. To clarify these effects, we show the wage premia assigned by equation (9.5) to the different population subgroups. A woman working in the *maquila* sector, for example, will receive a market premium equal to $\delta_1 + \delta_2 + \delta_3$ (with respect to men outside the *maquila* sector) controlling for the market remuneration to her personal characteristics $\sum_j \beta_j x_{i,j}$. The wage premium of women working in the *maquila* sector with respect to women in the other sectors will be equal to $(\delta_1 + \delta_2 + \delta_3) - \delta_1 = \delta_2 + \delta_3$.

So far the analysis has not incorporated any time dimension. As noted earlier, from a theoretical point of view, trade reforms can be seen as a shock redistributing resources across the different sectors of the economy. This redistribution process is concomitant to price changes or changes in market returns to personal characteristics. We are interested in the welfare effects brought about by change in *maquila* employment, the change in the premia given to workers in the *maquila* sector, changes in the overall gender gap, and in particular the interactive effect capturing the gender wage gap differential between the export-oriented sector and other sectors. The change in the wage premia can be easily measured by introducing a time dimension to equation (9.5). Define t as time dummies, and redefine $D_w = D_1$, $D_m = D_2$, and $D_w D_m = D_3$ as follows:

$$(9.6) \quad \ln(w_i^t) = \sum_{j=1}^{J} \beta_j x_{i,j}^t + \sum_{k=1}^{3} \delta_k D_k^t + \sum_{t=2}^{T} \phi_t t + \sum_{k=1}^{3} \sum_{t=2}^{T} \lambda_k^t D_k^t t + v_i^t.$$

The first term on the right-hand side of equation (9.6) captures the returns to personal characteristics; the second term captures the effects shown in table 9.5; the third term shows time controls; the fourth term allows for time-varying gender, *maquila*, and interactive effects; and the last term is a normally distributed random component. Parameters λ_k^t (called difference-in-difference estimators) reveal how the premia shown in table 9.5 vary over time.[9] If the trade reforms in Honduras had a greater positive effect on women in the *maquila* sector (making their real wages increase faster than wages in other categories over time), λ_k^t should be significantly different from zero and positive.

Results

The poverty effects of a boom in the *maquila* sector are estimated using data from the Encuesta Permanente de Hogares de Propósitos Múltiples (EPHPM)—Honduras' nationally representative household survey—for 1991, 1995, 2001, and 2006. The time span covered by these surveys (1991–2006) captures a period of significant tariff reduction and strong growth of the *maquila* industry (see figure 9.1).

All of the regression results for the four specifications of equation (9.6) account for EPHPM's survey design (that is, clustering, stratification, and expansion factors on point estimators and standard errors); all of the results presented show heteroskedastic-robust standard errors and control for year and industry fixed effects (table 9.6).[10] The first specification shows the result of a standard human capital equation, with the log of wages a function of years of schooling and its squared form, experience and experience squared, and a dummy variable for urban workers. The results of this specification are as expected. One additional year of schooling yields a 10 percent increase in wages; experience has a positive, though marginally decreasing, effect on earnings; and urban wages are about 16 percent higher than rural wages. Female wage-earners in Honduras earn 27 percent less than men, once observable characteristics are taken into account. Regardless of their gender, *maquila* workers earn a conditional wage premium of 31 percent over workers outside the sector. These results are robust, both qualitatively and quantitatively, to differences in model specification.

The second specification includes three dummy variables capturing the gender wage gap, a *maquila*-specific wage premium, and a premium associated with women in the *maquila* sector, respectively. Recall that the interactive term measures the difference in the gender wage gap inside and outside the *maquila* sector. Between 1991 and 2006, women earned average wages that were 28.7 percent lower than those of men. The average wage of workers in the *maquila* sector was more than 20 percent higher than that of workers outside the sector. Controlling for observable characteristics, female workers in the *maquila* sector earned 9.5 percent ($\approx -28.7 + 21.6 + 16.6$) more than men working outside the *maquila*

Table 9.6 Regression Results

Item	Specification 1	Specification 2	Specification 3a	Specification 3b
Core variable				
Schooling	0.0953***	0.0954***	0.0956***	0.0956***
Schooling squared	0.0020***	0.0020***	0.0019***	0.0019***
Experience	0.0192***	0.0185***	0.0185***	0.0185***
Experience squared	−0.0000***	−0.0000***	−0.0000***	−0.0000***
Urban dummy	0.1630***	0.1632***	0.1635***	0.1635***
Maquila and women controls				
Women dummy (δ_1)	−0.2710***	−0.2871***	−0.3684***	—
Maquila dummy (δ_2)	0.3139***	0.2157***	0.2276***	—
Women * *maquila* (δ_3)		0.1664***	0.2578***	—
Dynamic effects				
Women				
1991			—	−0.3684***
1995			0.0447	−0.3237***
2001			0.0727***	−0.2957***
2006			0.1650***	−0.2034***

Maquila				
1991			—	0.2276***
1995			−0.1815**	0.0461
2001			0.0117	0.2393***
2006			0.0367	0.2643***
*Women * maquila*				
1991			—	0.2578***
1995			0.0799	0.3377***
2001			−0.0742	0.1836***
2006			−0.2280***	0.0298
Year controls	Yes	Yes	Yes	Yes
Industry controls	Yes	Yes	Yes	Yes
Constant	6.4083***	6.4260***	6.5318***	6.1634***

Source: Authors.

Note: The dependent variable is the log of wages. Schooling is measured as the years of formal education. — Symbolizes the intentional exclusion of these variables to avoid perfect multicollinearity. Industry controls include dummy-variables for each of the nine industries at the one-digit level of industrial aggregation; the agricultural sector was chosen as the base category. Specifications 3a and 3b are two different ways of presenting the same equation. Sample size of 43,268 and R-squared is 0.47 in all specifications.

*** Significant at the 1 percent level; ** significant at the 5 percent level.

sector and 38 percent ($\approx 28.7 + 9.5$) more than women working outside the sector (table 9.7).[11]

The results for specification 2 reveal another important feature of the *maquila* sector: the fact that the gender wage gap is 16.6 percentage points smaller than the gap observed in industries outside the sector. For this reason, the increase in the importance of the *maquila* industry in total employment had a gender-equalizing effect.

The wage premia shown in table 9.7 are the average over the entire period of analysis; these estimates do not consider any time dimension, as observations from the four household surveys are pooled in a single sample. One of the hypotheses outlined earlier was that the *maquila* boom of the 1990s resulted in a growing wage premium for workers in the sector. To test this hypothesis, we formulate specification 3a in table 9.6, which allows for dynamic effects (that is, the wage premia related to gender, the *maquila* sector, and the interaction between the two can take different values over time). All the time-interacting terms, or difference-in-difference (DID) estimators, take 1991 as the base year, capturing the change in the parameter over time with respect to the initial year. Consider first the DID estimator for the premium received by workers in *maquila*. The lack of statistical significance for this estimator indicates that the *maquila* premium remained constant during the time period analyzed here, except in 1995. This is not the case for the gender wage gap, which decreased over time (significantly so in 2001 and 2006). The reduction in the gender wage gap outside the *maquila* sector partly explains the lack of significant dynamic effects on wage premia for women working in *maquila*. In fact, the DID estimator on the interactive term is negative and significant in 2006, implying that women did not receive a wage premium for working in the *maquila* sector in 2006 (that is, the gender wage gap was the same in and out of the *maquila* sector).

The lack of significant dynamic effects deserves some explanation. Although the results on *maquila* wage premia suggest some level of labor market segmentation, a minimum degree of labor

Table 9.7 Wage Premium Results from Specification 2 (percent)

Item	Maquila	Non-maquila
Men	$\delta_2 = 21.5$	Control
Women	$\delta_1 + \delta_2 + \delta_3 = 9.5$	$\delta_1 = -28.7$
Wage gap (men/women)	$-(\delta_1 + \delta_3) = 12$	$-\delta_1 = 28.7$

Source: Authors.

Note: All parameters are significant at the 1 percent level.

mobility would be enough to offset any long-term trend in wage differentials between the *maquila* and other sectors. As shown by the identical specifications 3a and 3b, *maquila* workers earned wages that were about 24 percent higher than workers outside the sector in all years but 1995. This differential may be enough to attract the workers the industry needs, creating no incentives for entrepreneurs to raise it over time. With some labor mobility, the trade-mandated increase in female labor demand would not only manifest itself as an increase in wages of women in the *maquila* industry but also expand to the rest of the economy, thereby reducing the overall gender wage gap. The long-term reduction in the gender wage gap (which had fallen 7.3 percent from the 1991 baseline by 2001 and 16.5 percent by 2006) can thus be at least partly explained by an increase in female labor demand in the *maquila* sector.

The Poverty Impact of a Growing Maquila *Sector*

To measure the poverty effects of the *maquila* boom documented above, we construct a distribution of hypothetical household per capita income that captures what the poverty level in Honduras would have been if the *maquila* industry had ceased to operate in any given year. The short-term income effect of a sudden elimination of the sector can be decomposed into two separate impacts: wage premia and employment. This section presents two simulations, one examining what the poverty level in Honduras would have been had the *maquila* industry not paid a wage premium and one examining what the poverty level would have been if all *maquila* jobs had been eliminated. These counterfactuals illustrate the short-term poverty impact of income changes originating in the *maquila* sector. We ignore the long-term or general equilibrium effects of the *maquila* boom.[12]

To formalize the simulation process, we redefine equation (9.2) in terms of the results from specification (4) in table 9.6:

$$(9.7) \quad \begin{aligned} Y_h &= \sum_{g=1}^{G} w_{g,h} + Y_h^o \\ w_i^t &= \exp\left\{ \sum_{j=1}^{J} \hat{\beta}_j x_{i,j}^t + \sum_{t=2}^{T} \hat{\phi}_t t + \sum_{k=1}^{3} \sum_{t=1}^{T} \hat{\lambda}_k^t D_k^t t + \hat{v}_i^t \right\}. \end{aligned}$$

The wage equation in equation (9.7) allows for different gender, *maquila*, and *maquila*–gender effects for each year.[13] Hypothetical wages can be constructed based on expression (9.7), assuming that, say, the premia for workers in the *maquila* sector, $\lambda_2^t t = (1991, 1995,$

2001, 2006) are equal to zero or that wages for all *maquila* workers
are set to zero. In 1991, for example, the simulated wages for
workers in the *maquila* sector would have been 22.7 percent lower
than their observed level (see specification 3b in table 9.6). Adding
the simulated wages to the exogenous household incomes (Y_h^o) and
dividing the sum by the number of household members yields the
simulated household per capita incomes, $y_h^i = Y_h^i/G_h$ These values
are used to compute hypothetical poverty indices:

$$(9.8) \qquad P_\alpha^i = \frac{1}{N} \sum_{b=1}^{N} \left(\frac{z - y_h^i}{z} \right)^\alpha \qquad \forall (y_h \le z).$$

The difference between the observed and simulated poverty,
$P_\alpha^i - P_\alpha$, can be thought of as the amount of poverty reduction
attributed to the *maquila* premia, employment, or both, depending
on the simulation.[14] Because both the *maquila* premia and the jobs
created by this sector had positive income effects, it will come as no
surprise that these impacts reduce poverty. The aim of the exercise
is to quantify the importance of the *maquila* industry for poverty
alleviation in Honduras.

Three simulations are run, two of which capture the poverty
effects attributable to the *maquila* wage premia (as shown in specification 3b in table 9.6) and one of which creates a hypothetical
world in which Honduras had no *maquila* jobs. In the first simulation, the year-specific *maquila* sector wage premia are subtracted
from wages of all *maquila* workers (table 9.8). This counterfactual
captures the difference between the observed poverty headcount and
the headcount ratio that would have prevailed in Honduras had
maquila workers not enjoyed a premium like the one shown by
specification (3b) in table 9.6. The second simulation captures the
poverty effects of the *maquila* sector wage premium, including its
effect through gender. In this simulation both sets of *maquila* premia
(the *maquila* effect and the *women**maquila effect in table 9.6) are
subtracted from the wages of women in the *maquila* sector.[15]

Given that all parameters measuring wage premia in the *maquila*
sector are nonnegative, it is not surprising that eliminating them
increases poverty. If the *maquila* sector had not paid a premium,
the moderate national poverty headcount in 2001 would have
been 71.5 percent instead of the observed level of 70.9 percent; if
the premium enjoyed by women in the *maquila* sector had also
been eliminated (together with the interaction effect), the poverty
headcount would have risen to 71.6 percent. By itself the *maquila*
premium accounted for 0.31 poverty points in the national poverty
level (0.44 when allowing for gender-specific effects).

Table 9.8 Estimated Poverty Headcounts in the Absence of *Maquila* Effects, 1991–2006

(percentage of poor)

Headcount ratio	1991	1995	2001	2006
Actual	79.9	75.1	70.9	67.0
Without *maquila* premium	80.0	75.1	71.5	67.6
Without *maquila* and gender premia	80.1	75.3	71.6	67.6
Without premia and *maquila* employment	80.5	75.9	73.0	69.4

Source: Authors.

Note: Poverty is measured using the moderate poverty line set by the Instituto Nacional de Estadísticas. Simulations are based on estimated parameters from specification 3a in table 9.6.

A third simulation captures the cumulative poverty effects of *maquila* premia and employment. This simulation sets the wage of all *maquila* workers equal to zero in order to produce a rough idea of how important the *maquila* sector is for poverty alleviation in Honduras.[16] The results show that had there been no *maquila* jobs in Honduras in 2001, the moderate poverty headcount would have been almost 2 percentage points higher on average (73.0 percent instead of 70.9 percent).

The results presented in table 9.8 are complemented by the presentation of the marginal contribution of each component (*maquila, maquila * women,* and employment) shown in figure 9.3.[17] On average the *maquila* sector accounts for almost 1.45 percentage point reduction in the poverty headcount, of which 1.00 point is attributable to employment creation, 0.35 points to *maquila* wage premium, and 0.10 point to the wage premium of women working in the *maquila* sector.

These poverty effects seem rather small. One has to bear in mind, however, the limited impact of the *maquila* sector for overall household income. Wages paid in the *maquila* sector account for less than 4 percent of total household income in Honduras. Furthermore, the incidence of poverty among *maquila* workers is lower than the national average (see table 9.3). Finally, as shown by the results of the dynamic model (specification 3b in table 9.6), the premia paid in the *maquila* sector did not increase as a result of the boom. These factors explain why the reduction of poverty attributable to the additional premium paid to workers in the *maquila* sector (including the women's premium) is on average less than 0.5 percent.

Over time, this premium contributed more and more to poverty reduction: in 1991 it accounted for 0.2 percent of the decline in

Figure 9.3 Percentage of Total Poverty Headcount
Attributable to Various Factors

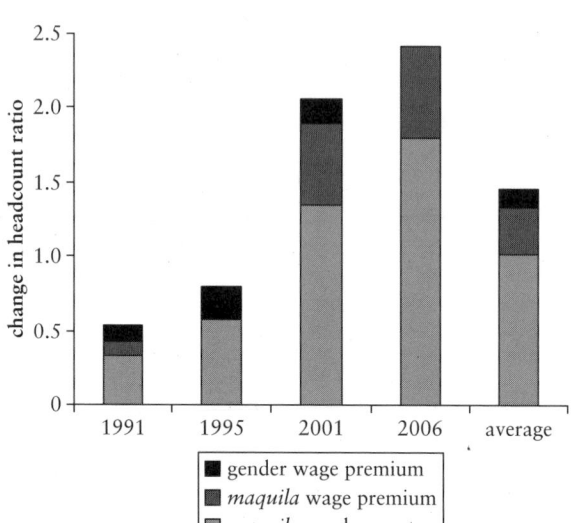

Source: Authors' simulations, based on estimation results from specification 3a in table 9.6.

Note: Percentages are computed as the marginal difference in the poverty headcount shown by the cumulative effects displayed in table 9.8.

poverty; by 2006 it had contributed 0.6 percent. Expansion of the *maquila* sector means that more people benefit from the additional gender-*maquila* premia and more individuals escape poverty. Although the *maquila* boom of the 1990s did not have a significant effect on wage premia, given the jobs it created, particularly jobs for women, it certainly helped alleviate poverty in Honduras.

Conclusions

Between 1990 and 2006, Honduras experienced significant poverty reduction and a booming *maquila* sector, a sector intensive in the employment of female workers. This chapter identifies and estimates the strength of the reduction in poverty caused by the improved opportunities the expanding sector offered to women.

The analysis shows that after controlling for observable characteristics, workers in the *maquila* sector earned wages that were about 30 percent higher than those of workers outside the sector. This gap was fairly stable over time. Firms in the *maquila* sector appear to be less discriminatory, as suggested by a gender wage gap that is 16 percent smaller than the gap outside the *maquila* sector.[18] This result is in line with the literature on labor market discrimination, which posits that firms operating in more competitive product markets should be less discriminatory in their hiring or remunerating policies. Because of the intensity of its use of female labor, the expanding *maquila* sector contributed to the economywide reduction in gender wage gap in Honduras.

A simulation exercise shows that, at a given point in time, poverty in Honduras would have been 1.5 percentage points higher had the *maquila* sector not existed. Of this increase in poverty, 0.35 percentage points is attributable to the wage premium paid to *maquila* workers, 0.1 percentage points to the wage premium received by women in the *maquila* sector, and 1 percentage point to employment creation. Given that female *maquila* workers represent only 1.1 percent of the active population in Honduras, this contribution to poverty reduction is significant.

Annex 9A: Main Factors behind Expansion of the *Maquila* Industry in Honduras

U.S. Trade Preferences

Outward processing is essentially a preferential trade arrangement that exempts from import duties the value of materials from a preference-giving country used in foreign assembly (that is, a *maquila*). The outward-processing programs in apparel and textiles under the Caribbean Basin Initiative (CBI) are among the most successful preferential trade arrangements; since the 1980s they have become an important part of U.S. apparel imports. The CBI, established in 1983, originally left in place custom duties on a small group of products, including textiles and clothing. In 1986 the United States instituted the Special Access Program (SAP), which encouraged outward-processing trade in apparel and textiles with the beneficiary countries of the CBI. It also provided preferential market access and maintained the rules of origin. In 2000 the United States adopted the Caribbean Basin Trade Partnership Act of 2000 (CBTPA), which improved preferential treatment of outward-processing apparel from CBI countries. The new act eliminated all tariffs (which averaged 5.8 percent in 1998–99) and maintained the SAP requirements on the usage of U.S.–made materials from import duties (see Skripnitchenko and Abbott 2003). The CBTPA spurred the *maquila* industry in the CBI region, offsetting the effect of "NAFTA parity."

Export Incentives, Logistics, and the Cost of Labor

The development of the *maquila* industry has been supported by a special legal framework that provides incentives such as temporary import and duty-free import on inputs for exports, originated in 1976 with the adoption of the law establishing the free zone of Puerto Cortés (Decree No. 356 of July 1976). A second law (the Decree No. 30 of December 20, 1984) created the temporary import regime. The law establishing export processing zones (Decree No. 37–87 of April 1987) enhanced the expansion of the *maquila* industry, providing incentives to develop large private industrial parks in which to establish *maquila* enterprises. Decree No. 130–98 of May 20, 1998, amended the law establishing the free trade zone of Puerto Cortés to allow the organization of free trade zones in any part of Honduras. These export-supporting schemes are subject to the disciplines of the World Trade Organization (WTO) Agreement on Subsidies and Countervailing Measures. However, as a developing country listed in Annex VII (b) of the Agreement, Honduras can apply to maintain these schemes beyond 2009 if per capita GNP does not surpass $1,000 in constant 1990 dollars for three consecutive years. Honduras' relatively short end-to-end logistic time, good facilities in free export zones, the largest port in Central America, and fairly low wages are important assets for the continued growth of Honduras' *maquila* industry. In March 2006 Honduran and U.S. authorities signed the Container Security Initiative (CSI), a partnership that should help accelerate the entry of cargo from Puerto Cortés into the United States.

The Dominican Republic–Central America Free Trade Agreement (DR–CAFTA) and the WTO

The DR–CAFTA spurred the *maquila* sector in Central America. However, the January 1, 2005 inclusion of textiles and apparel in the WTO rules has resulted in declining demand in the United States for CBI outward-processing apparel, which faces strong competition from countries such as Bangladesh, China, and Vietnam. In addition, the negotiations within the deferred Doha Round that are expected to reduce tariffs in the industrial sector (known as NAMA, for nonagricultural market access) are likely to result in the erosion of the DR-CAFTA market access preference for textile and clothing. Low, Piermartini, and Richtering (2005) argue that Honduras will be one of the developing countries most severely affected by the erosion preferences in NAMA, indicating that an important part of the erosion would come from the textile and apparel sector.

Annex 9B: Identifying Employees in the *Maquila* Industry from Honduras's Household Surveys

Before 2006, the Honduras household survey (EPHPM) did not include information on *maquila* labor participation. This annex shows how workers were classified into *maquila* versus non-*maquila* before 2006.

The 2006 EPHPM indicates that textile and apparel *maquila* are highly concentrated in a few departments (or provinces) in Honduras (Cortes, Atlántida, Francisco Morazán, Yoro, Santa Bárbara, and Comayagua). In all years the EPHPM provides information on workers manufacturing textiles, working in knitting mills, and manufacturing wearing apparel other than footwear, as classified by the UN International Standard Industrial Classification of all Economics Activities, Third Revision (ISIC Rev. 3). For years other than 2006, when respondents were not asked whether they worked in a *maquila*, a worker was classified as being part of the *maquila* industry if he or she was currently employed by a private firm in the textile and apparel industry that employed 10 or more workers and was located in a department in which *maquila* operate.

In order to evaluate the goodness of fit of these criteria of classification, we classified workers into *maquila* and non-*maquila* in 2006 following the procedure described above and then compared the outcome with the results of the 2006 EPHPM. In 98 percent of cases, this procedure correctly identified workers in textile and apparel *maquilas*, giving us a high level of confidence in the approach.

Notes

Rafael E. De Hoyos is the corresponding author; his e-mail address is rdehoyos@sems.gob.mx.

1. Authors' computations based on data from INE (2006).

2. A manufacturing firm is defined as a *maquila* when it operates within a fiscal regime that allows it to import intermediate goods on a duty-free or tariff-free basis, process or assemble them (labor value-added), and then reexport the final good, usually to the originating country.

3. The average implicit tariff was calculated as import tariff revenue/ imports fob, excluding oil.

4. For an estimation of the ex ante poverty effects of trade liberalization in Honduras focusing on the agricultural sector, see República de Honduras (2005).

5. For a brief description of the main factors behind the increase in Honduras' *maquila* exports, see annex 9A.

6. People in rural areas, particularly poor small-scale farmers, were seriously affected by Hurricane Mitch.

7. A similar methodology, with an application to Mexico, can be found in Artecona and Cunningham (2002) and De Hoyos (2005 and 2006).

8. Given data restrictions, the textile and apparel industry is used as a proxy for *maquila* sector. In 2006, the industry accounted for 77 percent of the total labor force and 79 percent of value added of the *maquila* sector (Banco Central de Honduras 2007). For more details, see annex 9B.

9. In strict sense, these are triple difference estimators, because they capture differences between men and women, between workers inside and outside of the *maquila* sector, and over time.

10. The industries included are mining; manufacturing; electricity, gas, and water; construction; commerce; restaurants and hotels; transport and communication; financial services; and other services. The excluded category is the agricultural sector.

11. Consider the case of a woman employed outside the *maquila* sector. According to specification 2 of table 9.6, she earns 28.7 percent less than her male counterpart. Because she is not working in the *maquila* sector, she does not benefit from the 9.5 percent premium that women in the sector enjoy. Therefore, on average, a woman employed outside the sector earns 38 percent less than a woman employed in the sector.

12. Using a dynamic CGE model, Morley, Nakasone, and Piñeiro (2007) estimate the ex ante general equilibrium poverty effects of CAFTA in Honduras.

13. The wage equation in equation (9.7) includes the estimated individual-specific residuals $\hat{v}_i^t$ using the results from specification 3a in table 9.6.

14. Nicita and Razzas (2003) estimate a model with enough economic structure to capture the employment effects associated with a boom in the textile and apparel industry. They find that for each new job created in the textile industry, 4.5 people experience an increase in their purchasing power.

15. Because only significant parameters were taken into account in this microsimulation, the *maquila* effect in 1995 is equal to zero.

16. This simulation is not a counterfactual of how the Honduras economy would have looked in the absence of a *maquila* sector. Creating such a scenario would require estimates of the general equilibrium effects of the sector. This simulation should therefore be seen as an upper-bound estimate of the poverty-reduction effects of the *maquila* boom.

17. The poverty effects attributable to the different components are equal to the marginal difference in the poverty headcount shown by the cumulative effects presented in table 9.8. There is an obvious problem of path dependency in our simulations.

18. The difference declined in 2006.

References

Arbache, J. S., and M. H. Santos. 2005. "Trade Openness and Gender Discrimination." Available from the Social Science Research Network: ssrn.com/abstract=812564.

Artecona, R., and W. Cunningham.2002. "Effects of Trade Liberalization on the Gender Wage Gap in Mexico." Policy Research Report on Gender and Development Working Paper 21, World Bank, Washington, DC.

Banco Central de Honduras. 2006. *Balanza de pagos y comercio exterior de Honduras.* Tegucigalpa.

———. 2007. *Actividad maquiladora en Honduras 2006 y expectativas 2007.* Tegucigalpa.

Becker, G. S. 1971. *The Economics of Discrimination.* Chicago: University of Chicago Press.

De Hoyos, R. E. 2005. "The Microeconomics of Poverty, Inequality and Market Liberalizing Reforms." UNU-WIDER Research Paper 2005/63, United Nations University–World Institute for Economic Research, Helsinki.

———. 2006. "Structural Modelling of Female Labour Participation and Occupation Decisions." Cambridge Working Paper in Economics 0611, Faculty of Economics, University of Cambridge.

Foster, J., J. Greer, and E. Thorbecke. 1984. "A Class of Decomposable Poverty Measures." *Econometrica* 52 (3) 761–66.

INE (Instituto Nacional de Estadísticas). Various years. *Encuesta permanente de hogares de propósitos múltiples.* Tegucigalpa.

Jansen, Hans G. P., Samuel Morley, Gloria Kessler, Valeria Pineiro, Marco Sánchez, and Maximo Torero. 2007. *The Impact of the Central America Free Trade Agreement on the Central American Textile Maquila Industry.* IFPRI Discussion Paper 720, International Food Policy Research Institute, Washington, DC.

Low, Patrick, Roberta Piermartini, and Jurgen Richtering. 2005. "Multilateral Solutions to the Erosion of Non-Reciprocal Preferences in NAMA." WTO Working Paper ERSD–2005–05, World Trade Organization, Geneva.

Morley, S., E. Nakasone, and V. Piñeiro. 2008. *The Impact of CAFTA on Employment, Production and Poverty in Hondruas.* IFPRI Discussion Paper 748, International Food Policy Research Institute, Washington, DC.

Nicita, Alessandro, and Susan Razzaz. 2003. "Who Benefits and How Much? How Gender Affects Welfare Impacts of a Booming Textile Industry." Policy Research Working Paper 3029, World Bank, Washington, DC.

República de Honduras. 2005. "Estimación del impacto del DR-CAFTA en el bienestar de los hogares." Documento de Trabajo, Secretaria de Estado del Despacho Presidencial, Tegucigalpa.

Skripnitchenko, A., and P. Abbott. 2003. *Trade in Apparel to the U.S. under the Caribbean Basin Initiative: A Dynamic Investment Approach.* Paper presented at the international conference "Agricultural Policy Reform and the WTO: Where Are We Heading?" Capri, Italy, June 23–26.

Index

Boxes, figures, notes, and tables are indicated by b, f, n, and t, respectively.

GENDER ASPECTS OF THE TRA~
MAIN

AND POVERTY NEXUS

A Macro-Micro Approach